lonely planet

French

PHRASEBOOK & DICTIONARY

Acknowledgments

Associate Publisher Tali Budlender

Managing Editors Annelies Mertens, Angela Tinson

Editors Samantha Forge, Branislava Vladisavljevic, Laura Crawford, Robyn Loughnane

Series Designer Mark Adams

Managing Layout Designer Chris Girdler

Layout Designers Carol Jackson, Kerrianne Southway, Joseph Spanti

Production Support Yvonne Kirk, Glenn van der Knijff

CD Production Labsonics

Language Writers Michael Janes, Jean-Pierre Masclef, Jean-Bernard Carillet

Thanks

Jane Atkin, Sasha Baskett, Yvonne Bischofberger, Helen Christinis, Brendan Dempsey, Indra Kilfoyle, Nic Lehman, Naomi Parker, Trent Paton, Piers Pickard, Averil Robertson, Jacqui Saunders, John Taufa, Juan Winata

Published by Lonely Planet Publications Pty Ltd
ABN 36 005 607 983

2nd Edition – October 2012
ISBN 978 1 74220 965 4
Text © Lonely Planet 2012
Cover Image Mark Avellino – Lonely Planet Images

Printed in China 10 9 8 7 6 5 4 3

Contact lonelyplanet.com/contact

MIX
Paper from
responsible sources
FSC™ C021741
www.fsc.org

HOW TO USE THIS BOOK

Look out for the following icons throughout the book:

'Shortcut' Phrase
Easy-to-remember alternative to the full phrase

Q&A Pair
Question-and-answer pair – we suggest a response to the question asked

Look For
Phrases you may see on signs, menus etc

Listen For
Phrases you may hear from officials, locals etc

Language Tip
An insight into the foreign language

Culture Tip
An insight into the local culture

How to read the phrases:
- Coloured words and phrases throughout the book are phonetic guides to help you pronounce the foreign language.
- Lists of phrases with tinted background are options you can choose to complete the phrase above them.

These abbreviations will help you choose the right words and phrases in this book:

a	adjective	m	masculine	pol	polite
f	feminine	n	noun	sg	singular
inf	informal	pl	plural	v	verb
lit	literal				

Contents

PAGE 178

Menu Decoder
Dishes and ingredients explained –
order with confidence and try new foods.

PAGE 196

Two-Way Dictionary
Quick reference vocabulary guide –
3500 words to help you communicate.

INTRO

French

français fron·say

Who Speaks French?
Official Language

CARIBBEAN
FRENCH GUIANA
GUADELOUPE
MARTINIQUE
HAITI

EUROPE
FRANCE
SWITZERLAND
LUXEMBOURG
BELGIUM
MONACO

AFRICA
DEMOCRATIC REPUBLIC OF
CONGO · GABON · CENTRAL
AFRICAN REPUBLIC · CHAD
NIGER · MALI · BURKINA FASO
CÔTE D'IVOIRE · TOGO · BENIN
CAMEROON · CONGO · RWANDA
BURUNDI · SENEGAL · GUINEA
COMOROS · MAYOTTE
MADAGASCAR · RÉUNION
SEYCHELLES · DJIBOUTI
GABON

SOUTH PACIFIC
FRENCH POLYNESIA
NEW CALEDONIA
WALLIS & FUTUNA
VANUATU

CANADA
(QUEBEC)

Widely Understood Algeria – Andorra – Egypt
Lebanon – Mauritania – Mauritius – Morocco – Tunisia

Why Bother

You may be told of a cosy vineyard way off the tourist track, or discover that there's little merit in the stereotype about the French being rude.

Distinctive Sounds

Throaty r, silent h, nasal vowels (pronounced as if you're trying to force the sound 'through the nose').

French in the World

French is the official language of a number of international organisations (including the UN and the International Olympic Committee). French films are

80 MILLION
speak French as their
first language

50 MILLION
speak French as their
second language

internationally renowned, and France has won the Nobel Prize in Literature more times than any other country.

French in France

Speaking a language other than their own is an emotional affair for the French, as attested by the online Musée des Horreurs (Museum of Horrors) of the Paris-based Défense de la Langue Française (DLF; Defence of the French Language; www.langue -francaise.org, in French).

False Friends

Warning: many French words look like English words but have a different meaning altogether, eg *menu* me·new is a set lunch, not a menu (which is *carte* kart in French).

Language Family

Romance (developed from the Latin spoken by the Romans during their conquest of the 1st century BC). Close relatives include Italian, Spanish, Portuguese and Romanian.

Must-Know Grammar

French has a formal and informal word for 'you' (*vous* voo and *tu* tew respectively); it distinguishes between masculine and feminine forms of words, eg *beau/belle* bo/bel m/f (beautiful).

Donations to English

Numerous – thanks to the Norman invasion of England in the 11th century, some estimate that three-fifths of everyday English vocabulary arrived via French. You may recognise *café*, *déjà vu*, *bon vivant*, *cliché*...

5 Phrases to Learn Before You Go

 What are the opening hours?
Quelles sont les heures d'ouverture?
kel son lay zer doo·vair·tewr

French business hours are governed by a maze of regulations, so it's a good idea to check before you make plans.

 I'd like the set menu, please.
Je voudrais le menu, s'il vous plait.
zher voo·dray ler mer·new seel voo play

The best-value dining in France is the two- or three-course meal at a fixed price. Most restaurants have one on the chalkboard.

 Which wine would you recommend?
Quel vin vous conseillez?
kel vun voo kon·say·yay

Who better to ask for advice on wine than the French?

 Can I address you with 'tu'?
Est-ce que je peux vous tutoyer?
es ker zher per voo tew·twa·yay

Before you start addressing someone with the informal 'you' form, it's polite to ask permission first.

 Do you have plans for tonight/tomorrow?
Vous avez prévu quelque chose ce soir/demain?
voo za·vay pray·vew kel·ker shoz ser swar/der·mun

To arrange to meet up without sounding pushy, ask friends if they're available rather than inviting them directly.

10 Phrases to Sound Like a Local

Cool!	**Génial!**	zhay·nyal
No worries.	**Pas de soucis.**	pa der soo·see
Sure.	**D'accord.**	da·kor
No way!	**Pas question!**	pa kay·styon
Just joking!	**Je plaisante!**	zher play·zont
Too bad.	**Tant pis.**	tom pee
What a shame.	**Quel dommage.**	kel do·mazh
What's up?	**Qu'est-ce qu'il y a?**	kes keel ya
Well done!	**Bien joué!**	byun zhoo·ay
Not bad.	**Pas mal.**	pa mal

ABOUT FRENCH

Pronunciation

The sounds used in spoken French can almost all be found in English. There are a few exceptions: nasal vowels, the 'funny' u sound and that deep-in-the-throat r, but throwing caution to the wind and mimicking every French accent you've heard can be surprisingly effective.

Vowel Sounds

Generally, French vowel sounds are short and don't glide into other vowels. As you order another coffee, listen to fellow patrons and note some of the differences in their pronunciation, like the ay in *café*. It's close to the English sound, but it's shorter and sharper.

SYMBOL	ENGLISH EQUIVALENT	FRENCH EXAMPLE	TRANSLITERATION
a	run	tasse	tas
ai	aisle	travail	tra·vai
air	fair	faire	fair
ay	say	musée	mew·zay
e	red	est	est
ee	bee	lit	lee
er	her	deux	der
ew	ee with rounded lips	tu	tew
o	pot	pomme	pom
oo	moon	chou	shoo

Nasal Vowel Sounds

Nasal vowels are pronounced as if you're trying to force the sound out of your nose rather than your mouth. It's easier than it sounds! English also has nasal vowels to some extent – when you say 'sing' in English, the 'i' is nasalised by the 'ng'. In French, though, nasal vowels cause the nasal consonant sound that follows them to be omitted, but a 'hint' of what the implied consonant is can sometimes be heard. We've used nasal consonant sounds (m, n, ng) with the nasal vowel to help you produce the sound with more confidence. Although there are four nasal vowels in French, our pronunciation guides use only two: o and u. These approximate the actual sounds. The four nasal sounds can be quite close, so to get you out there speaking, we've simplified it in the following way:

SYMBOL	ENGLISH EQUIVALENT	FRENCH EXAMPLE	TRANSLITERATION
om	like 'pot' + nasal consonant sound	mouton	moo·ton
on			
ong			
um	similar to 'bat' + nasal consonant sound	magasin	ma·ga·zun
un			
ung			

Consonant Sounds

Swallow deeply and prepare for just one sticking point when it comes to pronouncing French consonants: the r sound. It's made in the back of the throat, a little like a growl. Using an English 'r' sound will get you by, but it's one of the French sounds that will really help you sound natural – it's well worth working on. The other consonant sounds can all be found in English.

SYMBOL	ENGLISH EQUIVALENT	FRENCH EXAMPLE	TRANSLITERATION
b	big	billet	bee·yay
d	din	date	dat
f	fun	femme	fam
g	go	grand	gron
k	kick	carte	kart
l	loud	livre	leev·rer
m	man	merci	mair·see
n	no	non	non
ng	sang	cinquante	sung·kont
ny	canyon	signe	see·nyer
p	pig	parc	park
r	run	rue	rew
s	so	si	see
sh	show	changer	shon·zhay
t	tin	tout	too
v	van	verre	vair
w	win	oui	wee
y	yes	payer, billet	pay·yay, bee·yay
z	is	vous avez	voo za·vay
zh	pleasure	je	zher

Word Stress & Rhythm

Syllables in French words are, for the most part, equally stressed. English speakers tend to stress the first syllable, which is definitely unusual in French, so try adding a light stress on the final syllable to compensate.

The rhythm of a French sentence is based on breaking the phrase into meaningful sections, then stressing the final syllable in each. The stress at these points is characterised by a slight rise in intonation. The 'beat' of the sentence is quite regular because of these stressed syllables (in italics in the example following).

French pronunciation, unlike that of English, is quite easy.

La prononciation du français, à la différence de l'anglais, est assez facile.
la pro·non·see·a·syon dew fron·*say* a la dee·*fair*·rons der long·*glay* ay ta·say fa·*seel*

Intonation

A rising intonation in French is used when asking a question. There is also a rise in intonation when listing items: your voice goes up after each item until you say the final item in the list, at which point your voice falls.

Reading & Writing

Writing French is a little more complicated than speaking it. The spelling of verb endings is a great example: sometimes an ending might consist of up to five letters and sound the same as a two-letter ending (eg both -*aient* and -*ai* sound like ay). Take heart though: the French themselves have difficulty with spelling – the annual national spelling competition attests to that.

If you try to compare the written French and the pronunciation guides in this book, you'll start to notice some of the relationships between sound and writing.

FRENCH ALPHABET

A a a	**B b** bay	**C c** say
D d day	**E e** er	**F f** ef
G g zhay	**H h** ash	**I i** ee
J j zhee	**K k** ka	**L l** el
M m em	**N n** en	**O o** o
P p pay	**Q q** kew	**R r** air
S s es	**T t** tay	**U u** ew
V v vay	**W w** doo·bler·vay	**X x** iks
Y y ee·grek	**Z z** zed	

ABOUT FRENCH

Grammar

This chapter is designed to explain the main grammatical structures you need in order to make your own sentences. Look under each heading – listed in alphabetical order – for information on functions which these grammatical categories express in a sentence. For example, demonstratives are used for giving instructions, so you'll need them to tell the taxi driver where your hotel is. A glossary of grammatical terms is included at the end of the chapter to help you.

Adjectives & Adverbs

Describing People/Things • Doing Things

As a rule, adjectives come after the noun in French. There are exceptions, however, such as *grand* gron (big) and *petit* per·tee (small), which come before the noun.

| **an expensive hotel** | un hôtel cher (lit: a hotel expensive-m-sg) |
| | un o·tel shair |

In French, adjectives agree with the noun in gender (see also **gender**). Generally, for the feminine form of an adjective just add an -e to the end. Note though that this ending usually causes the consonant before it to be pronounced, or it may change the final vowel sound or the preceding consonant.

	~ MASCULINE ~		~ FEMININE ~	
small	petit	per·tee	petite	per·teet
next	prochain	pro·shun	prochaine	pro·shen
white	blanc	blong	blanche	blonsh

Adjectives whose masculine form ends in -*e* don't change form for gender, eg *jeune* zhern (young) or *riche* reesh (rich). Other adjectives differ more significantly in their masculine and feminine form, eg *beau/belle* m/f bo/bel (beautiful).

Adjectives also agree with the noun in number. In general, to make an adjective plural, add -*s* to the end (see also **plurals**).

gay venue	boîte gaie	bwat gay
gay venues	boîtes gaies	bwat gay

To form adverbs in French, you generally add the ending -*ment* mon (just like you add '-ly' in English) to the feminine form of the adjective, or to the masculine form if it ends in a vowel. Adverbs are placed after the verb they modify (see also **verbs**).

slow	lent(e) m/f	lon(t)
to speak slowly	parler lentement	par·lay lon·ter·mon

Articles

Naming People/Things

French has three words for the definite article (ie 'the' in English), depending on the noun's gender and number (see **gender** and **plurals**). Both *le* and *la* become *l'* before a word beginning with a vowel or *h*, eg *l'hôtel* lo·tel (hotel) or *l'eau* lo (water).

		~ DEFINITE ARTICLES ~		
m sg	le	ler	**the steak**	le biftek	ler beef·tek
f sg	la	la	**the tart**	la tarte	la tart
pl	les	lay	**the snails**	les escar-gots	lay zes·kar·go

ABOUT FRENCH GRAMMAR

Similarly, there are three words for the indefinite article (ie 'a' or 'an' in English) to match the gender and number of the noun.

~ INDEFINITE ARTICLES ~

m	un	un	**a ticket**	un ticket	un tee·kay
f	une	ewn	**a postcard**	une carte postale	ewn kart pos·tal
pl	des	day	**some apples**	des pommes	day pom

Be

Describing People/Things • Making Statements

The verb *être* e·trer (be) changes form depending on the subject, just as in English. For information on negative forms, see **negatives**.

~ ÊTRE (BE) – PRESENT TENSE ~

I am	je suis	zher swee
you are sg inf	tu es	tew ay
you are sg pol	vous êtes	voo zet
he/she is	il/elle est	eel/el ay
we are	nous sommes	noo som
you are pl	vous êtes	voo zet
they are	ils/elles sont m/f	eel/el son m/f

Demonstratives

Giving Instructions • Indicating Location • Pointing Things Out

The easiest way to point something out in French is to use the phrase *c'est* say (lit: it-is).

That's the right train.	C'est le bon train. (lit: it-is the-**m-sg** good-**m-sg** train)
	say ler bon trun

The demonstrative adjectives 'this' and 'that' are translated with the same word in French – *ce* ser for masculine singular nouns and *cette* set for feminine singular nous. The plural form of both words is *ces* say (these/those). See also **gender** and **plurals**.

this/that group	ce groupe	se groop
this/that woman	cette femme	set fam
these/those people	ces gens	say zhon

Gender

Naming People/Things

In French, all nouns (words which denote a thing, person or idea) have either masculine or feminine gender. You can recognise the noun's gender by the article, demonstrative, possessive or any other adjective accompanying the noun, as they change form to agree with the noun's gender (see **adjectives & adverbs**, **articles**, **demonstratives**, **possessives**). The gender of words is also indicated in the dictionary, but here are some general rules:

» A word is masculine/feminine if it refers to a man/woman.
» Words ending in a consonant, *-acle, -age, -ème* or *-isme* are generally masculine.
» Words ending in *-e, -ion* or *-aison* are usually feminine.

The masculine and feminine forms of words are indicated with **m** and **f** throughout this phrasebook where relevant. See also the boxed text, p129.

Have

Possessing

Possession can be indicated in various ways in French (see also **possessives**). One way is by using the verb *avoir* a·vwar (have). For information on negative forms, see **negatives**.

~ AVOIR (HAVE) – PRESENT TENSE ~

I have	j'ai	zhay
you have sg inf	tu as	tew a
you have sg pol	vous avez	voo za·vay
he/she has	il/elle a	eel/el a
we have	nous avons	noo za·von
you have	vous avez	voo za·vay
they have	ils/elles ont m/f	eel/el zon m/f

Negatives

Negating

To make a sentence negative, French uses two words – *ne* ner and *pas* pa, both meaning 'not' – around the verb:

I don't know.   Je ne sais pas. (lit: I not know not)
zher ner say pa

If there are two verbs or two words that make up the verb, the *ne ... pas* goes around the first verb or first part of the verb:

I don't want to go.   Je ne veux pas aller. (lit: I not want not go)
zher ner ver pa za·lay

With another negative word in the sentence, *pas* is omitted:

I have nothing to declare.	Je n'ai rien à déclarer. (lit: I not-have nothing to declare) zher nay ryun a day·kla·ray

The word *pas* pa (not) is used alone when there is no verb:

| **Not yet.** | Pas encore. | pa ong·kor |
| **Not bad.** | Pas mal. | pa mal |

Personal Pronouns

Making Statements • Naming People/Things

Personal pronouns ('I', 'you' etc) change form in French depending on whether they're the subject or the object in a sentence, just like English has 'I' and 'me' as the subject and object pronouns (eg 'I see her' and 'She sees me'). The subject pronoun *on* on (one) is often used to refer to a nonspecific subject:

French is spoken here.	On parle français ici. (lit: one speaks French here) on parl fron·say ee·see

~ SUBJECT PRONOUNS ~

I	je	zher	**we**	nous	noo
you sg inf	tu	tew	**you** pl	vous	voo
you sg pol	vous	voo			
he/it	il	eel	**they**	ils m	eel m
she/it	elle	el		elles f	el f

When talking to someone familiar or younger than you, use the informal form of 'you', *tu* tew, rather than the polite form, *vous* voo. Phrases in this book use the form of 'you' that is appropriate to the situation. Where both forms are used, they are indicated by pol and inf. See also the boxed text, p99.

me	me	mer	us	nous	noo
you sg inf	te	ter	you pl	vous	voo
you sg pol	vous	voo			
him/it	le/lui	ler/lwee	them	les/leur	lay/ler
her/it	la/lui	la/lwee			

~ OBJECT PRONOUNS ~

In the table above, the French forms separated by a slash are direct/indirect object pronouns.

The direct and indirect object pronouns differ only for the third person ('he', 'she', 'it', 'they').

| **I see him.** | Je le vois. (lit: I him see) zher ler vwa |
| **I gave him the ticket.** | Je lui ai donné le billet. (lit: I to-him have given the-m-sg ticket) zher lwee ay do·nay ler bee·yay |

The object pronouns are placed before the verb. The direct object pronoun comes before the indirect object pronoun.

| **I gave it to him.** | Je le lui ai donné. (lit: I it-m-sg to-him have given) zher ler lwee ay do·nay |

Plurals

Naming People/Things

To form the plural of a noun in French, an -s is added to the noun in writing (though there are exceptions), but it's often not pronounced. In spoken language, the easiest way to indicate plural is to use words like *beaucoup de* bo·koo der (a lot of), numbers or the plural articles *les* lay and *des* day (see **articles**).

I'd like two tickets.	Je voudrais deux billets. (lit: I would-like two tickets)
	zher voo·dray der bee·yay

Possessives

Possessing

A common way of indicating possession is by using possessive adjectives before the noun they refer to. Like other adjectives, they agree with the noun in number, and sometimes also in gender (see also **gender** and **plurals**).

~ POSSESSIVE ADJECTIVES ~

my	mon/mes m ma/mes f	mon/may m ma/may f	**our**	notre/nos	no·trer/no
your sg inf	ton/tes m ta/tes f	ton/tay m ta/tay f	**your** pl	votre/vos	vo·trer/vo
your sg pol	votre/vos	vo·trer/vo			
his/her/its	son/ses m sa/ses f	son/say m sa/say f	**their**	leur/leurs	ler/ler

In the table above, the French forms separated by a slash are used with a singular/plural noun.

When a singular noun begins with 'h' or a vowel, *mon, ton* and *son* are used, regardless of the noun's gender:

my team	mon équipe (lit: my team-f-sg)
	mon ay·keep

Another way to indicate possession is by using possessive pronouns, which also agree in number and sometimes gender with the noun. The corresponding definite article is used before the possessive pronoun (see **articles**).

That bag is mine.	Ce sac est le mien. (lit: that-m-sg bag is the-m-sg mine-m-sg)
	ser sak ay ler myun

~ POSSESSIVE PRONOUNS ~

mine	mien/ miens m mienne/ miennes f	myun/ myun m myen/ myen f	ours	nôtre/ nôtres	no·trer/ no·trer
yours sg inf	tien/tiens m tienne/ tiennes f	tyun/tyun m tyen/ tyen f	yours pl	vôtre/ vôtres	vo·trer/ vo·trer
yours sg pol	vôtre/ vôtres	vo·trer/ vo·trer			
his/hers/ its	sien/siens m sienne/ siennes f	syun/syun m syen/ syen f	theirs	leur/ leurs	ler/ ler

In the table above, the French forms separated by a slash are used with a singular/plural noun.

You can also indicate ownership by using the verb *avoir* a·vwar (see **have**) or with '*de* der (of) + noun', just as in English:

Marie's bag

le sac de Marie (lit: the-m-sg bag of Marie)
ler sak der ma·ree

Prepositions

Giving Instructions • Indicating Location •
Pointing Things Out

Like English, French uses prepositions to explain where things are in time or space. Common prepositions are listed in the table opposite; for more prepositions, see the **dictionary**.

~ PREPOSITIONS ~

after	après	a·pray	from	de	der
at (time)	à	a	in (place)	dans	don
before	avant	a·von	to	à	a

Questions

Asking Questions • Negating

The easiest way to ask a 'yes/no' question in French is to make a statement and add a rise in your intonation as you speak. Alternatively, you can use *est-ce que* es ker (lit: is-it that) in front of a statement.

Is this the right train?
Est-ce que c'est le bon train? (lit: is-it that it-is the-**m-sg** good-**m-sg** train)
es ker say ler bon trun

Another way to ask a 'yes/no' question is to put the verb before the subject of the sentence, as in English, and link them with a hyphen.

Do you have a car?
As-tu une voiture? (lit: have-you-**sg-inf** a-**f-sg** car)
a·tew ewn vwa·tewr

Just as in English, there are also question words for asking more specific questions. These words are used at the start of the sentence in French.

~ QUESTION WORDS ~

how	comment	ko·mon	where	où	oo
what	qu'est-ce que	kes ker	who	qui	kee
when	quand	kon	why	pourquoi	poor·kwa

To answer 'yes' after a question in the affirmative, use *oui* wee, and to answer 'yes (I do)' after a question in the negative, use *si* see. The negative answer is *non* non (no).

Verbs

Doing Things

There are three verb categories in French – those whose infinitive (dictionary form) ends in *-ir, -er* or *-re*, eg *finir* fee·neer (finish), *parler* par·lay (speak), *vendre* von·drer (sell). Tenses are formed by adding various endings for each person to the verb stem (the part of the verb that remains after removing *-ir, -er* or *-re*), and for most verbs these endings follow regular patterns according to the verb category. The verb endings for the present and future tenses are shown in the following tables. For negative forms of verbs, see **negatives**.

~ PRESENT TENSE ~

		finir	parler	vendre
I	je	finis	parle	vends
you sg inf	tu	finis	parles	vends
you sg pol	vous	finissez	parlez	vendez
he/she	il/elle	finit	parle	vend
we	nous	finissons	parlons	vendons
you pl	vous	finissez	parlez	vendez
they	ils/elles m/f	finissent	parlent	vendent

The main past tense in French, used for a completed action, is a compound tense, which means it is made up of an auxiliary verb – either *être* e·trer (be) or *avoir* a·vwar (have) – in the present tense, plus a form of the main verb, called 'past participle' (see also **be** and **have**). The past participle is formed by replacing the infinitive endings *-ir, -er* or *-re* with *-i, -é* or *-u* respectively (some past participles are irregular). Past participles of the verbs taking *être* must agree with the subject in gender and number, while past participles of the verbs taking *avoir* don't change form.

We arrived.	Nous sommes arrivées. (lit: we are arrived-f-pl) noo som za·ree·vay

| **They saw.** | Elles ont vu. (lit: they-f have seen) |
| | el zon vew |

	~ INFINITIVE ~		~ PAST PARTICIPLE ~	
finish	finir	fee·neer	fini	fee·nee
speak	parler	par·lay	parlé	par·lay
sell	vendre	von·drer	vendu	von·dew

In the future tense, the endings follow the same pattern for all three verb categories, and they are simply added to the infinitive (dictionary form of the verb), not the verb stem. For verbs ending in -*re* the final *e* is dropped before adding the new endings.

~ FUTURE TENSE ~		**finir**	**parler**	**vendre**
I	je	finirai	parlerai	vendrai
you sg inf	tu	finiras	parleras	vendras
you sg pol	vous	finirez	parlerez	vendrez
he/she	il/elle	finira	parlera	vendra
we	nous	finirons	parlerons	vendrons
you pl	vous	finirez	parlerez	vendrez
they	ils/elles m/f	finiront	parleront	vendront

Word Order

Making Statements

The basic word order in French is subject-verb-object, just as in English. See also **negatives** and **questions**.

| **I speak French.** | Je parle français. (lit: I speak French) |
| | zher parl fron·say |

~ GRAMMAR GLOSSARY ~

adjective	a word that describes something – 'there are five **basic** types of cheese in France'
adverb	a word that explains how an action is done – 'that are **usually** displayed in cheese shops'
article	the words 'a', 'an' and 'the'
demonstrative	a word that means 'this' or 'that'
direct object	the thing or person in the sentence that has the action directed to it – 'you can sample **them**'
gender	classification of *nouns* into classes (like masculine and feminine), requiring other words (eg *adjectives*) to belong to the same class
indirect object	the person or thing in the sentence that is the recipient of the action – 'and the merchants will often give **you** advice'
infinitive	dictionary form of a *verb* – 'on what **to choose**'
noun	a thing, person or idea – 'it's a **matter** of **taste**'
number	whether a word is singular or plural – 'and the **choices** on offer can be overwhelming'
personal pronoun	a word that means 'I', 'you' etc
possessive adjective	a word that means 'my', 'your' etc
possessive pronoun	a word that means 'mine', 'yours' etc
preposition	a word like 'for' or 'before'
subject	the thing or person in the sentence that does the action – '**you** should also consider'
tense	form of a *verb* that tells you whether the action is in the present, past or future – eg 'eat' (present), 'ate' (past), 'will eat' (future)
verb	a word that tells you what action happened – 'which wine **goes** best with each type of cheese'
verb stem	part of a *verb* that doesn't change – eg '**sampl**' in '**sampl**ing' and '**sampl**ed'

Basics

Understanding

KEY PHRASES

Do you speak English?	Vous parlez anglais?	voo par·lay ong·glay
I don't understand.	Je ne comprends pas.	zher ner kom·pron pa
What does (that) mean?	Qu'est-ce que (ça) veut dire ?	kes·ker sa ver deer

1a Q **Do you speak English?**
Vous parlez anglais?
voo par·lay ong·glay

A **I speak a little.**
Je parle un peu.
zher parl um per

1b Q **Do you understand?**
Vous comprenez?
voo kom·prer·nay

1c A **I understand.**
Je comprends.
zher kom·pron

1d A **I don't understand.**
Je ne comprends pas.
zher ner kom·pron pa

I need an interpreter who speaks English.
J'ai besoin d'un interprète de langue anglaise.
zhay ber·zwun dun nun·tair·pret der long ong·glay·zer

I'd like to practice French.
Je voudrais parler en français.
zher voo·dray par·lay on fron·say

2a **What does (that) mean?**
Qu'est-ce que (ça) veut dire?
kes·ker sa ver deer

2b **How do you pronounce this?**
Comment ça se prononce?
ko·mon sa se pro·nons

LANGUAGE TIP

False Friends

Many French words look like English words but have a different meaning altogether – beware!

Here are a few:

car
kar
coach/bus (not 'car', which is *voiture* vwa·tewr)

information
un·for·ma·syon
news (not 'information', which is *renseignement* ron·sen·yer·mon)

introduire
un·tro·dweer
insert (not 'introduce', which is *présenter* pray·zon·tay)

librairie
lee·bray·ree
book shop (not 'library', which is *bibliothèque* bee·blee·o·tek)

menu
me·new
set menu (not 'menu', which is *carte* kart)

prune
prewn
plum (not 'prune', which is *pruneau* prew·no)

vacance
va·kons
holidays (not 'vacancy', which is *poste vacant* post va·kon)

How do you write ...?	Comment est-ce qu'on écrit ...? ko·mon es kon ay·kree ...
2c Could you please repeat that?	Pourriez-vous répéter, s'il vous plaît? poo·ree·yay·voo ray·pay·tay seel voo play
2d Could you please write it down?	Pourriez-vous l'écrire, s'il vous plaît? poo·ree·yay·voo lay·kreer seel voo play

BASICS

UNDERSTANDING

LANGUAGE TIP

Reading French

In written French, you'll often see an *l'* in front of a word beginning with a vowel or a silent *h:* this replaces a *le* or a *la* (the) and is pronounced as a single word starting with an *l*, eg, *l'orange* lo·ronzh.

Generally, you don't pronounce a consonant at the end of a word, eg *faux* fo. There's one exception – final 'c', eg *sec* sek. Also, you do pronounce a final consonant if the next word starts with a vowel or an *h*, eg *faux ami* fo zami.

2e	Could you please speak more slowly?	Pourriez-vous parler plus lentement, s'il vous plaît? poo·ree·yay·voo par·lay plew lon·ter·mon seel voo play

---

✂	Slowly, please!	Lentement, s'il vous plaît!	lon·ter·mon seel voo play

Numbers & Amounts

KEY PHRASES

How many/much?	Combien?	kom·byun
all	tout	too
none	rien	ryun

Cardinal Numbers

3a	0	zéro	zay·ro
3b	1	un	un
3c	2	deux	der
3d	3	trois	trwa
3e	4	quatre	ka·trer
3f	5	cinq	sungk
3g	6	six	sees
3h	7	sept	set
3i	8	huit	weet
3j	9	neuf	nerf
3k	10	dix	dees
	11	onze	onz
	12	douze	dooz
	13	treize	trez
	14	quatorze	ka·torz
	15	quinze	kunz
	16	seize	sez
	17	dix-sept	dee·set
	18	dix-huit	dee·zweet

BASICS NUMBERS & AMOUNTS

	19	dix-neuf	deez·nerf
4a	20	vingt	vung
	21	vingt et un	vung tay un
	22	vingt-deux	vung·der
4b	30	trente	tront
4c	40	quarante	ka·ront
4d	50	cinquante	sung·kont
4e	60	soixante	swa·sont
4f	70	soixante-dix	swa·son·dees
4g	80	quatre-vingts	ka·trer·vung
4h	90	quatre-vingt-dix	ka·trer·vung·dees
4i	100	cent	son
4j	1000	mille	meel
4k	1,000,000	un million	um meel·yon

Ordinal Numbers

1st	premier/première m/f	prer·myay/prer·myair
2nd	deuxième	der·zyem
3rd	troisième	trwa·zyem

Useful Amounts

How many/much?	Combien?	kom·byun
a quarter	un quart	ung kar
a third	un tiers	un tyair
a half	un demi	un der·mee
all	tout	too
none	rien	ryun

For other useful amounts, see **self-catering** (p169).

Time & Dates

KEY PHRASES

What time is it?	Quelle heure est-il?	kel er ay·teel
At what time?	À quelle heure?	a kel er
At ...	À ...	a

Telling the Time

The 24-hour clock is usually used when telling the time in French. After the half hour, use the next hour minus (*moins* mwun) the minutes until that hour arrives.

5a Q What time is it?	Quelle heure est-il? kel er ay·teel
5b A It's (one) o'clock.	Il est (une) heure. ee lay (ewn) er
A It's (10) o'clock.	Il est (dix) heures. ee lay (deez) er
Quarter past (one).	Il est (une) heure et quart. ee lay (ewn) er ay kar
Twenty past (one).	Il est (une) heure vingt. ee lay (ewn) er vung
Half past (one).	Il est (une) heure et demie. ee lay (ewn) er ay der·mee
Twenty to (one).	Il est (une) heure moins vingt. ee lay (ewn) er mwun vung
Quarter to (one).	Il est (une) heure moins le quart. ee lay (ewn) er mwun ler kar

Q	At what time?	À quelle heure? a kel er
A	At ...	À ... a ...

6a	morning	le matin	ler ma·tun
	day	le jour	ler zhoor
	midday	le midi	ler mee·dee
6b	afternoon	l'après-midi	la·pray·mee·dee
6c	evening	le soir	ler swar
	night	la nuit	la nwee
	midnight	le minuit	ler mee·nwee

The Calendar

7a	Monday	lundi m	lun·dee
7b	Tuesday	mardi m	mar·dee
7c	Wednesday	mercredi m	mair·krer·dee
7d	Thursday	jeudi m	zher·dee
7e	Friday	vendredi m	von·drer·dee
7f	Saturday	samedi m	sam·dee
7g	Sunday	dimanche m	dee·monsh

8a	January	janvier m	zhon·vyay
8b	February	février m	fayv·ray
8c	March	mars m	mars
8d	April	avril m	a·vreel
8e	May	mai m	may
8f	June	juin m	zhwun
8g	July	juillet m	zhwee·yay
8h	August	août m	oot
8i	September	septembre m	sep·tom·brer
8j	October	octobre m	ok·to·brer

| 8k November | novembre m | no·vom·brer |
| 8l December | décembre m | day·som·brer |

9a spring	printemps m	prun·tom
9b summer	été m	ay·tay
9c autumn	automne m	o·ton
9d winter	hiver m	ee·vair

What day is it today?	C'est quel jour aujourd'hui? say kel zhoor o·zhoor·dwee
10a Q **What date is it today?**	Quelle est la date aujourd'hui? kel ay la dat o·zhoor·dwee
A **It's (18 October).**	C'est le (dix-huit octobre). say ler (dee·zwee tok·to·brer)

Present

10b today	aujourd'hui	o·zhoor·dwee
this morning	ce matin	ser ma·tun
this afternoon	cet après-midi	say ta·pray·mee·dee
10c tonight	ce soir	ser swar
this week	cette semaine	set ser·men
this month	ce mois	ser mwa
this year	cette année	set a·nay

Past

half an hour ago	une demi-heure avant ewn de·mee·er a·von
(three) days ago	il y a (trois) jours eel ya (trwa) zhoor
(five) years ago	il y a (cinq) ans eel ya (sungk) on
11a yesterday	hier ee·yair

BASICS TIME & DATES

BASICS

TIME & DATES

yesterday morning	hier matin ee·yair ma·tun
yesterday afternoon	hier après-midi ee·yair a·pray·mee·dee
yesterday evening	hier soir ee·yair swar
11a last week	la semaine dernière la ser·men dair·nyair
11b last month	le mois dernier ler mwa dair·nyay
11c last year	l'année dernière la·nay dair·nyair

Future

in (five) minutes	dans (cinq) minutes don (sungk) mee·newt
within an hour	d'ici une heure dee·see ewn er
in (six) days	dans (six) jours don (see) zhoor
12a tomorrow	demain der·mun
tomorrow morning	demain matin der·mun ma·tun
tomorrow afternoon	demain après-midi der·mun a·pray·mee·dee
tomorrow evening	demain soir der·mun swar
12b next week	la semaine prochaine la se·men pro·shen
12c next month	le mois prochain ler mwa pro·shen
12d next year	l'année prochaine la·nay pro·shen

Practical

Transport

KEY PHRASES

What time's the next bus?	Le prochain bus part à quelle heure?	ler pro·shun bews par a kel er
One ticket, please.	Un billet, s'il vous plaît.	um bee·yay seel voo play
Please tell me when we get to ...?	Prévenez-moi, s'il vous plaît, quand on arrivera à...	prev·nay·mwar seel voo play kont on a·ree·vra a...
Please take me to this address.	Conduisez-moi à cette adresse, s'il vous plaît.	kon·dwee·zay·mwa a set a·dres seel voo play

Getting Around

What time does the ... leave?	À quelle heure part ...? a kel er par ...

boat	le bateau	ler ba·to
bus	le bus	ler bews
plane	l'avion	la·vyon
train	le train	ler trun
tram	le tramway	ler tram·way

13a **What time's the first bus?** Le premier bus part à quelle heure?
ler prer·myay bews par a kel er

13b What time's the last bus?	Le dernier bus part à quelle heure? ler dair·nyay bews par a kel er
13c What time's the next bus?	Le prochain bus part à quelle heure? ler pro·shun bews par a kel er
What time does it arrive?	À quelle heure est-ce qu'il arrive? a kel er es keel a·ree·ve
Which platform does it depart from?	Il part de quel quai? eel par der kel kay
Which bus goes to (Bordeaux)?	Quel bus va à (Bordeaux)? kel bews va a (bor·do)
13d That's my seat.	C'est ma place. say ma plas
13e Is this seat available?	Est-ce que cette place est libre? es ker set plas ay lee·brer

✂ **Is it available?** | C'est libre? | say lee·brer

For bus numbers, see **numbers & amounts** (p31).

Can we get there by public transport?	Peux-t-on s'y rendre en transport publique? per·ton see ron·dre on trons·por pewb·leek
I'd prefer to walk there.	Je préfère y marcher. zhe pray·fair ee mar·shay
Can I take my car on the boat?	Je peux transporter ma voiture sur ce bateau? zher per trons·por·tay ma vwa·tewr sewr ser ba·to
Can I take my bike?	Je peux amener mon vélo? zher per am·nay mon vay·lo

PRACTICAL TRANSPORT

13f Please tell me when we get to...	Prévenez-moi, s'il vous plaît, quand on arrivera à...	prev·nay·mwar seel voo play kont on a·ree·vra a...
I want to get off at (Nantes).	Je veux descendre à (Nantes).	zher ver day·son·drer a (nont)
I want to get off here.	Je veux descendre ici.	zher ver day·son·drer ee·see

For phrases for getting through customs and immigration, see **border crossing** (p50). For phrases on disabled access, see **senior & disabled travellers** (p93).

Buying Tickets

14a Where can I buy a ticket?	Où peut-on acheter un billet?	oo per·ton ash·tay um bee·yay
14b Do I need to book a seat?	Est-ce qu'il faut réserver une place?	es keel fo ray·zer·vay ewn plas
14c I'd like to cancel my ticket, please.	Je voudrais annuler mon billet, s'il vous plaît.	zher voo·dray a·new·lay mom bee·yay seel voo play
14d I'd like to change my ticket, please.	Je voudrais changer mon billet, s'il vous plaît.	zher voo·dray shon·zhay mom bee·yay seel voo play
How much is it?	C'est combien?	say kom·byun
It's full.	C'est complet.	say kom·play

Buying a Ticket

What time is the next ...?
À quelle heure part le prochain ...?
a kel er par ler pro·shun ...

boat
bateau
ba·to

bus
bus
bews

train
train
trun

One ... ticket, please.
Un billet ..., s'il vous plaît.
um bee·yay ... seel voo play

one-way
simple
sum·pler

return
aller et retour
a·lay ay rer·toor

I'd like a/an ... seat.
Je voudrais une place ...
zher voo·dray ewn plas ...

aisle
côté couloir
ko·tay koo·lwar

window
côté fenêtre
ko·tay fe·ne·trer

Which platform does it depart from?
Il part de quel quai?
eel par der kel kay

PRACTICAL TRANSPORT

One ... ticket (to Paris), please.	Un billet ... (pour Paris), s'il vous plaît.
	um bee·yay ... (poor pa·ree) seel voo play

1st-class	de première classe	der prem·yair klas
2nd-class	de seconde classe	der sgond klas
child's	au tarif enfant	o ta·reef on·fon
one-way	simple	sum·pler
return	aller et retour	a·lay ay rer·toor
student's	au tarif étudiant	o ta·reef ay·tew·dyon

I'd like a/an ... seat.	Je voudrais une place ...
	zher voo·dray ewn plas ...

aisle	côté couloir	ko·tay koo·lwar
nonsmoking	non-fumeur	non few·mer
smoking	fumeur	few·mer
window	côté fenêtre	ko·tay fe·ne·trer

Is there air-conditioning?	Est-qu'il y a la climatisation? es·keel ya la klee·ma·tee·za·syon
Is there a toilet?	Est-qu'il y a des toilettes? es·keel ya day twa·let
15a **How long does the trip take?**	Le trajet prend combien de temps? ler tra·zhay pron kom·byun der tom
15b **Is it a direct route?**	Est-ce que c'est direct? es ker say dee·rekt

Luggage

Where's the baggage claim?	Où est la livraison des bagages? oo ay la lee·vray·zon day ba·gazh
16a My luggage has been damaged.	Mes bagages ont été endommagés. may ba·gazh on tay·tay on·do·ma·zhay
16b My luggage has been lost.	Mes bagages ont été perdus. may ba·gazh on tay·tay per·dew
16c My luggage has been stolen.	Mes bagages ont été volés. may ba·gazh on tay·tay vo·lay

C'est quelle gare?
say kel gar
What station is this?

METROPOLITAIN

© JEAN-BERNARD CARILLET / LONELY PLANET IMAGES

Train

17a What station is this?	C'est quelle gare? *say kel gar*	
17b What's the next station?	Quelle est la prochaine gare? *kel ay la pro·shen gar*	
Does this train stop at (Amboise)?	Est-ce que ce train s'arrête à (Amboise)? *es ker se trun sa·ret a (om·bwaz)*	
Do I need to change trains?	Est-ce qu'il faut changer de train? *es keel fo shon·zhay der trun*	
17c How long will it been delayed?	Combien de retard y aura-t-il? *kom·byun der rer·tar ee o·ra teel*	
Which carriage is for (Bordeaux)?	C'est quelle voiture pour (Bordeaux)? *say kel vwa·tewr poor (bor·do)*	
Which is the dining car?	Où est le wagon-restaurant? *oo ay ler va·gon·res·to·ron*	

Boat

Are there life jackets?	Est-ce qu'il y a des gilets de sauvetage? *es keel ya day zhee·lay der sov·tazh*
What's the sea like today?	L'état de la mer est bon? *lay·ta der la mair ay bon*
I feel seasick.	J'ai le mal de mer. *zhay ler mal der mair*

Taxi

18a I'd like a taxi.	Je voudrais un taxi. zher voo·dray un tak·see
I'd like a taxi tomorrow.	Je voudrais un taxi demain. zher voo·dray un tak·see der·mun
Where's the taxi stand?	Où est la station de taxis? oo ay la sta·syon der tak·see
18b Is this taxi available?	Vous êtes libre? voo zet lee·brer
18c Please put the meter on.	Mettez le compteur en route, s'il vous plaît. me·tay ler kon·ter on root seel voo play
18d How much is it to...?	C'est combien pour aller à...? say kom·byun poor a·lay a...
19a Please take me to (this address).	Conduisez-moi à (cette adresse), s'il vous plaît. kon·dwee·zay·mwa a (set a·dres) seel voo play
How much is the final fare?	C'est combien en tout? say kom·byun on too
19b Please slow down.	Roulez plus lentement, s'il vous plaît. roo·lay plew lont·mon seel voo play
19c Please wait here.	Attendez ici, s'il vous plaît. a·ton·day ee·see seel voo play
Stop at the corner.	Arrêtez-vous au coin de la rue. a·ray·tay·voo o kwun der la rew
19d Please stop here.	Arrêtez-vous ici, s'il vous plaît. a·ray·tay·voo ee·see seel voo play

For other useful phrases, see **directions** (p52), and **money & banking** (p83).

Car & Motorbike

20a	I'd like to hire a car.	Je voudrais louer une voiture. zher voo·dray loo·way ewn vwa·tewr
20b	I'd like to hire a motorbike.	Je voudrais louer une moto. zher voo·dray loo·way ewn mo·to
20c	I'd like to hire a bicycle.	Je voudrais louer un vélo. zher voo·dray loo·way un vay·lo
20d	How much for daily hire?	Quel est le tarif par jour? kel ay ler ta·reef par zhoor
20e	How much for weekly hire?	Quel est le tarif par semaine? kel ay ler ta·reef par ser·men
	Does that include mileage?	Est-ce que le kilométrage est compris? es ker ler kee·lo·may·trazh ay kom·pree
	Does that include insurance?	Est-ce que l'assurance est comprise? es ker la·sew·rons ay kom·preez

🔍 LOOK FOR

Cédez la Priorité	say·day la pree·o·ree·tay	Give Way
Entrée	on·tray	Entrance
Péage	pay·azh	Toll
Sens Interdit	sons un·ter·dee	No Entry
Sens Unique	sons ew·neek	One-Way
Sortie	sor·tee	Exit
Stop	stop	Stop

Can I return it in another city?	Je peux la rendre dans une autre ville? zher per la ron·drer don zewn o·trer veel
What's the speed limit?	Quelle est la vitesse maximale permise? kel ay la vee·tes mak·see·mal per·meez
20f Is this the road to...?	C'est la route pour...? say la root poor...
(How long) Can I park here?	(Combien de temps) Est-ce que je peux stationner ici? (kom·byun der tom) es ker zher per sta·syo·nay ee·see

windscreen
pare-brise m
par·breez

petrol
essence f
es·sons

battery
batterie f
ba·tree

engine
moteur m
mo·ter

headlight
phare m
far

tyre
pneu f
pner

🔊 : LOOK FOR

diesel m	dyay·zel	diesel
au plomb	o plom	leaded
essence f	es·sons	petrol/gas
ordinaire	or·dee·nair	regular
sans plomb	son plom	unleaded

Where's a petrol station?	Où est-ce qu'il y a une station-service? oo es keel ya ewn sta·syon·ser·vees
Please fill it up.	Le plein, s'il vous plaît. ler plun seel voo play
I'd like (20) litres.	Je voudrais (vingt) litres. zher voo·dray (vung) lee·trer
21a I've run out of petrol.	Je suis en panne d'essence. zher swee zon pan de·sons
Please check the oil/water.	Contrôlez l'huile/l'eau, s'il vous plaît. kon·tro·lay lweel/lo seel voo play
21b I have a flat tyre.	Mon pneu est à plat. mom pner ay ta pla
21c I need a mechanic.	J'ai besoin d'un mécanicien. zhay ber·zwun dun may·ka·nee·syun
The car/motorbike has broken down (at Amboise).	La voiture/moto est tombée en panne (à Amboise). la vwa·tewr/mo·to ay tom·bay on pan (a om·bwaz)
I had an accident.	J'ai eu un accident. zhay ew un ak·see·don

Bicycle

Where can I ...?	Où est-ce que je peux ...?	
	oo es ker zher per ...	

have my bike repaired	faire réparer mon vélo	fair ray·pa·ray mon vay·lo
hire a bicycle	louer un vélo	loo·way un vay·lo
leave my bike	laisser mon vélo	lay·say mon vay·lo

Are there any bicycle paths?	Est-ce qu'il y a des pistes cyclables? es keel ya day peest see·kla·bler
Can I take my bike on the train?	Est-ce que ce train accepte les vélos à bord? es ker ser trun ak·sept lay vay·lo a bor
Can we get there by bike?	Peut-on s'y rendre en vélo? pe·ton see ron·dre on vay·lo
Do I have to wear a helmet?	Il faut porter un casque? eel fo por·tay ung kask
Is it within cycling distance?	On peut y aller à vélo? on per tee a·lay a vay·lo
Is there bicycle parking?	Y a-t'il une zone de stationnement pour bicyclettes? ya·teel ewn zon der sta·syon·mon poor bee·see·klet

CULTURE TIP **Bike Bag**
Travelling with a bicycle in France can be made a great deal easier if you have *une housse* ewn hoos – a bike bag. In such a bag, your bike can be transported on any train or coach, including the TGV (high-speed train).

Border Crossing

KEY PHRASES

I'm here for ... days.	Je suis ici pour ... jours.	zher swee zee·see poor ... zhoor
I'm staying at ...	Je loge à ...	zher lozh a ...
I have nothing to declare.	Je n'ai rien à déclarer.	zher nay ryun a day·kla·ray

Passport Control

22a I'm here on business.	Je suis ici pour affaires.	
	zher swee ee·see poor a·fair	
22b I'm here on holiday.	Je suis ici en vacances.	
	zher swee ee·see on va·kons	
I'm here for study.	Je suis ici pour les études.	
	zher swee zee·see poor lay zay·tewd	
I'm here for (two) days.	Je suis ici pour (deux) jours.	
	zher swee zee·see poor (der) zhoor	
I'm here for (two) months.	Je suis ici pour (deux) mois.	
	zher swee zee·see poor (der) mwa	
I'm here for (two) weeks.	Je suis ici pour (deux) semaines.	
	zher swee zee·see poor (der) ser·men	
I'm in transit.	Je suis ici de passage.	
	zher swee zee·see der pa·sazh	
I'm going to (Paris).	Je vais à (Paris).	
	zher vay a (pa·ree)	

🔊 LISTEN FOR

Votre passeport/visa, s'il vous plaît.	vo·trer pas·por/vee·za seel voo play Your passport/visa, please.
Vous voyagez en famille/groupe?	voo vwa·ya·zhay on fa·mee·yer/groop Are you travelling with a family/group?
Vous voyagez seul?	voo vwa·ya·zhay serl Are you travelling on your own?

I'm staying at ...	Je loge à ... zher lozh a ...

At Customs

22c	I have nothing to declare.	Je n'ai rien à déclarer. zher nay ryun a day·kla·ray
22d	I have something to declare.	J'ai quelque chose à déclarer. zhay kel·ker·shoz a day·kla·ray
	That's not mine.	Ce n'est pas à moi. ser nay pa a mwa
	I didn't know I had to declare it.	Je ne savais pas que je devais déclarer cela. zher ner sa·vay pa ker zher der·vay day·kla·ray ser·la

For phrases on payments and receipts, see **money & banking** (p83).

PRACTICAL

BORDER CROSSING

Directions

KEY PHRASES

Where's ...?	Où est-ce qu'il y a...?	oo es keel ya ...
What's the address?	C'est à quelle adresse?	say ta kel adres
How far away is it?	C'est loin?	say lwun

Where's (a bank)?	Où est-ce qu'il y a (une banque)? oo es keel ya (ewn bongk)
I'm looking for (a hotel).	Je cherche (un hôtel). zher shairsh (un o·tel)
23a **Can you show me on the map?**	Pouvez-vous m'indiquer sur la carte? poo·vay·voo mun·dee·kay sewr la kart
23b **What's the address?**	C'est à quelle adresse? say ta kel adres
23c **How do I get there?**	Comment faire pour y aller? ko·mon fair poor ee a·lay
23d **How far away is it?**	C'est loin? say lwun
24a **by bus**	en bus om bews
24b **by taxi**	en taxi on tak·see
24c **by train**	en train on trun

24d on foot	à pied	a pyay
25a Turn at the corner.	Tournez au coin.	toor·nay o kwun
25b Turn at the traffic lights.	Tournez aux feux.	toor·nay o fer
25c Turn left.	Tournez à gauche.	toor·nay a gosh
25d Turn right.	Tournez à droite.	toor·nay a drwat
26a It's far.	C'est loin d'ici.	say lwun dee·see
26b It's near.	C'est près d'ici.	say pray dee·see
26c It's next to ...	C'est à côté de ...	say a ko·tay der ...

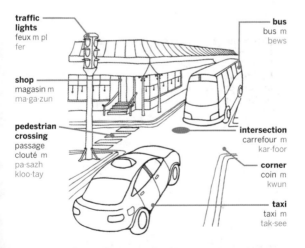

traffic lights
feux m pl
fer

shop
magasin m
ma·ga·zun

pedestrian crossing
passage clouté m
pa·sazh kloo·tay

bus
bus m
bews

intersection
carrefour m
kar·foor

corner
coin m
kwun

taxi
taxi m
tak·see

27a opposite	en face de
	on fas der

27b straight ahead	tout droit
	too drwa

27c here	ici
	ee·see

27d there	là
	la

27e north	nord
	nor

27f south	sud
	sewd

27g east	est
	est

27h west	ouest
	west

It's ...	C'est ...
	say ...

(10) minutes	(dix) minutes	(dee) mee·newt
(100) metres	(cent) mètres	(son) me·trer
behind ...	derrière ...	dair·yair ...
beside ...	à côté de ...	a ko·tay der ...
in front of ...	devant ...	der·von ...
on the corner	au coin	o kwun

Accommodation

KEY PHRASES

Where's a hotel?	Où est-ce qu'on peut trouver un hôtel?	oo es kon per troo·vay un o·tel
Do you have a double room?	Avez-vous une chambre avec un grand lit?	a·vay·voo ewn shom·brer a·vek ung gron lee
How much is it per night?	Quel est le tarif pour une nuit?	kel ay ler ta·reef poor ewn nwee
Is breakfast included?	Le petit déjeuner est-il inclus?	ler per·tee day·zher·nay ay·teel un·klew
What time is checkout?	A quelle heure faut-il libérer la chambre?	a kel er fo·teel lee·bay·ray la shom·brer

Finding Accommodation

28a Where's a guesthouse?	Où est-ce qu'on peut trouver une pension? oo es kon per troo·vay ewn pon·syon	
28b Where's a hotel?	Où est-ce qu'on peut trouver un hôtel? oo es kon per troo·vay un o·tel	
28c Where's a youth hostel?	Où est-ce qu'on peut trouver une auberge de jeunesse? oo es kon per troo·vay ewn o·bairzh der zher·nes	

28d Can you recommend somewhere cheap?	Est-ce que vous pouvez recommander un logement pas cher? es ker voo poo·vay rer·ko·mon·day un lozh·mon pa shair
28e Can you recommend somewhere nearby?	Est-ce que vous pouvez recommander un logement près d'ici? es ker voo poo·vay rer·ko·mon·day un lozh·mon pray dee·see

For responses, see **directions** (p52).

Booking Ahead & Checking In

29a I'd like to book a room, please.	Je voudrais réserver une chambre, s'il vous plaît. zher voo·dray ray·zair·vay ewn shom·brer seel voo play
✂ **Are there rooms?**	Y a t'il des chambres? ya teel day shom·brer
29b I have a reservation.	J'ai une réservation. zhay ewn ray·zair·va·syon
There are (three) of us.	Nous sommes (trois). noo som (trwa)
I'd like to stay for (two) nights.	Je voudrais rester pour (deux) nuits. zher voo·dray res·tay poor (der) nwee
From (2 July) to (6 July).	Du (deux juillet) au (six juillet). dew (der zhwee·yay) o (see zhwee·yay)

Finding a Room

Do you have a ... room?
Avez-vous une chambre ...?
a·vay·voo ewn shom·brer ...

double
avec un grand lit
a·vek ung gron lee

single
à un lit
a un lee

How much is it per ...?
Quel est le prix par ...?
kel ay ler pree par ...

night
nuit
nwee

person
personne
per·son

Is breakfast included?
Le petit déjeuner est-il inclus?
ler per·tee day·zher·nay ay·teel un·klew

Can I see the room?
Est-ce que je peux voir la chambre?
es ker zher per vwar la shom·rer

I'll take it.

Je la prends.
zher la prond

I won't take it.

Je ne la prends pas.
zher ner la prond pa

PRACTICAL ACCOMMODATION

🔊 LISTEN FOR

Désolé, c'est complet.	day·zo·lay say kom·play I'm sorry, we're full.
Combien de nuits?	kom·byun der nwee For how many nights?
Votre passeport, s'il vous plaît.	vo·trer pas·por seel voo play Your passport, please.

Is breakfast included?	Le petit déjeuner est-il inclus? ler per·tee day·zher·nay ay·teel un·klew
Is there parking?	Y a-t'il un parking? ya·teel um par·keeng
30a Do you have a double room?	Avez-vous une chambre avec un grand lit? a·vay·voo ewn shom·brer a·vek ung gron lee
30b Do you have a single room?	Avez-vous une chambre à un lit? a·vay·voo ewn shom·brer a un lee
30c Do you have a twin room?	Avez-vous une chambre avec des lits jumeaux? a·vay·voo ewn shom·brer a·vek day lee zhew·mo
Can I see the room?	Est-ce que je peux voir la chambre? es ker zher per vwar la shom·brer
30d How much is it per night?	Quel est le tarif pour une nuit? kel ay ler ta·reef poor ewn nwee

30e How much is it per person?	Quel est le tarif par personne? kel ay ler tareef par per·son
Do I need to pay upfront?	Est-ce qu'il faut payer par avance? es keel fo pay·yay par a·vons

For other methods of payment, see **money & banking** (p83).

Requests & Queries

31a Where's breakfast served?	Où le petit déjeuner est-il servi? oo ler per·tee day·zher·nay ay·teel sair·vee
31b When's breakfast served?	Quand le petit déjeuner est-il servi? kon ler per·tee day·zher·nay ay·teel sair·vee
31c Please wake me at (seven).	Réveillez-moi à (sept) heures, s'il vous plaît. ray·vay·yay·mwa a (set) er seel voo play
Can I use the ...?	Est-ce que je peux utiliser ...? es ker zher per ew·tee·lee·zay ...

internet	l'Internet	lun·tair·net
kitchen	la cuisine	la kwee·zeen
laundry	la blanchisserie	la blon·shees·ree
telephone	le téléphone	ler tay·lay·fon

31d Is there an elevator?	Vous avez un ascenseur? voo zavay un a·son·ser
31e Is there a safe?	Vous avez un coffre-fort? voo zavay ung ko·frer·for

Do you change money here?	Echangez-vous l'argent ici? ay·shon·zhay·voo lar·zhon ee·see
Do you arrange tours here?	Organisez-vous des excursions ici? or·ga·nee·zay·voo day zeks·kewr·syon ee·see
Is there a message for me?	Vous avez un message pour moi? voo za·vay um me·sazh poor mwa
There's no hot water.	Il n'y a pas d'eau chaude. eel nya pa do shod
I'm locked out of my room.	Je me suis enfermé(e) dehors. m/f zher mer swee zon·fair·may der·or
The (bathroom) door is locked.	La porte (de la salle de bain) est verrouillée. la port (der la sal der bun) ay ver·roo·yay
There's no need to change my sheets.	Il n'y a pas besoin de changer mes draps. eel nee·ya pa be·zwun de shon·zhay may dra
Can I get another blanket?	Est-ce que je peux avoir une autre couverture? es ker zher per a·vwar ewn o·trer koo·vair·tewr
It's too ...	C'est trop ... say tro ...

cold	froid	frwa
dark	sombre	som·brer
expensive	cher	shair
noisy	bruyant	brew·yon
small	petit	per·tee

32a	The air conditioning doesn't work.	La climatisation ne fonctionne pas. la klee·ms·tee·za·syon ner fong·syon pa
32b	The fan doesn't work.	Le ventilateur ne fonctionne pas. ler von·tee·la·ter ner fong·syon pa
32c	The toilet doesn't work.	Les toilettes ne marchent pas. lay twa·let ner marsh pa

TV
télévision f
tay·lay·vee·zyon

fan
ventilateur m
von·tee·la·ter

air-conditioning
climatiseur m
klee·ma·tee·zer

bed
lit m
lee

key
clé f
klay

toilet
toilettes f
twa·let

bathroom
salle de bain f
sal der bun

Answering the Door

Who is it?	Qui est-ce? kee e·ser
Just a moment.	Un instant. un uns·ton
Come in.	Entrez. on·tray
Come back later, please.	Veuillez repasser plus tard, s'il vous plaît. ver·yay rer·pa·say plew tar seel voo play

Checking Out

33a What time is checkout?	A quelle heure faut-il libérer la chambre? a kel er fo·teel lee·bay·ray la shom·brer
Can I have a late checkout?	Pourrai-je régler plus tard? poo·rezh ray·glay plew tar
I'm leaving now.	Je pars maintenant. zher par mun·ter·non
Can you call a taxi for me (for 11 o'clock)?	Pouvez-vous appeler un taxi pour moi (pour onze heures)? poo·vay·voo a·play un tak·see poor mwa (poor on zer)
33b Can I leave my luggage here?	Puis-je laisser mes bagages ici? pweezh lay·say may ba·gazh ee see
I'll be back in (three) days.	Je retournerai dans (trois) jours. zher rer·toor·ner·ray on (trwa) zhur
33c Could I have my deposit, please?	Est-ce que je pourrais avoir ma caution, s'il vous plaît? es ker zher poo·ray a·vwar ma ko·syon seel voo play

33d Could I have my passport, please?	Est-ce que je pourrais avoir mon passeport, s'il vous plaît? es·ker zher poo·ray a·vwar mon pas·por seel voo play
33e Could I have my valuables, please?	Est-ce que je pourrais avoir mes objets de valeur, s'il vous plaît? es·ker zher poo·ray a·vwar may obzhay der valer seel voo play
I had a great stay, thank you.	J'ai fait un séjour magnifique, merci. zhay fay un say·zhoor ma·nyee·feek mair·see
I'll recommend it to my friends.	Je le recommanderai à mes amis. zher ler rer·ko·mon·dray a may za·mee
I'll be back on (Tuesday).	Je retournerai (mardi). zher rer·toor·ner·ray (mar·dee)

Camping

| **34a** Where's a camping ground? | Où est-ce qu'on peut trouver un terrain de camping? oo es kon per troo·vay un tay·run der kom·peeng |
| Where's the nearest ...? | Où est le ... le plus proche? oo ay ler ... ler plew prosh |

shop	magasin	ma·ga·zun
shower facility	bloc sanitaire	blok sa·nee·tair
toilet block	bloc toilettes	blok twa·let

| How much is it per ...? | C'est combien pour chaque ...? say kom·bee·un poor shak ... |

caravan	caravane	ka·ra·van
person	personne	pair·son
tent	tente	tont

Do you have ...?	Avez-vous ...?
	a·vay·voo ...

electricity	l'électricité	lay·lek·tree·see·tay
shower	un bloc	um blok
facilities	sanitaire	sa·nee·tair
a site	un emplacement	un om·plas·mon
tents for hire	des tentes à	day tont a
	louer	loo·ay

Is the water drinkable?	L'eau est-elle potable?
	lo ay·tel po·ta·bler

34b Am I allowed to camp here?	Est-ce qu'on peut camper ici?
	es kon per kom·pay ee·see

Who do I ask to stay here?	Je m'adresse où pour rester ici?
	zher ma·dres oo poor res·tay ee·see

Could I borrow a spade?	Est-ce que je pourrais emprunter une pelle?
	es ker zher poo·ray um·prun·tay ewn pel

Could I borrow a flashlight?	Est-ce que je pourrais emprunter une lampe de poche?
	es ker zher poo·ray um·prun·tay ewn lomp der posh

Renting

Do you have ... for rent?	Avez-vous ... à louer?
	a·vay·voo ... a loo·ay

an apartment	un appartement	un a·par·ter·mon
a house	une maison	ewn may·zon
a room	une chambre	ewn shom·brer
a villa	une villa	ewn vee·la

I'm here about the ... for rent.	Je suis ici au sujet de ... à louer. zher swee zee·see o sew·zhay der ... a loo·ay
How much is it for (one) week?	C'est combien pour (une) semaine? say kom·byun poor (ewn) ser·men
How much is it for (two) months?	C'est combien pour (deux) mois? say kom·byun poor (der) mwa
Is there a bond?	Faut-il verser une caution? fo·teel vair·say ewn ko·syon

Avez-vous un appartement à louer?

a·vay·voo un a·par·ter·mon a loo·ay

Do you have an apartment for rent?

Staying with Locals

Can I stay at your place?	Est-ce que je peux rester chez vous? es ker zher per ray·stay shay voo
I have my own sleeping bag.	J'ai un sac de couchage. zhay un sak der koo·shazh
Is there anything I can do to help?	Y a-t-il quelque chose que je peux faire pour aider? ya·teel kel·ker shoz ker zher per fair poor ay·day
Thanks for your hospitality.	Merci pour votre hospitalité. mair·see poor vo·trer os·pee·ta·lee·tay
Can I ...?	Puis-je ...? pwee·zher ...

bring anything for the meal	apporter quelque chose pour le repas	a·por·tay kel·ker shoz poor ler rer·pa
do the dishes	faire la vaisselle	fair la vay·sel
set the table	mettre la table	me·trer la ta·bler
take out the rubbish	sortir les poubelles	sor·teer lay poo·bel

To compliment your hosts' cooking, see **eating out** (p156). See also **making conversation** (p101).

Shopping

KEY PHRASES

I'd like to buy ...	Je voudrais acheter ...	zher voo·dray ash·tay ...
Can I look at it?	Est-ce que je peux le voir?	es ker zher per ler vwar
Can I try it on?	Puis-je l'essayer?	pwee·zher lay·say·yay
How much is it?	C'est combien?	say kom·byun
That's too expensive.	C'est trop cher.	say tro shair

Looking For ...

Where's (a supermarket)?	Où est-ce qu'il y a (un supermarché)? oo es keel ya (un sew·pair·mar·shay)
35a Where can I buy (a padlock)?	Où puis-je acheter (un cadenas)? oo pweezh ash·tay (un kad·na)

For additional shops and services, see the **dictionary**.

Making a Purchase

35b How much is it?	C'est combien? say kom·byun

✂ How much?	Combien?	kom·byun

I'd like to buy ...	Je voudrais acheter ... zher voo·dray ash·tay ...
35c I'm looking for ...	Je cherche ... zher shayrsh ...

🔊 LISTEN FOR

Non, nous n'en avons pas.	non noo non a·vom pa	No, we don't have any.
Autre chose?	o·trer shoz	Anything else?
Vous désirez?	voo day·zee·ray	Can I help you?
Vous en désirez combien?	voo zon day·zee·ray kom·byun	How much/many do you want?
Je vous l'emballe?	zher voo lom·bal	Would you like it wrapped?

What is this made of?	C'est fabriqué avec quoi? say fa·bree·kay a·vek kwa
I'm just looking.	Je regarde. zher rer·gard
36a Can you write down the price?	Vous pouvez écrire le prix? voo poo·vay ay·kreer ler pree
36b Do you have any others?	Vous en avez d'autres? voo zon a·vay do·trer
36c Can I look at it?	Est-ce que je peux le voir? es ker zher per ler vwar
I don't need a bag, thanks.	Je n'ai pas besoin de sac, merci. zher nay pa ber·zwun der sak mair·see
36d Do you accept credit cards?	Est-ce que je peux payer avec une carte de crédit? es ker zher per pay·yay a·vek ewn kart der kray·dee
36e Do you accept debit cards?	Est-ce que je peux payer avec une carte de débit? es ker zher per pay·yay a·vek ewn kart der day·bee

Making a Purchase

 I'd like to buy ...
Je voudrais acheter ...
zher voo·dray ash·tay ...

 How much is it?
C'est combien?
say kom·byun

OR

 Can you write the price?
Pouvez-vous écrire le prix?
poo·vay·voo ay·kreer ler pree

 Do you accept credit cards?
Est-ce que je peux payer avec une carte de crédit?
es ker zher per pay·yay a·vek ewn kart der kray·dee

 Could I have a ..., please?
Puis-je avoir un ..., s'il vous plaît?
pweezh a·vwar un ... seel voo play

 receipt
reçu
rer·sew

 bag
sac
sak

37a I'd like a bag, please.	Puis-je avoir un sac, s'il vous plaît? pweezh a·vwar un sak seel voo play
37b I'd like a receipt, please.	Puis-je avoir un reçu, s'il vous plaît? pweezh a·vwar un rer·sew seel voo play
Could I have it wrapped?	Pouvez-vous l'envelopper? poo·vay·voo lon·vlo·pay
37c Does it have a guarantee?	Est-ce qu'il y a une garantie? es keel ya ewn ga·ron·tee
Can I have it sent overseas?	Pouvez-vous me l'envoyer à l'étranger? poo·vay·voo mer lon·vwa·yay a lay·tron·zhay
Can I pick it up later?	Je peux passer le prendre plus tard? zher per pa·say ler pron·drer plew tar
37d It's faulty.	C'est défectueux. say day·fek·twer
37e I'd like my change, please.	Je voudrais ma monnaie, s'il vous plaît. zher voo·dray ma mo·nay seel voo play

🔊 LISTEN FOR

occasion f	o·ka·zyon	bargain
chercheur/ chercheuse m/f d'occasions	shair·sher/ shair·sherz do·ka·zyon	bargain hunter
arnaque f	ar·nak	rip-off
soldes m pl	sold	sales

© KRZYSZTOF DYDYNSKI / LONELY PLANET IMAGES

C'est combien?
say kom·byun
How much is it?

37f	I'd like a refund, please.	Je voudrais un remboursement, s'il vous plaît. zher voo·dray un rom·boors·mon seel voo play
37g	I'd like to return this, please.	Je voudrais rapporter ça, s'il vous plaît. zher voo·dray ra·por·tay sa seel voo play

Bargaining

38a	That's too expensive.	C'est trop cher. say tro shair
38b	Can you lower the price?	Vous pouvez baisser le prix? voo poo·vay bay·say ler pree

I'll give you ...	Je vous donnerai ... zher voo don·ray ...
Do you have something cheaper?	Avez-vous quelque chose de moins cher? a·vay·voo kel·ker shoz der mwun shair

Repairs

Can I have my camera repaired here?	Puis-je faire réparer mon appareil photo ici? pwee·zher fair ray·pa·ray mon a·pa·ray fo·to ee·see
Can I have my (sun) glasses repaired here?	Puis-je faire réparer mes lunettes (de soleil) ici? pwee·zher fair ray·pa·ray may lew·net (der so·lay) ee·see
39a When will it be ready?	Quand est-ce que cela sera prêt? kon es ker serla ser·ra pray

Clothes

I'm looking for shoes/ underwear.	Je cherche des chaussures/ sous-vêtements. zher shairsh day sho·sewr/ soo·vet·mon
39b Can I try it on?	Puis-je l'essayer? pwee·zher lay·say·yay
39c My size is (32).	Je fais du (trente-deux). zher fay dew (tront·der)
39d It doesn't fit.	Ce n'est pas la bonne taille. ser nay pa la bon tai
It's too big/small.	C'est trop grand/petit. say tro gron/per·tee

For items of clothing, see the **dictionary**. For sizes, see **numbers & amounts** (p31).

Books & Reading

Is there an English-language section?	Y a-t-il un rayon anglais? ya-teel un ray-yon ong-glay
I'd like a dictionary/newspaper.	Je voudrais un dictionnaire/journal. zher voo-dray un deek-syo-nair/zhoor-nal
Can you recommend a book for me?	Pouvez-vous me conseiller un roman? poo-vay-voo mer kon-say-yay un ro-mon
I'm looking for something by (Albert Camus).	Je cherche quelque chose de (Albert Camus). zher shairsh kel-ker shoz der (al-bair ka-mew)

For more on books and reading, see **interests** (p111).

Music & DVD

I'd like a CD/DVD.	Je voudrais un CD/DVD. zher voo-dray un say-day/day-vay-day
I'd like headphones.	Je voudrais un casque. zher voo-dray ung kask
What's his/her best recording?	Quel est son meilleur enregistrement? kel ay som may-yer on-rer-zhees-trer-mon
Will this work on any DVD player?	Est-ce que ça fonctionne quel que soit le lecteur de DVD? es ker sa fonk-syon kel ker swa ler lek-ter der day-vay-day

74

Video & Photography

PRACTICAL SHOPPING

40a	**Could you develop this film?**	Pouvez-vous développer cette pellicule? poo·vay·voo day·vlo·pay set pay·lee·kewl
40b	**I need a B&W film for this camera.**	J'ai besoin d'une pellicule noir et blanc pour cet appareil. zhay ber·zwun dewn pay·lee·kewl nwar ay blong poor say ta·pa·ray
40c	**I need a colour film for this camera.**	J'ai besoin d'une pellicule couleur pour cet appareil. zhay ber·zwun dewn pay·lee·kewl koo·ler poor say ta·pa·ray
	Can you print digital photos?	Pourriez-vous imprimer des photos numériques? poo·ree·yay·voo um·pree·may day fo·to new·may·reek
	Can you transfer my photos from camera to CD?	Pourriez-vous transférer mes photos de la carte mémoire vers un CD? poo·ree·yay·voo trons·fay·ray may fo·to der la kart may·mwar vair un say·day
	Do you have (a) ... for this camera?	Avez-vous ... pour cet appareil? a·vay·voo ... poor set ta·pa·ray

batteries	des piles	day peel
flash (bulb)	un flash	un flash
memory cards	des cartes mémoire	day kart may·mwar
zoom (lens)	un objectif	un nop·zhek·teef

I need a cable to connect my camera to a computer.	J'ai besoin d'un câble pour connecter mon appareil photo à un ordinateur. zhay ber·zwun dung ka·bler poor ko·nek·tay mong na·pa·ray fo·to a un nor·dee·na·ter
I need a cable to recharge this battery.	J'ai besoin d'un câble pour recharger cette pile. zhay ber·zwun dung ka·bler poor rer·shar·zhay set peel
Can you recharge the battery for my digital camera?	Pourriez-vous recharger les piles de mon appareil numérique? poo·ree·yay·voo rer·shar·zhay lay peel der mon na·pa·ray new·may·reek
I need a video cassette for this camera.	J'ai besoin d'une cassette vidéo pour cet appareil. zhay ber·zwun dewn ka·set vee·day·yo poor set ta·pa·ray
Do you have one-hour processing?	Vous faites le développement en une heure? voo fet ler day·vlop·mon on ewn er
I need a passport photo taken.	J'ai besoin d'une photo d'identité. zhay ber·zwun dewn fo·to dee·don·tee·tay
I'm not happy with these photos.	Je ne suis pas content(e) de ces photos. m/f zher ner swee pa kon·ton(t) der say fo·to

Communications

KEY PHRASES

Where's the local internet cafe?	Il y a un cybercafé près d'ici?	eel ya un see·bair·ka·fay pray dee·see
I'd like to check my email.	Je voudrais consulter mon courrier électronique.	zher voo·dray kon·sewl·tay mong koor·yay ay·lek·tro·neek
I'd like a SIM card for your network.	J'aimerais une carte SIM pour le réseau.	zhem ray ewn kart seem poor ler ray·zo

Post Office

41a	**I want to send a postcard.**	Je veux envoyer une carte postale. zher ver on·vwa·yay ewn kart postal
41b	**I want to send a parcel.**	Je veux envoyer un colis. zher ver on·vwa·yay ung ko·lee
41c	**I want to buy an envelope.**	Je veux acheter une enveloppe. zher ver ash·tay ewn on·vlop
41d	**I want to buy stamps.**	Je veux acheter des timbres. zher ver ash·tay day tum·brer
	Where's the poste restante section?	Où est le service de poste restante? oo ay ler sair·vees der post res·tont

🔊 LISTEN FOR

déclaration en douane f	day·kla·ra·syon on doo·wan	customs declaration
national(e) m/f	na·syo·nal	domestic
fragile	fra·zheel	fragile
international(e) m/f	un·tair·na·syo·nal	international
boîte aux lettres f	bwat o lay·trer	mailbox
adresse postale f	a·dres pos·tal	postal address
code postal m	kod pos·tal	postcode

Is there any mail for me?	Y a-t-il du courrier pour moi? ya·teel dew koor·yay poor mwa
Please send it (to Australia) by ...	Envoyez-le (en Australie) ..., s'il vous plaît. on·vwa·yay·ler (on os·tra·lee) ... seel voo play

airmail	par avion	par a·vyon
express post	en exprès	on neks·pres
registered mail	en recommandé	on rer·ko·mon·day
sea mail	voie maritime	vwa ma·ree·teem

It contains ...	Cela contient ... ser·la kon·tyun ...

Phone

42a Q	**What's your phone number?**	Quel est votre numéro de téléphone? kel ay vo·trer new·may·ro der tay·lay·fon
A	**The number is ...**	Le numéro est ... ler new·may·ro ay ...

🔊 LISTEN FOR

À qui voulez-vous parler?	a kee voo·lay·voo par·lay	Who do you want to speak to?
Désolé, vous vous trompez de numéro.	day·zo·lay voo voo trom·pay der new·may·ro	Sorry, wrong number.
Qui est-ce?	kee ay·ser	Who's calling?
Non, il/elle n'est pas là.	non eel/el nay pa la	No, he/she is not here.
Je peux prendre un message?	zher per pron·drer um may·sazh	Can I take a message?

42b Where's the nearest public phone?	Où est le téléphone public le plus proche? oo ay ler tay·lay·fon pewb·leek ler plew prosh	
I'd like to know the number for ...	Je voudrais connaître le numéro de ... zher voo·dray ko·nay·trer ler new·may·ro der ...	
I want to make a local call.	Je veux passer un appel téléphonique local. zher ver pa·say un na·pel tay·lay·fo·neek lo·kal	
I want to make a call to (Singapore).	Je veux téléphoner avec préavis à (Singapour). zher ver tay·lay·fo·nay a·vek pray·a·vee a (sung·ga·poor)	
I want to make a reverse-charge/collect call.	Je veux téléphoner en PCV. zher ver tay·lay·fo·nay om pay·say·vay	
42c I'd like to buy a phone card.	J'aimerais acheter une télécarte. zhem·ray ash·tay ewn tay·lay·kart	

Do you have international prepaid phone cards?	Avez-vous des cartes téléphoniques prépayées pour les appels à l'international? a·vay·voo day kart tay·lay·fo·neek pray·pay·yay poor lay za·pel a lun·tair·na·syo·nal
How much is a (three)-minute call?	Quel est le prix d'une communication de (trois) minutes? kel ay ler pree dewn ko·mew·nee·ka·syon der (trwa) mee·newt
What's the area/country code for ...?	Quel est l'indicatif pour ...? kel ay lun·dee·ka·teef poor ...

Quel est votre numéro de téléphone?

kel ay vo·trer new·may·ro der tay·lay·fon

What's your phone number?

It's busy.	La ligne est occupée. la lee·nyer ay to·kew·pay
I've been cut off.	J'ai été coupé(e). **m/f** zhay ay·tay koo·pay
The connection is bad.	La ligne est mauvaise. la lee·nyer ay mo·vayz
Can I leave a message?	Je peux laisser un message? zher per lay·say um may·sazh
I'll call back later.	Je rappellerai plus tard. zher ra·pel·ray plew tar
My number is ...	Mon numéro est ... mon new·may·ro ay ...

For telephone numbers, see **numbers & amounts** (p31).

Mobile/Cell Phone

| **42d** I'd like a SIM card for
your network. | J'aimerais une carte SIM
pour le réseau.
zhem·ray ewn kart seem
poor ler ray·zo |
| I'd like a/an ... | Je voudrais ...
zher voo·dray ... |

adaptor plug	une prise multiple	ewn preez mewl·tee·pler
charger for my phone	un chargeur pour mon portable	un shar·zher poor mom por·ta·bler
prepaid recharge card	une carte prépayée rechargeable	ewn kart pray·pay·yay rer·shar·zha·bler

| What are the rates? | Quels sont les tarifs?
kel son lay ta·reef |

The Internet

43a Where's the local internet cafe?	Il y a un cybercafé près d'ici?	eel ya un see·bair·ka·fay pray dee·see
43b I'd like to get internet access.	J'aimerais me connecter à l'internet.	zhem·ray mer ko·nek·tay a lun·tair·net
Is there wireless internet access here?	Avez-vous le wifi ici?	a·vay·voo ler wee·fee ee·see
Can I connect my laptop here?	Est-ce que je peux utiliser mon ordinateur portable ici?	es ker zher per ew·tee·lee·zay mong or·dee·na·ter por·ta·bler ee·see
Do you have headphones (with a microphone)?	Avez-vous un casque (avec un micro)?	a·vay·voo ung kask (a·vek un mee·kro)
43c I'd like to use a printer.	J'aimerais utiliser une imprimante.	zhem·ray ew·tee·lee·zay ewn um·pree·mont
I'd like to ...	Je voudrais ...	zher voo·dray ...

PRACTICAL COMMUNICATIONS

burn a CD	brûler un CD	brew·lay un se·de
check my email	consulter mon courrier électronique	kon·sewl·tay mong koor·yay ay·lek·tro·neek
download my photos	télécharger mes photos	tay·lay·shar·zhay may fo·to
use a scanner	utiliser un scanner	ew·tee·lee·zay un ska·nair
use Skype	utiliser Skype	ew·tee·lee·zay skaip

43d How much is it per hour?	Quel est le tarif horaire? key ay ler ta·reef horayr
How much per page?	C'est combien la page? say kom·byun la pazh
How do I log on?	Comment faire pour me con·necter? ko·mon fair poor mer ko·nek·tay
Can you help me change to English-language preference?	Pouvez-vous m'aider à choisir l'anglais comme langue de préférence? poo·vay·voo may·day a shwa·zeer long·glay kom long der pray·fay·rons
It's crashed.	C'est tombé en panne. say tom·bay om pan
I've finished.	J'ai terminé. zhay tair·mee·nay
Can I connect my ... to this computer?	Est-ce que je peux brancher ... sur cet ordinateur? es ker zher per bron·shay ... sewr set or·dee·na·ter

camera	mon appareil photo	mon na·pa·ray fo·to
iPod/iPhone/ iPad	mon iPod/ iPhone/iPad	mon nai·pot/ nai·fon/nai·pet
media player (MP3)	mon lecteur MP3	mon lek·ter em·pay·trwa
portable hard drive	mon disque dur portable	mon disk dewr por·ta·bler
memory stick	ma clé USB	ma klay ew·es·bay

Money & Banking

KEY PHRASES

How much is it?	Ça fait combien?	sa fay kom·byun
What's the exchange rate?	Quel est le taux de change?	kel ay ler to der shonzh
Where's an ATM?	Où est-ce qu'il y a un guichet automatique?	oo es keel ya un gee·shay o·to·ma·teek

Paying the Bill

Q How much is it?	Ça fait combien? sa fay kom·byun
A It's free.	C'est gratuit. say gra·twee
A It's (12) euros.	C'est (douze) euros. say (dooz) er·ro
Can you write down the price?	Pouvez-vous écrire le prix? poo·vay·voo ay·kreer ler pree
44a There's a mistake in the bill.	Il y a une erreur dans la note. eel ya ewn ay·rer don la not
Do you want to sign or use your PIN?	Vous préférez signer ou utiliser votre code? voo pray·fay·ray see·nyay oo ew·tee·lee·zay vo·trer kod
Do you accept credit/ debit cards?	Est-ce que je peux payer avec une carte de crédit/débit? es ker zher per pay·yay a·vek ewn kart der kray·dee/day·bee

44b **Do you accept travellers cheques?**	Est-ce que je peux payer avec des chèques de voyages?
	es ker zher per pay·yay a·vek day shek der vwa·yazh
I'd like my change, please.	Je voudrais ma monnaie, s'il vous plaît.
	zher voo·dray ma mo·nay seel voo play
I'd like a receipt, please.	Je voudrais un reçu, s'il vous plaît.
	zher voo·dray un rer·sew seel voo play

At the Bank

Where can I arrange a transfer?	Où est-ce que je peux faire un virement?
	oo es ker zher per fair un veer·mon
45a **I'd like to change money.**	Je voudrais changer de l'argent.
	zher voo·dray shon·zhay der lar·zhon
45b **I'd like to withdraw money.**	Je voudrais retirer de l'argent.
	zher voo·dray rer·tee·ray der lar·zhon
45c **I'd like to cash a cheque.**	Je voudrais encaisser un chèque.
	zher voo·dray ong·kay·say un shek
45d **I'd like to change travellers cheques.**	Je voudrais changer des chèques de voyage.
	zher voo·dray shon·zhay day shek der vwa·yazh
Has my money arrived yet?	Est-ce que mon argent est arrivé?
	es ker mon ar·zhon ay ta·ree·vay

🔊 LISTEN FOR

Dans quatre jours ouvrables.	don ka·trer zhoor oo·vra·bler	In four working days.
Il ne vous reste plus d'argent.	eel ner voo rest plew dar·zhon	You have no funds left.
Notez-le.	no·tay·ler	Write it down.
papiers d'identité	pa·pyay dee·don·tee·tay	ID
Signez ici.	see·nyay ee·see	Sign here.

46a What time does the bank open?	À quelle heure ouvre la banque? a kel er oo·vrer la bongk
46b Where's an ATM?	Où est-ce qu'il y a un guichet automatique? oo es keel ya un gee·shay o·to·ma·teek
46c Where's a foreign exchange office?	Où est-ce qu'il y a un bureau de change? oo es keel ya un bew·ro der shonzh
The automatic teller machine took my card.	Le guichet automatique a avalé ma carte de crédit. ler gee·shay o·to·ma·teek a a·va·lay ma kart der kray·dee
I've forgotten my PIN.	J'ai oublié mon code confidentiel. zhay oo·blee·yay mong kod kon·fee·don·syel
46d What's the exchange rate?	Quel est le taux de change? kel ay ler to der shonzh
What's the charge for that?	Quel est le tarif pour cela? kel ay ler ta·reef poor ser·la

Business

KEY PHRASES

I'm attending a conference.	Je participe à une conférence.	zhe par·tee·seep a ewn kon·fay·rons
I have an appointment with ...	J'ai rendez-vous avec ...	zhay ron·day·voo a·vek ...
Can I have your business card?	Pourriez-vous me laisser votre carte de visite?	poo·ree·yay·voo mer lay·say vo·trer kart der vee·zeet

As you'd expect, doing business in France could be the topic of a whole book. As a starting point though, remember to use polite forms when speaking to clients and colleagues (until invited to use the familiar form – see p99) and it's probably best to save cheek-kisses for *very* successful meetings...

I'm attending a ...	Je participe à un/une ... m/f zhe par·tee·seep un/ewn ...
Where's the ...?	Où est le/la ...? m/f oo ay ler/la...

conference	conférence f	kon·fay·rons
course	stage m	stazh
meeting	réunion f	ray·ew·nyon
trade fair	foire commerciale f	fwar ko·mair·syal

I'm with my colleague(s).	Je suis avec mon/mes collègue(s). sg/pl zher swee a·vek mong/may ko·leg

I'm alone.	Je suis seul(e). m/f zher swee serl
I'm with (two) others.	Je suis avec (deux) autres. zher swee a·vek (der) o·trer
I need an interpreter.	J'ai besoin d'un interprète. zhay ber·zwun dun un·tair·pret
Q Can I have your business card?	Pourriez-vous me laisser votre carte de visite? poo·ree·yay·voo mer lay·say vo·trer kart der vee·zeet
A Here's my business card.	Voici ma carte. vwa·see ma kart
I have an appointment with ...	J'ai rendez-vous avec ... zhay ron·day·voo a·vek ...
I'm expecting a fax/call.	Je attends un fax/appel. zha·ton un faks/a·pel
I'd like a connection to the internet.	Je voudrais me connecter à l'Internet. zher voo·dray mer ko·nek·tay a lun·tair·net
I'd like to use a computer.	Je voudrais utiliser un ordinateur. zher voo·dray ew·tee·lee·zay un or·dee·na·ter
Is there a data projector?	Y a-t-il un projecteur data? ya·teel um pro·zhek·ter da·ta
Is there a laser pointer?	Y a-t-il un pointeur laser? ya·teel un pwun·ter la·zair
That went very well.	Ça c'est très bien passé. sa say tray byun pa·say
Thank you for your time/interest.	Merci pour votre temps/attention. mair·see poor vo·trer tom/a·ton·syon

PRACTICAL SIGHTSEEING

Sightseeing

KEY PHRASES

I'd like a guide.	Je voudrais un guide.	zher voo·dray ung geed
Can I take a photo?	Je peux prendre des photos?	zher per pron·drer day fo·to
When's the museum open?	Le musée ouvre à quelle heure?	ler mew·zay oo·vrer a kel er

---

47a I'd like to see ...
J'aimerais voir ...
zhem·ray vwar ...

Do you have information on ... sights?
Avez-vous des renseignements sur les sites ... à visiter?
a·vay·voo day ron·sen·yer·mon sewr lay seet ... a vee·zee·tay

free	gratuits	gra·twee
historical	historiques	ees·to·reek
local	locaux	lo·ko
natural	naturels	na·tew·rel

I'd like to hire a local guide.
Je voudrais faire appel aux services d'un guide.
zher voo·dray fair a·pel o sair·vees dung geed

47b What's that?
Qu'est-ce que c'est?
kes ker say

How old is it?	Ça date de quand?	
	sa dat der kon	
47c Can I take a photo?	Je peux prendre des photos?	
	zher per pron·drer day fo·to	
I'll send you the photograph.	Je vous enverrai la photo.	
	zher voo zon·vay·ray la fo·to	
47d I'd like a local map.	Je voudrais une carte de la région.	
	zher voo·dray ewn kart der la ray·zhyon	
I'd like a/an ...	Je voudrais ...	
	zher voo·dray ...	

audio set	un écouteur	un ay·koo·ter
city map	un plan de la ville	um plon der la veel
guide	un guide	ung geed

Getting In

48a What's the admission charge?	Combien coûte l'entrée?	
	kom·byun koot lon·tray	
48b What time does it open?	Ça ouvre à quelle heure?	
	sa oovrer a kel er	
48c What time does it close?	Ça ferme à quelle heure?	
	sa ferm a kel er	
48d Is there a discount for children?	Il y a une réduction pour les enfants?	
	eel ya ewn ray·dewk·syon poor lay zon·fon	
48e Is there a discount for students?	Il y a une réduction pour les étudiants?	
	eel ya ewn ray·dewk·syon poor lay zay·tew·dyon	

Galleries & Museums

When's the gallery open?	La galerie ouvre à quelle heure? la gal·ree oo·vrer a kel er
When's the museum open?	Le musée ouvre à quelle heure? ler mew·zay oo·vrer a kel er
Q What's in the collection?	Qu'est-ce qu'il y a dans la collection? kes keel·ya don la ko·lek·syon
A It's a/an ... exhibition.	C'est une exposition ... set ewn ek·spo·zee·syon ...
I like the works of ...	J'aime l'œuvre de ... zhem ler·vrer der ...
It reminds me of ...	Cela me rappelle ... ser·la mer ra·pel ...
... art	l'art ... lar ...

contemporary	contemporain	kon·tom·po·run
impressionist	impressionniste	um·pray·syo·neest
modernist	moderniste	mo·dair·neest
Renaissance	de la Renaissance	der la rer·nay·sons

Tours

Are there (organised) walking tours?	Y a-t-il des visites guidées (organisées) à pied? ya·teel day vee·zeet gee·day (or·ga·nee·zay) a pyay

I'd like to do cooking/ language classes.	Je voudrais suivre des cours de cuisine/langue. zher voo·dray swee·vrer day koor der kwee·zeen/long
Can you recommend a tour?	Pouvez-vous me recommander une excursion? poo·vay·voo mer rer·ko·mon·day ewn eks·kewr·syon
49a When's the next day trip?	Quand est la prochaine excursion d'une journée? kon ay la pro·shen eks·kewr·syon dewn zhoor·nay

PRACTICAL SIGHTSEEING

Je peux prendre des photos?
zher per pron·drer day fo·to
Can I take photographs?

PRACTICAL SIGHTSEEING

🔊 LISTEN FOR

Il y a (pas) beaucoup à voir.	eel ya (pa) bo·koo a vwar There is (not) a lot to see.
des escrocs	day zes·kro rip-off merchants
trop de touristes	tro der too·reest too many tourists
Le meilleur moment pour partir c'est en (décembre).	ler may·yer mo·mon poor par·teer se ton (day·som·brer) The best time to go is (December).

Is accommodation included?	Est-ce que le logement est inclus? es ker ler lozh·mon ay tung·klew
49b Is food included?	Est-ce que la nourriture est comprise? es ker la noo·ree·tewr ay kom·preez
49c Is transport included?	Est-ce que le transport est compris? es ker ler trons·por ay kom·preez
49d How long is the tour?	L'excursion dure combien de temps? leks·kewr·syon dewr kom·byun der tom
49e What time should we be back?	On doit rentrer à quelle heure? on dwa ron·tray a kel er
I've lost my group.	J'ai perdu mon groupe. zhay pair·dew mon groop

Senior & Disabled Travellers

KEY PHRASES

I need assistance.	J'ai besoin d'aide.	zhay ber·zwun ded
Is there wheelchair access?	Y a-t-il un accès pour fauteuil roulant?	ya·teel un ak·say poor fo·ter·yer roo·lon
Are there toilets for people with a disability?	Est-ce qu'il y a des toilettes pour handicapés?	es keel ya day twa·let poor on·dee·ka·pay

I have a disability.	Je suis handicapé(e). m/f zher swee zon·dee·ka·pay
I need assistance.	J'ai besoin d'aide. zhay ber·zwun ded
Is there wheelchair access?	Y a-t-il un accès pour fauteuil roulant? ya·teel un ak·say poor fo·ter·yer roo·lon
How many steps are there?	Il y a combien de marches? eel ya kom·byun der marsh
Is there a lift?	Est-ce qu'il y a un ascenseur? es keel ya un a·son·ser
Are guide dogs permitted?	Est-ce que les chiens d'aveugle sont permis? es ker lay shyun da·ver·gler son pair·mee

Is there somewhere I can sit down?	Est-ce qu'il y a un endroit où on peut s'asseoir? es keel ya un on·drwa oo on per sa·swar
Are there toilets for people with a disability?	Est-ce qu'il y a des toilettes pour handicapés? es keel ya day twa·let poor on·dee·ka·pay
Are there rails in the bathroom?	Est-ce qu'il y a des barres dans la salle de bain? es keel ya day bar don la sal der bun
Are there parking spaces for people with a disability?	Est-ce qu'il y a des emplacements pour handicapés? es keel ya day zom·plas·mon poor on·dee·ka·pay
Could you call me a taxi for the disabled?	Pouvez-vous appeler un taxi pour personne handicapée? poo·vay·voo a·play un tak·see poor pair·son on·dee·ka·pay
Could you help me cross this street?	Pouvez-vous m'aider à traverser cette rue? poo·vay·voo may·day a tra·vair·say set rew
crutches	béquilles f pl bay·kee·yer
guide dog	chien d'aveugle m shyun da·ver·gler
ramp	rampe f romp
walking frame	déambulateur m day·om·bew·la·ter
walking stick	canne f kan
wheelchair	fauteuil roulant m fo·ter·yee roo·lon

Travel with Children

KEY PHRASES

Are children allowed?	Les enfants sont permis?	lay zon·fon son pair·mee
Is there a child discount?	Y a-t-il un tarif réduit pour les enfants?	ya teel un ta·reef ray·dwee poor lay zon·fon
Is there a baby change room?	Y a-t-il un endroit pour changer le bébé?	ya teel un on·drwa poor shon·zhay ler bay·bay

I need a ... J'ai besoin ...
zhay ber·zwun ...

child seat	d'un siège-enfant	dun syezh·on·fon
cot	d'un lit pour bébé	dun lee poor bay·bay
potty	d'un pot de bébé	dum po der bay·bay
stroller	d'une poussette	dewn poo·set

Do you sell ...? Avez-vous ...?
a·vay·voo ...

baby wipes	des lingettes pour bébé	day lun·zhet poor bay·bay
disposable nappies/ diapers	des couches jetables	day koosh zher·ta·bler
milk formula	du lait maternisé	dew lay ma·tair·nee·say

PRACTICAL TRAVEL WITH CHILDREN

Is there a/an ...?	Y a-t-il ...? ya teel ...	
baby change room	un endroit pour changer le bébé	un on·drwa poor shon·zhay ler bay·bay
child discount	un tarif réduit pour les enfants	un ta·reef ray·dwee poor lay zon·fon
child-minding service	une garderie	ewn gar·dree
children's menu	un menu pour enfant	un mer·new poor on·fon
creche	une crèche	ewn kresh
high chair	une chaise haute	ewn shay zot

Can I breastfeed here?	Je peux allaiter mon bébé ici? zher per a·lay·tay mon bay·bay ee·see
Are children allowed?	Les enfants sont permis? lay zon·fon son pair·mee
Is this suitable for (six)-year-old children?	Cela convient-il aux enfants de (six) ans? ser·la kon·vyun·teel o zon·fon der (seez) on

If your child is sick, see **health** (p146).

Social

Meeting People

KEY PHRASES

My name is ...	Je m'appelle ...	zher ma·pel ...
I'm from ...	Je suis de ...	zher swee der ...
I work in ...	Je travaille dans ...	zher tra·vai don ...
I'm ... years old.	J'ai ... ans.	zhay ... on
I'm pleased to meet you.	Enchanté(e). m/f	on·shon·tay

Basics

50a Yes.	Oui.	wee
50b No.	Non.	non
50c Please.	S'il vous plaît.	seel voo play
50d Thank you.	Merci.	mair·see
50e You're welcome.	Je vous en prie. pol	zher voo zon pree
50f Excuse me.	Excusez-moi.	ek·skew·zay·mwa
50g Sorry.	Pardon.	par·don

Greetings

A kiss on each cheek remains a common greeting in France, though between men (and when meeting a man or a woman for the first time) a handshake is more usual.

51a Hello.	Bonjour. bon·zhoor
Hi.	Salut. sa·lew
Good morning/afternoon.	Bonjour. bon·zhoor
Good evening/night.	Bonsoir. bon·swar
51b See you later.	À bientôt. a byun·to
51c Goodbye.	Au revoir. o rer·vwar

LANGUAGE TIP

Addressing People

When talking to people familiar to you, or to children, it's usual to use the informal form of you, *tu* tew, rather than the plural or polite form, *vous* voo. The verb ending also changes. Phrases in this book are generally in the polite form, but where you see inf, you have a casual option to use where appropriate. If you feel you've become familiar enough to start using the informal form, you can ask if it's OK to use it:

Est-ce que je peux   es ker zher per
vous tutoyer?   voo tew·twa·yay

See also **personal pronouns** (p19) in the **grammar** chapter.

52a	Q How are you?	Comment allez-vous? pol ko·mon ta·lay·voo
52b	Q How are you?	Ça va? inf sa va
52c	A Good, thanks,	Bien, merci. pol/inf byun mair·see
53a	Q What's your name?	Comment vous appelez-vous? pol ko·mon voo za·play·voo
53b	Q What's your name?	Comment tu t'appelles? inf ko·mon tew ta·pel
53c	A My name is ...	Je m'appelle ... zher ma·pel ...
53d	I'm pleased to meet you.	Enchanté(e). m/f on·shon·tay
	I'd like to introduce you to ...	Je vous présente ... pol zher voo pray·zont ...

✂	This is ...	Voici ...	vwa·see ...

The French can seem very formal about addressing people they don't know. They use *Monsieur* (M), *Madame* (Mme) or *Mademoiselle* (Mlle) where English speakers would use no term of address at all.

54a	Mr	Monsieur mer·syer
54b	Mrs	Madame ma·dam
54c	Miss	Mademoiselle mad·mwa·zel

Making Conversation

Sport and culture are safe areas of conversation and food is a sure way to get a French person speaking, but money talk (prices, income, etc) is best avoided.

Do you speak English?	Parlez-vous anglais? pol	par·lay·voo ong·glay
Do you live here?	Vous habitez ici? pol	voo za·bee·tay ee·see
Q Do you like it here?	Ça vous plaît ici? pol	sa voo play ee·see
A I love it here.	Ça me plaît beaucoup ici.	sa mer play bo·koo ee·see
Where are you going?	Où allez-vous? pol	oo a·lay·voo
What are you doing?	Que faites-vous? pol	ker fet·voo
Can I take a photo (of you)?	Je peux (vous) prendre en photo? pol	zher per (voo) pron·drer on fo·to
That's (beautiful), isn't it?	C'est (beau), non?	say (bo) non

SOCIAL   MEETING PEOPLE

🔊 LISTEN FOR

Ça ira mieux la prochaine fois.	sa ee·ra myer la pro·shen fwa	Better luck next time.
Quelle chance.	kel shons	How lucky!
C'est marrant.	say ma·ron	It's strange.
Pas de problème.	pa der pro·blem	No problem.
Tant pis.	tom pee	Too bad.
Quel dommage.	kel do·mazh	What a shame.
Qu'est-ce qu'il y a?	kes keel ya	What's up?

🔊 LISTEN FOR

Hé!	ay	Hey!
Formidable!	for·mee·da·bler	Great!
D'accord.	da·kor	Sure.
Peut-être.	per·te·trer	Maybe.
Pas question!	pa kay·styon	No way!
(C'est) bien.	(say) byun	(It's) OK.

Q Are you here on holiday?	Vous êtes ici pour les vacances? pol voo zet ee·see poor lay va·kons
A I'm here for a holiday.	Je suis ici pour les vacances. zher swee zee·see poor lay va·kons
A I'm here on business.	Je suis ici pour le travail. zher swee zee·see poor ler tra·vai
A I'm here to study.	Je suis ici pour les études. zher swee zee·see poor lay zay·tewd
This is my first trip (to France).	C'est la première fois que je viens (en France). say la prer·myair fwa ker zher vyun (on frons)
I'm here for ... days/ weeks.	Je reste ici ... jours/semaines. zher rest ee·see ... zhoor/ser·men
How long have been here?	Vous êtes ici depuis quand? pol voo zet ee·see der·pwee kon
Have you ever been (to England)?	Est-ce-que vous êtes déjà allé(e) (en Angleterre)? m/f pol es ker voo zet day·zha a·lay (on ong·gler·tair)
Do you want to come out with me?	Voulez-vous sortir avec moi? pol voo·lay·voo sor·teer a·vek mwa

Nationalities

What part of ... do you come from?	D'où est-ce que vous venez en ...? pol	
	doo es ker voo ver·nay on ...	
	D'où est-ce que tu viens en ...? inf	
	doo es ker tew vyun on ...	
55a **Q** **Where are you from?**	D'où êtes-vous? pol	
	doo ayt voo	
55b **Q** **Where are you from?**	D'où es-tu? inf	
	doo ay tu	
55c **A** **I'm from (Singapore).**	Je suis de (Singapour).	
	zher swee der (sung·ga·poor)	
A **I'm from ...**	Je suis ...	
	zher swee ...	

Australia	d'Australie	dos·tra·lee
Canada	du Canada	dew ka·na·da
England	d'Angleterre	dong·gle·tair
New Zealand	de la	der la
	Nouvelle-Zélande	noo·vel·zay·lond
the USA	des USA	day zew·es·a

For more countries, see the **dictionary**.

Age

56a **Q** **How old are you?**	Quel âge avez-vous? pol	
	kel azh a·vay·voo	
56b **Q** **How old are you?**	Quel âge as-tu? inf	
	kel azh a·tew	
56c **A** **I'm (25) years old.**	J'ai (vingt-cinq) ans.	
	zhay (vung·sungk) on	
A **Too old!**	Trop vieux/vieille! m/f	
	tro vyer/vyay	

SOCIAL MEETING PEOPLE

| Q How old is your son/daughter? | Quel âge a votre fils/fille? pol
kel azh a vo·trer fees/fee·yer |
| A He/She is ... years old. | Il/Elle a ... ans.
eel/el a ... on |

For your age, see **numbers & amounts** (p31).

Occupations & Study

Q What's your occupation?	Vous faites quoi comme métier? pol voo fet kwa kom may·tyay Tu fais quoi comme métier? inf tew fay kwa kom may·tyay
A I'm a chef.	Je suis un(e) cuisinier/cuisinière. m/f zher swee zun/zewn kwee·zee·nyay/kwee·zee·nyair
A I'm a student.	Je suis un(e) étudiant(e). m/f zher swee zun/zewn ay·tew·dyon(t)
A I work in (education).	Je travaille dans (l'enseignement). zher tra·vai don (lon·sen·yer·mon)
A I work in health.	Je travaille dans la santé. zher tra·vai don la son·tay
A I'm retired.	Je suis retraité(e). m/f zher swee rer·tray·tay
A I'm self-employed.	Je suis indépendant(e). m/f zher swee un·day·pon·don(t)
A I'm unemployed.	Je suis chômeur/chômeuse. m/f zher swee sho·mer/sho·merz

Q What are you studying?	Que faites-vous comme études? pol ker fet·voo kom ay·tewd Que fais-tu comme études? inf ker fay·tew kom ay·tewd
A I'm studying engineering.	Je fais des études d'ingénieur. zher fay day zay·tewd dun·zhay·nyer
A I'm studying French.	Je fais des études de français. zher fay day zay·tewd der fron·say

For more occupations and fields of study, see the **dictionary**.

Family

Q Do you have a ...?	Vous avez ...? pol voo·za·vay ... Tu as ...? inf tew a ...
A I have a ...	J'ai ... zhay ...
A I don't have a ...	Je n'ai pas ... zher nay pa ...

boyfriend	un petit ami	um per·tee ta·mee
brother	un frère	un frair
child	un/une enfant m/f	un/ewn on·fon
family	une famille	ewn fa·mee·yer
father	un père	um pair
girlfriend	une petite amie	ewn per·tee ta·mee
husband	un mari	um ma·ree
mother	une mère	ewn mair
partner	un/une partenaire m/f	um/ewn par·ter·nair
sister	une sœur	ewn ser
wife	une femme	ewn fam

57a Q Are you married?	Est-ce que vous êtes marié(e)? m/f pol	es ker voo zet mar·yay
57b Q Are you married?	Est-ce que tu es marié(e)? m/f inf	es ker tew ay mar·yay
57c A I'm married.	Je suis marié(e). m/f	zher swee mar·yay
57d A I'm single.	Je suis célibataire.	zher swee say·lee·ba·tair
A I live with my ...	J'habite avec mon/ma/ mes ... m/f/pl	zha·beet a·vek mon/ma/ may ...
A I live with someone.	Je vis avec quelqu'un.	zher vee a·vek kel·kun

Talking with Children

What's your name?	Comment tu t'appelles?	ko·mon tew ta·pel
How old are you?	Quel âge as-tu?	kel azh a·tew
Do you like school?	L'école te plaît?	lay·kol ter play
Do you learn English?	Tu apprends l'anglais?	tew a·pron long·glay

Farewells

Are you on Facebook?	Es-tu sur Facebook? inf	ay·tew sewr fays·book
58a Q What's your address?	Quel est votre adresse? pol	kel ay vo·trer a·dres

58b Q What's your address?	Quel est ton adresse? inf kel ay ton a·dres
58c A Here's my address.	Voici mon adresse. vwa·see mon a·dres
A Here's my ...	Voici mon ... vwa·see mon ...

email	e-mail	ay·mel
mobile number	numéro de portable	new·may·ro der por·ta·bler
phone number	numéro de téléphone	new·may·ro der tay·lay·fon

If you ever visit (Laos), come and visit us.	Si vous voyagez au (Laos), il faut nous rendre visite. pol see voo vwa·ya·zhay o (low) eel fo noo ron·drer vee·zeet
Keep in touch!	Reste en contact! inf rest ong kon·takt
It's been great meeting you!	Ravi d'avoir fait ta connaissance! inf ra·vee da·vwar fay ta ko·nay·sons

Well-Wishing

Congratulations!	Félicitations! fay·lee·see·ta·syon
Happy birthday!	Joyeux anniversaire! zhwa·yer za·nee·ver·sair
Merry Christmas!	Joyeux Nöel! zhwa·yer no·el
Happy Easter!	Joyeuses Pâques! zhwa·yerz pak

Interests

KEY PHRASES

What do you do in your spare time?	Que fais-tu pendant tes loisirs?	ker fay·tew pon·don tay lwa·zeer
Do you like ...?	Tu aimes ...?	tew em ...
I like ...	J'aime ...	zhem ...

In this section, phrases are given in an informal form. If you're unsure about what this means, see the box, p99.

Common Interests

What do you do in your spare time?	Que fais-tu pendant tes loisirs? ker fay·tew pon·don tay lwa·zeer
59a Q Do you like ...?	Vous aimez ...? pol voo zaymay ...
59b Q Do you like ...?	Tu aimes ...? inf tew em ...
59c A I like ...	J'aime ... zhem ...
59d A I don't like ...	Je n'aime pas ... zher nem pa ...
Q Do you like art?	Tu aimes l'art? tew em lar
A I like hiking.	J'aime la randonnée. zhem la ron·do·nay

For sporting interests, see **sports** (p132) and the **dictionary**.

Music

Do you like to go to concerts?	Aimes-tu aller aux concerts? em·tew a·lay o kon·sair
Do you like to listen to music?	Aimes-tu écouter de la musique? em·tew ay·koo·tay der la mew·zeek
Have you heard the latest album by ...?	As tu entendu le dernier album de ...? a tew on·ton·dew ler dair·nyay al·bom der ...
Which bands do you like?	Quels groupes aimes-tu? kel groop em·tew
Which music do you like?	Quels genres de musique aimes-tu? kel zhon·rer der mew·zeek em·tew
Where can I buy this music?	Où puis-je trouver ce type de musique? oo pweezh troo·vay ser teep der mew·zeek

See also **going out** (p117).

Cinema & Theatre

I feel like going to a movie.	J'aimerais bien voir un film. zhem·ray byun vwar un feelm
I feel like going to a play.	J'aimerais bien voir une pièce de théâtre. zhem·ray byun vwar ewn pyes der tay·a·trer
What's showing at the cinema tonight?	Qu'est-ce qui passe au cinéma ce soir? kes kee pas o see·nay·ma ser swar

Does it have subtitles?	C'est sous-titré? say soo·tee·tray
Is it dubbed in English/French?	Ce film est-il doublé en anglais/français? ser feelm ay·teel doo·blay on ong·glay/fron·say
Is there a cloakroom?	Y a-t-il un vestiaire? ya·teel un vest·yair
Is there an intermission?	Y a-t-il un entracte? ya·teel un on·trakt
Is there a programme?	Y a-t-il un programme? ya·teel un pro·gram
Where can I get a cinema/theatre guide?	Où pourrais-je trouver un programme de cinéma/théâtre? oo poo·rezh troo·vay um pro·gram der see·nay·ma/tay·atrer
Are those seats taken?	Est-ce que ces places sont prises? es ker say plas son preez
Have you seen ...?	As-tu vu ...? a·tew vew ...
Q **Who's in it?**	Qui joue dans ce film? kee zhoo don ser feelm
A **It stars ...**	... est la vedette du film. ... ay la ver·det dew feelm
Q **Did you like the film?**	As-tu aimé le film? a·tew ay·may ler feelm
Q **Did you like the play?**	As-tu aimé la pièce? a·tew ay·may la pyes

A I thought it was excellent.	Je l'ai trouvé excellent. zher lay troo·vay ek·say·lon
A I thought it was long.	Je l'ai trouvé long. zher lay troo·vay long
I don't like (action movies).	Je n'aime pas les (films d'action). zher nem pa lay (feelm dak·syon)
I like (French films).	J'aime (les films français). zhem (lay feelm fron·say)

Reading

Q What kind of books do you read?	Quel genre de livres lis-tu? kel zhon·rer der lee·vrer lee·tew
Q Have you read ...?	As-tu lu ...? a·tew lew ...
A I read ...	Je lis ... zher lee ...
Q Who's your favourite author?	Quel est ton auteur préféré? kel ay ton o·ter pray·fay·ray
Q Which (French) author do you recommend?	Quel auteur (français) peux-tu recommander? kel o·ter (fron·say) per·tew rer·ko·mon·day
A I recommend ...	Je peux recommander ... zher per rer·ko·mon·day ...
Where can I exchange books?	Où puis-je échanger des livres? oo pweezh ay·shon·zhay day lee·vrer

For more on books and reading, see **shopping** (p67).

SOCIAL INTERESTS

Feelings & Opinions

KEY PHRASES

Are you tired?	Vous êtes fatigué? pol	voo zayt fatigay
I'm tired.	J'ai sommeil.	zhay so·may
I'm not tired.	Je n'ai pas sommeil.	zher nay pa so·may
What did you think of it?	Qu'est-ce que vous en avez pensé? pol	kes ker voo zon na·vay pon·say
I thought it was OK.	Je l'ai trouvé bien.	zher lay troo·vay byun
Did you hear about ...?	Vous avez entendu parler de ...? pol	voo za·vay on·ton·dew par·lay der ...

Feelings

Feelings are described with either nouns or adjectives: the nouns use 'have' in French (eg 'I have hunger') and the adjectives use 'be' (like in English).

60a Q **Are you cold?**	Vous avez froid? pol voo zavay fwa
60b A **I'm cold.**	J'ai froid. zhay fwa
60c A **I'm not cold.**	Je n'ai pas froid. zher nay pa fwa

61a Q Are you hot?	Vous avez chaud? pol voo zavay sho
61b A I'm hot.	J'ai chaud. zhay sho
61c A I'm not hot.	Je n'ai pas chaud. zher nay pa sho
62a Q Are you hungry?	Vouz avez faim? pol voo zavay fum ...
62b A I'm hungry.	J'ai faim. zhay fum
62c A I'm not hungry.	Je n'ai pas faim. zher nay pa fum
63a Q Are you thirsty?	Vouz avez soif? pol voo zavay swaf.
63b A I'm thirsty.	J'ai soif. zhay swaf
63c A I'm not thirsty.	Je n'ai pas soif. zher nay pa swaf
64a Q Are you tired?	Vous êtes fatigué? pol voo zayt fatigay
64b A I'm tired.	J'ai sommeil. zhay so·may
64c A I'm not tired.	Je n'ai pas sommeil. zher nay pa so·may
65a Q Are you OK?	Ça va? inf sa va
65b A I'm OK.	Je vais bien. zher vay byun
65c A I'm not OK.	Je ne vais pas bien. zher ner vay pa byun

If you're not feeling well, see **health** (p146).

SOCIAL FEELINGS & OPINIONS

114

SOCIAL FEELINGS & OPINIONS

🔊 LISTEN FOR

un peu	um per	a little
Je suis un peu triste.	zher swee zum per treest	I'm a little sad.
vraiment	vray·mon	really
Je suis vraiment navré.	zher swee vray·mon na·vray	I'm really sorry.
très	tray	very
Je me sens très vulnérable.	zher mer son tray vewl·nay·ra·bler	I feel very vulnerable.

Opinions

❓ **What did you think of it?**	Qu'est-ce que vous en avez pensé? pol kes ker voo zon na·vay pon·say
❓ **Did you like it?**	Cela vous a plu? pol ser·la voo za plew
💬 **I thought it was ...**	Je l'ai trouvé ... zher lay troo·vay ...
💬 **It's ...**	C'est ... say ...

beautiful	beau	bo
better	mieux	myer
great	formidable	for·mee·da·bler
horrible	horrible	o·ree·bler
OK	bien	byun
strange	étrange	ay·tronzh
weird	bizarre	bee·zar
worse	pire	peer

Politics & Social Issues

Q Who do you vote for?
Pour qui votez-vous? pol
poor kee vo·tay·voo

A I support the ... party.
Je soutiens le parti ...
zher soo·tyun ler par·tee ...

communist	communiste	ko·mew·neest
conservative	conservateur	kon·sair·va·ter
democratic	démocrate	day·mo·krat
green	écologiste	ay·ko·lo·zheest
labour	travailliste	tra·va·yeest
republican	républicain	ray·pew·blee·kun
social	social	so·syal
democratic	démocrate	day·mo·krat
socialist	socialiste	so·sya·leest

Did you hear about ...?	Vous avez entendu parler de ...? pol voo za·vay on·ton·dew par·lay der ...
How do people feel about ...?	Qu'est-ce qu'on pense de ...? kes kom pons der ...
Q Do you agree with it?	Êtes-vous d'accord avec cela? pol et·voo da·kor a·vek ser·la
A I (don't) agree with ...	Je (ne) suis (pas) pour .... zher (ner) swee (pa) poor ...
Q Are you in favour of (it)?	Êtes-vous pour (cela)? pol et·voo poor (ser·la)
A I'm against (it).	Je suis contre (cela). zher swee kon·trer (ser·la)
economy	économie f ay·ko·no·mee
environment	environnement m on·vee·ron·mon

SOCIAL   FEELINGS & OPINIONS

116

SOCIAL FEELINGS & OPINIONS

> **CULTURE TIP**
> **Famous Quotes**
> **'Comment est-il possible de gouverner un pays qui produit plus de trois cent soixante-dix fromages différents?'** (Charles de Gaulle)
> ko·mon ay·teel po·see·bler der goo·vair·nay un pay·ee kee pro·dwee plews der trwa·son swa·son·dees fro·mazh dee·fay·ron
> 'How is it possible to govern a country that produces more than 370 different cheeses?'

immigration	immigration f ee·mee·gra·syon
the war in ...	la guerre f en ... la gair on ...

The Environment

Is there an environmental problem here?	Y a-t-il un problème d'environnement ici? ya·teel un pro·blem don·vee·ron·mon ee·see
Is this a protected forest/species?	C'est une forêt/espèce protégée? set ewn fo·ray/es·pes pro·tay·zhay
Where can I recycle this?	Où est-ce que je peux recycler ceci? oo es ker zhe per re·see·klay se·see
climate change	changement climatique m shon·zhe·mon klee·ma·teek
pollution	pollution f po·lew·syon
recycling	recyclage m rer·see·klazh

Going Out

SOCIAL GOING OUT

KEY PHRASES

What's on tonight?	Qu'est-ce qu'on joue ce soir?	kes kon zhoo ser swar
What time shall we meet?	On se retrouve à quelle heure?	on ser rer·troov a kel er
Where will we meet?	On se retrouve où?	on ser rer·troov oo

In this section, phrases are given in an informal form. If you're unsure about what this means, see the box, p99.

Where to Go

What's on today?	Qu'est-ce qu'on joue aujourd'hui? kes kon zhoo o·zhoor·dwee
What's on tonight?	Qu'est-ce qu'on joue ce soir? kes kon zhoo ser swar
What's on this weekend?	Qu'est-ce qu'on joue ce week-end? kes kon zhoo ser week·end
Where are the ...?	Où sont les ...? oo son lay ...

clubs	clubs	klerb
discos	discothèques	dees·ko·tek
gay venues	boîtes gaies	bwat gay
places to eat	restaurants	res·to·ron
pubs	pubs	perb

	Is there a local entertainment/film guide?	Y a-t-il un programme des spectacles/films? ya·teel un pro·gram day spek·ta·kler/feelm
66a	**Where can I find a gay venue?**	Où sont les boîtes gaies? oo son lay bwat gay
	What's there to do in the evenings?	Qu'est-ce qu'on peut faire le soir? kes kon per fair ler swar
66b	**Where can I find a pub?**	Où est-ce qu'il y a un pub? oo es keel ya un pub
66c	**I feel like going to a concert.**	Je voudrais aller à un concert. zher voo·dray a·lay a ung kon·sair
66d	**I feel like going to the movies.**	Je voudrais aller voir un film. zher voo·dray a·lay vwar un feelm
66e	**I feel like going to a party.**	Je voudrais aller à une fête. zher voo·dray a·lay a ewn fayt
66f	**I feel like going to the theatre.**	Je voudrais aller au théâtre. zher voo·dray a·lay o tay·a·trer

Invitations

What are you doing right now?	Que fais-tu maintenant? ker fay·tew mun·ter·non
What are you doing this evening?	Que fais-tu ce soir? ker fay·tew ser swar
What are you doing this weekend?	Que fais-tu ce week-end? ker fay·tew ser week·end

Would you like to go?	Tu voudrais aller? tew voo·dray a·lay
Would you like to go for a coffee?	Tu voudrais aller boire un café? tew voo·dray a·lay bwar ung ka·fay
My round.	C'est ma tournée. say ma toor·nay
Do you know a good restaurant?	Tu connais un bon restaurant? tew ko·nay un bon res·to·ron
Do you want to come to the concert with me?	Tu veux aller au concert avec moi? tew ver a·lay o kon·sair a·vek mwa
We're having a party.	Nous allons faire une fête. noo za·lon fair ewn fet
You should come.	Tu dois venir. tew dwa ver·neer

SOCIAL GOING OUT

Responding to Invitations

Sure!	D'accord! da·kor
Yes, I'd love to.	Je viendrai avec plaisir. zher vyun·dray a·vek play·zeer
Where shall we go?	Où aller? oo a·lay
No, I'm afraid I can't.	Non, désolé, je ne peux pas. non day·zo·lay zher ner per pa
What about tomorrow?	Et demain? ay der·mun

Arranging to Meet

Q **What time shall we meet?**	On se retrouve à quelle heure? on ser rer·troov a kel er
A **Let's meet at (eight o'clock).**	On peut se retrouver à (huit heures). on per ser rer·troo·vay a (wee ter)
Q **Where will we meet?**	On se retrouve où? on ser rer·troov oo
A **Let's meet at the (entrance).**	On peut se retrouver devant (l'entrée). on per ser rer·troo·vay der·von (lon·tray)
I'll pick you up (at seven).	Je viendrai te chercher (à sept heures). zher vyun·dray ter shair·shay (a set er)
If I'm not there by (nine), don't wait for me.	Si je ne suis pas là avant (neuf heures), ne m'attends pas. see zher ner swee pa la a·von (ner ver) ner ma·ton pa
I'm looking forward to our meeting.	J'attends notre rendez-vous avec impatience. zha·ton no·trer ron·day·voo a·vek um·pa·syons
Agreed/OK!	D'accord! da·kor
I'll see you then.	Allez, salut! a·lay sa·lew
See you later.	À plus tard. a plew tar
See you tomorrow.	À demain. a der·mun

Sorry I'm late.	Désolé d'être en retard.
	day·zo·lay de·trer on rer·tar
Never mind.	Ce n'est pas grave.
	ser nay pa grav

Nightclubs & Bars

Are there any nightclubs here?	Est-ce qu'il y a des boîtes de nuit ici?
	es keel ya day bwat der nwee ee·see
Where can we go (salsa) dancing?	Où est-ce qu'on peut danser (la salsa)?
	oo es kom per don·say (la sal·sa)

Je m'amuse bien!
zher ma·mewz byun
I'm having a great time!

SOCIAL   GOING OUT

What time does the show start?	Le spectacle commence à quelle heure? ler spek·ta·kler ko·mons a kel er
How do I get there?	Comment y aller? ko·mon ee a·lay
What's the cover charge?	C'est combien le couvert? say kom·byun ler koo·vair
Come on!	Allez! a·lay
Q What type of music do you like?	Quel genre de musique aimes-tu? kel zhon·rer der mew·zeek em·tew
A I like (reggae).	J'aime (le reggae). zhem (ler ray·gay)
This place is great!	C'est formidable ici! say for·mee·da·bler ee·see
I'm having a great time!	Je m'amuse bien! zher ma·mewz byun
I don't like the music here.	Je n'aime pas la musique ici. zher nem pa la mew·zeek ee·see
Let's go somewhere else.	Allons ailleurs. a·lon za·yer
Do you want to go closer to the stage?	Tu veux bien t'approcher de la scène? tew ver byun ta·pro·shay der la sen
Do you want to sit at the front?	Tu veux bien t'asseoir au premier rang? tew ver byun ta·swar o prer·myay rong

Do you want to sit at the back?	Tu veux bien t'asseoir au dernier rang? tew ver byun ta·swar o dair·nyay rong
What a fantastic concert/ group!	Quel concert/groupe fantastique! kel kon·sair/groop fon·ta·steek
What a great singer!	Quel(le) chanteur/chanteuse formidable! m/f kel shon·ter/shon·terz for·mee·da·bler

For more on bars, drinks and partying, see **eating out** (p156).

Drugs

I don't take drugs.	Je ne touche pas à la drogue. zher ner toosh pa a la drog
I take ... occasionally.	Je prends du ... occasionnellement. zher pron dew ... o·ka·zyo·nel·mon
Do you want to have a smoke?	Tu veux fumer? tew ver few·may
Do you have a light?	Vous avez du feu? voo za·vay dew fer

If the police are talking to you about drugs, see **police** (p144), for useful phrases.

Romance

KEY PHRASES

Do you want to go out with me?	Veux-tu sortir avec moi?	ver·tew sor·teer a·vek mwa
Do you love me?	Tu m'aimes?	tew mem
I love you.	Je t'aime.	zher tem
Leave me alone!	Laissez-moi tranquille!	lay·say·mwa trong·keel

In this section, phrases are given in an informal form – if you're unsure about what this means, see the box, p99.

Asking Someone Out

Q **Would you like to do something?**	Est-ce que tu aimerais faire quelque chose? es ker tew em·ray fair kel·ker shoz
A **Yes, I'd love to.**	Oui, j'aimerais bien. wee zhem·ray byun
A **I'm sorry, I can't.**	Non, je suis désolé(e), je ne peux pas. **m/f** non zher swee day·zo·lay zher ner per pa
A **No chance!**	Jamais de la vie! zha·may der la vee

Pick-Up Lines

You look like someone I know.	Tu me fais penser à quelqu'un que je connais. tew mer fay pon·say a kel·kun ker zher ko·nay
Would you like a drink?	Si on buvait quelque chose? see on bew·vay kel·ker shoz
What star sign are you?	Tu es de quel signe? tew ay der kel see·nyer
Shall we get some fresh air?	Nous allons prendre l'air? noo za·lon pron·drer lair
You're a fantastic dancer.	Tu danses vraiment bien. tew dons vray·mom byun
Do you come here often?	Tu viens ici souvent? tew vyun ee·see soo·von
Can I ...?	Puis-je ...? pweezh ...

dance with you	danser avec toi	don·say a·vek twa
see you again	te revoir	ter rer·vwar
sit here	m'asseoir ici	ma·swar ee·see
take you home	te raccompagner	ter ra·kom·pa·nyay

Do you have a boyfriend?	Est-ce que tu as un petit ami? es ker tew a um per·tee ta·mee
Do you have a girlfriend?	Est-ce que tu as une petite amie? es ker tew a ewn per·teet a·mee
Do you have a light?	Est-ce que tu as du feu? es ker tew a dew fer

SOCIAL

ROMANCE

You have (a) beautiful ...	Tu as ...	
	tew a ...	

body	un beau corps	um bo kor
eyes	de beaux yeux	der bo zyer
hands	de belles mains	der bel mun
laugh	un beau sourire	um bo soo·reer
personality	une belle personnalité	ewn bel pair·so·na·lee·tay

Will you take me home?	Tu veux bien me ramener à la maison? tew ver byun mer ram·nay a la may·zon
Do you want to come inside for a while?	Tu veux entrer un instant? tu ver on·tray un un·ston

Rejections

Excuse me, I have to go now.	Excusez-moi, je dois partir maintenant. ek·skyew·zay·mwa zher dwa par·teer mun·ter·non
No, thank you.	Non, merci. non mair·see
I'd rather not.	Je n'ai pas très envie. zher nay pa tray zon·vee
Your ego is out of control!	Tu es complètement imbu(e) de toi-même! m/f tew ay kom·plet·mon um·bew der twa·mem
Leave me alone!	Laissez-moi tranquille! lay·say·mwa trong·keel
Don't touch me!	Ne me touchez pas! ner mer too·shay pa

> **LANGUAGE TIP**
>
> **Swear Word Warning**
> The word for 'a kiss' in French is *un baiser* un bay·zay, but the *un* word is the key here – without it, the word becomes a certain strong swear word. The verb 'kiss' is *embrasser* om·bra·say.

I'm not interested.	Ça ne m'intéresse pas. sa ner mun·tay·res pa
Get lost!	Va te faire voir! va ter fair vwar
You're disturbing me.	Tu me gênes. tew mer zhen

Getting Closer

Q Do you like me too?	Tu m'aimes aussi? tew mem o·see
A I like you very much.	Je t'aime beaucoup. zher tem bo·koo
You're very attractive.	Tu es très beau/belle. m/f tew ay tray bo/bel
I'm interested in you.	Je m'intéresse vraiment à toi. zher mun·tay·res vray·mon a twa
You're great.	Tu es formidable. tew ay for·mee·da·bler
Can I kiss you?	Je peux t'embrasser? zher per tom·bra·say

Sex

I want to make love to you.	Je veux faire l'amour avec toi. zher ver fair la·moor a·vek twa
Let's use (a condom).	On va utiliser (un préservatif). on va ew·tee·lee·zay (um pray·zair·va·teef)
I think we should stop now.	Il faut arrêter maintenant. eel fo a·ray·tay mun·ter·non
Let's go to bed!	On va se coucher. on va ser koo·shay
Kiss me.	Embrasse-moi. om·bras·mwa
I want you.	Je te veux. zher ter ver
Q Do you like this?	Ça te plaît? sa ter play
A I like that.	J'aime ça. zhem sa
A I don't like that.	Je n'aime pas ça. zher nem pa sa
That's great.	C'est sensationnel. say son·sa·syo·nel
Stop!	Arrête! a·ret
Don't stop!	N'arrête pas! na·ret pa
Oh yeah!	Chouette alors! shwet a·lor

LANGUAGE TIP

Masculine & Feminine
In this book, masculine forms appear before the feminine forms. If a letter has been added to denote the feminine form (often an -*e*), it will appear in parentheses. If the change involves more than the addition of a letter, two words are given, separated by a slash. For more information, see **gender** in the **grammar** chapter (p17).

Easy tiger!	Vas-y mollo! va·zee mo·lo
That was amazing/weird.	C'était excellent/bizarre. say·tay ek·say·lon/bee·zar

Love

Q Do you love me?	Tu m'aimes? tew mem
A I love you.	Je t'aime. zher tem
Do you want to go out with me?	Veux-tu sortir avec moi? ver·tew sor·teer a·vek mwa
Let's move in together!	Vivons ensemble! vee·von on·som·bler
Will you marry me?	Veux-tu m'épouser? ver·tew may·poo·zay

Beliefs & Culture

KEY PHRASES

What's your religion?	Quelle est votre/ta religion? pol/inf	kel ay vo·trer/ta rer·lee·zhyon
I'm ...	Je suis ...	zher swee ...
I'm sorry, it's against my religion.	Je m'excuse, c'est contraire à ma religion.	zher mek·skewz say kon·trair a ma rer·lee·zhyon

Religion

Q What's your religion?	Quelle est votre/ta religion? pol/inf kel ay vo·trer/ta·ray·lee·zhyon
A I'm ...	Je suis ... zher swee ...
A I'm not ...	Je ne suis pas ... zher ner swee pa ...

agnostic	agnostique	ag·no·steek
atheist	athée	a·tay
practising	pratiquant(e) m/f	pra·tee·kon(t)
religious	croyant(e) m/f	krwa·yon(t)

For religions, see the **dictionary**.

I (don't) believe in God.	Je (ne) crois (pas) en Dieu. zher (ner) krwa (pa) on dyer

Where can I attend mass?	Où est-ce qu'on peut aller à la messe? oo es kom per a·lay a la mes
Where can I attend a service?	Où est-ce qu'on peut aller à l'office? oo es kom per a·lay a lo·fees
Where can I pray?	Où est-ce qu'on peut faire ses dévotions? oo es kom per fair say day·vo·syon

Cultural Differences

Is this a local custom?	Est-ce que c'est une coutume locale? esk ker say·tewn koo·tewm lo·kal
I didn't mean to do anything wrong.	Mes propos n'avaient rien de blessant. may pro·po na·vay ryun der blay·son
I'll try it.	Je vais essayer ça. zher vay ay·say·yay sa
I'd rather not join in.	Je ne veux pas participer. zher ner ver pa par·tee·see·pay
I'm sorry, it's against my culture/religion.	Je m'excuse, c'est contraire à ma culture/religion. zher mek·skewz say kon·trair a ma kewl·tewr/rer·lee·zhyon
This is very different/ interesting.	Ceci est très différent/ intéressant. ser·see ay tray dee·fay·ron/ zun·tay·ray·son

For phrases relating to cultural differences and food, see **vegetarian & special meals** (p174).

SOCIAL BELIEFS & CULTURE

SOCIAL SPORTS

Sports

Which sport do you play?	Quel sport faites-vous? pol	kel spor fet·voo
Who's your favourite team?	Quelle est votre équipe favorite? pol	kel ay vo·trer ay·keep fa·vo·reet
What's the score?	Quel est le score?	kel ay ler skor

Sporting Interests

Do you like sport?	Vous aimez le sport? voo zay·may ler spor
I prefer watching sport.	Je préfère regarder le sport. zher pray·fair rer·gar·day le spor
Which sport do you play?	Quel sport faites-vous? pol kel spor fet·voo
Q Which sports do you like?	Quels sports aimez-vous? pol kel spor ay·may·voo
A I like (football/soccer).	J'aime (le football). zhem (ler foot·bol)
Who's your favourite sportsperson?	Quel(le) est votre sportif/ sportive favori(te)? m/f pol kel ay vo·trer spor·teef/ spor·teev fa·vo·ree(t)
Who's your favourite team?	Quelle est votre équipe favorite? pol kel ay vo·trer ay·keep fa·vo·reet

For more sports, see the **dictionary**.

Going to a Game

Would you like to go to a game?	Vous voulez aller voir un match? pol voo voo·lay a·lay vwar um matsh
Who's playing?	Qui joue? kee zhoo
Who's winning?	Qui est en train de gagner? kee ay ton trun der ga·nyay
🅠 **What was the final score?**	Quel est le score final? kel ay ler skor fee·nal
🅐 **It was a draw.**	Ils ont fait match nul. eel zon fay matsh newl
That was a good/bad game.	C'était vraiment un bon/mauvais match. say·tay vray·mon um bon/mo·vay matsh
What's the score?	Quel est le score? kel ay ler skor

Playing Sport

🅠 **Do you want to play?**	Vous voulez jouer? pol voo voo·lay zhoo·ay
🅐 **Yes, that'd be great.**	Oui, ça serait excellent. wee sa se·ray tek·say·lon
🅐 **I have an injury.**	Je suis blessé. zher swee blay·say
Can I join in?	Je peux participer? zher per par·tee·see·pay
Your/My point.	Un point pour vous/moi. pol um pwun poor voo/mwa

SOCIAL

SPORTS

SOCIAL SPORTS

match nul	matsh newl	draw/even
égalité	ay·ga·lee·tay	tie
balle de match	bal der matsh	match point
zéro	zay·ro	nil/zero

Kick/Pass it to me!	Passez-le-moi! pol pa·say·ler·mwa
Thanks for the game.	Merci d'avoir joué avec moi. mair·see da·vwar zhoo·ay a·vek mwa
Where's the best place to jog around here?	Où peut-on faire du jogging? oo per·ton fair dew zho·geeng
Where's a nearby gym?	Où y a t-il un gymnase par ici? oo ya teel un zheem·naz par ee·see
Where's a nearby swimming pool?	Où y a t-il une piscine par ici? oo ya teel ewn pee·seen par ee·see
Where's a nearby tennis court?	Où y a t-il un terrain de tennis par ici? oo ya teel un tay·run der tay·nees par ee·see
Can I rent a locker, please?	Puis-je louer un casier, s'il vous plaît? pol pweezh loo·way ung ka·zyay seel voo play
Can I see the gym, please?	Puis-je voir le gymnase, s'il vous plaît? pol pweezh vwar ler zheem·naz seel voo play

What's the charge per ...?	Quel est le prix ...?	kel ay ler pree ...

day	par jour	par zhoor
game	de la séance	der la say·ons
hour	de l'heure	der ler
visit	de la visite	der la vee·zeet

Can I hire a bicycle?	Puis-je louer un vélo?
	pwee·zher loo·way un vay·lo
Can I hire a tennis court?	Puis-je louer un terrain de tennis?
	pwee·zher loo·way un tay·run der tay·nees
Can I hire a racquet?	Puis-je louer une raquette?
	pwee·zher loo·way ewn ra·ket
Where are the changing rooms?	Où sont les vestiaires?
	oo son lay vays·tyair

Cycling

Where does the race finish?	Où finit la course?
	oo fee·nee la koors
Where does it pass through?	Ça passe par où?
	sa pas par oo
Who's winning?	Qui est en train de gagner?
	kee ay ton trun der ga·nyay
Is today's leg very hard?	Est-ce que l'étape d'aujourd'hui est très difficile?
	es ker lay·tap do·zhoor·dwee ay tray dee·fee·seel

SOCIAL

SPORTS

cyclist	cycliste m&f	
	see·kleest	
hill stage	fortes côtes f	
	fort kot	
leg (in race)	étape f	
	ay·tap	
time trial	course contre la montre f	
	koors kon·trer la mon·trer	
winner	gagnant(e) m/f	
	ga·nyon(t)	
the yellow jersey	le maillot jaune m	
	ler ma·yo zhon	

For phrases on getting around by bicycle, see **transport** (p38).

Soccer

He's a great (player).	C'est un (joueur) formidable.
	say tun (zhoo·er)
	for·mee·da·bler
Which team is at the top of the league?	Quelle équipe est en tête du championnat?
	kel ay·keep ay ton tet dew
	shom·pyo·na

🔊 LISTEN FOR

corner m	kor·nair	corner
faute f	fot	foul
coup franc m	koo frong	free kick
gardien de but m	gar·dyun der bewt	goalkeeper
hors jeu m	or zher	offside
penalty m	pay·nal·tee	penalty

Outdoors

KEY PHRASES

Do we need a guide?	A-t-on besoin d'un guide?	a·tom ber·zwun dung geed
I'm lost.	Je suis perdu(e). m/f	zher swee pair·dew
What's the weather like?	Quel temps fait-il?	kel tom fay·teel

Hiking

Where can I ...?　　Où est-ce que je peux ...?
oo es ker zher per ...

buy supplies	acheter des provisions	ash·tay day pro·vee·zyon
find out about hiking trails	me renseigner sur les sentiers à suivre	mer ron·se·nyay sewr lay son·tyay a swee·vrer
find someone who knows this area	trouver quelqu'un qui connaît la région	troo·vay kel·kun kee ko·nay la ray·zhyon
get a map	trouver une carte	troo·vay ewn kart
hire hiking gear	louer du matériel de randonnée	loo·way dew ma·tay·ryel der ron·do·nay

Do I need to take food?　　Est-ce qu'il faut apporter des vivres?
es keel fo a·por·tay day vee·vrer

Do I need to take water?	Est-ce qu'il faut apporter de l'eau? es keel fo a·por·tay der lo
How long is the trail?	Le chemin fait combien de kilomètres? ler shmun fay kom·byun der kee·lo·me·trer
Do we need a guide?	A-t-on besoin d'un guide? a·tom ber·zwun dung geed
Are there guided treks?	Est-ce qu'il y a des marches organisées? es keel ya day marsh or·ga·nee·zay
Is it safe?	C'est sans danger? say son don·zhay
Is there a hut there?	Y a-t-il une cabane là-bas? ya·teel ewn ka·ban la·ba
When does it get dark?	À quelle heure fait-il nuit? a kel er fay·teel nwee
Where's the nearest village?	Où est le village le plus proche? oo ay ler vee·lazh ler plew prosh
Which is the easiest route?	Quel est l'itinéraire le plus facile à suivre? kel ay lee·tee·nay·rair ler plew fa·seel a swee·vrer
Which is the most interesting route?	Quel est l'itinéraire le plus intéressant? kel ay lee·tee·nay·rair ler plew zun·tay·ray·son
Where have you come from?	Vous êtes parti d'où? pol voo zet par·tee doo

How long did it take?	Ça a pris combien de temps? sa a pree kom·byun der tom
Does this path go to ...?	Est-ce que ce sentier mène à ...? es ker ser son·tyay men a ...
Can we go through here?	On peut passer par ici? on per pa·say par ee·see
Is the water OK to drink?	Est-ce que l'eau est potable? es ker lo ay po·ta·bler
I'm lost.	Je suis perdu(e). m/f zher swee pair·dew

At the Beach

Where's the nearest beach?	Où est la plage la plus proche? oo ay la plazh la plew prosh
Is it safe to dive/swim here?	On peut plonger/nager sans danger? on per plon·zhay/na·zhay son don·zhay
What time is high/low tide?	À quelle heure est la marée haute/basse? a kel er ay la ma·ray ot/bas
How much for a chair?	Combien coûte une chaise longue? kom·byun koot ewn shez long·ger

🔍 **LOOK FOR**

| Baignade Interdite! | be·nyad un·ter·deet | No Swimming! |

SOCIAL OUTDOORS

🔊 LISTEN FOR

Attention au courant sous-marin.	a·ton·syon o koo·ron soo·ma·run Be careful of the undertow.
C'est dangereux.	say don·zhrer It's dangerous.

How much for a hut?	Combien coûte une cabine de bain? kom·byun koot ewn ka·been der bun
How much for an umbrella?	Combien coûte un parasol? kom·byun koot um pa·ra·sol

Weather

67a Q	What's the weather like?	Quel temps fait-il? kel tom fay·teel
67b A	It's cold.	Il fait froid. eel fay frwa
67c A	It's hot.	Il fait chaud. eel fay sho
A	It's windy.	Il fait du vent. eel fay dew von
67d A	It's raining.	Il pleut. eel pler
A	It's snowing.	Il neige. eel nezh
A	It's cloudy.	Le temps est couvert. ler tom ay koo·vair
	What's the weather forecast?	Quelles sont les prévisions météo? kel son lay pray·vee·zyon may·tay·yo

Safe Travel

Emergencies

KEY PHRASES

Help!	Au secours!	o skoor
There's been an accident.	Il y a eu un accident.	eel ya ew un ak·see·don
It's an emergency!	C'est urgent!	say tewr·zhon

68a Help!	Au secours! o skoor	
68b Stop!	Arrêtez! pol a·ray·tay	
68c Go away!	Allez-vous-en! pol a·lay·voo·zon	
68d Thief!	Au voleur! o vo·ler	
68e Fire!	Au feu! o fer	
69a Watch out!	Attention! pol a·ton·syon	
69b It's an emergency!	C'est urgent! say tewr·zhon	
69c Call the police!	Appelez la police! pol a·play la po·lees	
69d Call a doctor!	Appelez un docteur! pol a·play un dok·ter	
69e Call an ambulance!	Appelez une ambulance! pol a·play ewn om·bew·lons	
There's been an accident.	Il y a eu un accident. eel ya ew un ak·see·don	

Do you have a first-aid kit?	Avez-vous une trousse de première urgence? pol	a·vay·voo ewn troos der prer·myair ewr·zhons
70a Can you help me, please?	Est-ce que vous pourriez m'aider, s'il vous plaît? pol	es ker voo poo·ryay may·day seel voo play
70b I have to use the telephone.	Je dois utiliser le téléphone.	zher dwa ew·tee·lee·zay ler tay·lay·fon
70c I'm lost.	Je suis perdu(e). m/f	zher swee pair·dew
70d Where's the toilet?	Où sont les toilettes?	oo son lay twa·let

SAFE TRAVEL

EMERGENCIES

LANGUAGE TIP

Code Language

As in any language, French words can have a number of meanings that can lead to some funny, or possibly strange, sentences. How about this for an account of a (sure, unlikely) run-in with the law:

Madame Aubergine a posé un papillon sur ma Renault, et les poulets m'ont ramené dans un panier à salade.

ma·dam o·bair·zheen a po·say un pa·pee·yon sewr ma re·no ay lay poo·lay mon ra·me·nay dons un pan·yay a sa·lad

(Lit: Mrs Eggplant put a butterfly on my Renault, and the chickens came and took me away in a salad basket.) A more useful translation of this might be: 'A parking inspector stuck a ticket on my car, then the cops came and took me away in a paddy wagon.'

SAFE TRAVEL   **POLICE**

Police

KEY PHRASES

Where's the police station?	Où est le commissariat de police?	oo ay ler ko·mee·sar·ya der po·lees
I want to contact my embassy.	Je veux contacter mon ambassade.	zher ver kon·tak·tay mon om·ba·sad
My ... was stolen.	On m'a volé	on ma vo·lay ...

71a Where's the police station?	Où est le commissariat de police? oo ay ler ko·mee·sar·ya der po·lees	
71b I want to report an offence.	Je veux signaler un délit. zher ver see·nya·lay un day·lee	
71c I've been raped.	J'ai été violé(e). m/f zhay ay·tay vyo·lay	
I've been assaulted.	J'ai été violenté(e). m/f zhay ay·tay vyo·lon·tay	
He/She has been raped.	Il/Elle a été violé(e). m/f eel/el a ay·tay vyo·lay	
71d I've been robbed.	On m'a volé. on ma vo·lay	
He/She has been robbed.	Il/Elle s'est fait voler. eel/el say fay vo·lay	
It was him/her.	C'est lui/elle. say lwee/el	

72a I've lost my bags.	J'ai perdu mes sacs. zhay pair·dew may sak
72b I've lost my money.	J'ai perdu mon argent. zhay pair·dew mon ar·zhon
72c I've lost my passport.	J'ai perdu mon passeport. zhay pair·dew mom pas·por
My ... was stolen.	On m'a volé ... on ma vo·lay ...

backpack	mon sac à dos	mon sak a do
handbag	mon sac à main	mon sak a mun
wallet	mon portefeuille	mom por·ter·fer·yer

What am I accused of?	Je suis accusé(e) de quoi? m/f zher swee a·kew·zay der kwa
I didn't realise I was doing anything wrong.	Je ne croyais pas que je faisais quelque chose de mal. zher ner krwa·yay pa ker zher fer·zay kel·ker shoz de mal
I'm innocent.	Je suis innocent(e). m/f zher swee zee·no·son(t)
73a I want to contact my embassy.	Je veux contacter mon ambassade. zher ver kon·tak·tay mon om·ba·sad
73b I want to contact my consulate.	Je veux contacter mon consulat. zher ver kon·tak·tay mon kon·sew·la
Can I have a lawyer (who speaks English)?	Je peux avoir un avocat (qui parle anglais)? zher per a·vwar un a·vo·ka (kee parl ong·glay)
Can I have a copy, please?	Puis-je en avoir un exemplaire? pwee·zhon a·vwar un eg·zom·plair

SAFE TRAVEL · POLICE

Health

KEY PHRASES

Where's the nearest hospital?	Il y a un hôpital par ici?	eel ya un o·pee·tal par ee·see
I'm sick.	Je suis malade.	zher swee ma·lad
I need a doctor.	J'ai besoin d'un médecin.	zhay ber·zwun dun mayd·sun
I'm on medication for ...	Je prends des médicaments pour ...	zher pron day may·dee·ka·mon poor ...
I'm allergic to ...	Je suis allergique à ...	zher swee a·lair·zheek a ...

74a Where's the nearest doctor?	Il y a un médecin par ici? eel ya un mayd·sun par ee·see	
74b Where's the nearest dentist?	Il y a un dentiste par ici? eel ya un don·teest par ee·see	
74c Where's the nearest hospital?	Il y a un hôpital par ici? eel ya un o·pee·tal par ee·see	
74d Where's the nearest (night) pharmacist?	Il y a une pharmacie (de nuit) par ici? eel ya ewn far·ma·see (der nwee) par ee·see	
75a I need a doctor.	J'ai besoin d'un médecin. zhay ber·zwun dun mayd·sun	

75b Could I see a female doctor?	Est-ce que je peux voir une femme médecin? es ker zher per vwar ewn fam mayd·sun
Can the doctor come here?	Est-ce que le médecin peut venir ici? es ker ler mayd·sun per ver·neer ee·see
75c I've run out of my medication.	Je n'ai plus de médicaments. zher nay plew der may·dee·ka·mon
I don't want a blood transfusion.	Je ne veux pas de transfusion sanguine. zher ner ver pa der trons·few·zyon song·geen
Please use a new syringe.	Je vous prie d'utiliser une seringue neuve. pol zher voo pree dew·tee·lee·zay ewn ser·rung nerv
He/She has been vaccinated for ...	Il/Elle s'est fait vacciner contre ... eel/el say fay vak·see·nay kon·trer ...

LANGUAGE TIP **French Idioms**
Here are a couple of colourful expressions referring to body parts:

J'ai l'estomac dans les talons.	zhay les·to·ma don lay ta·lon I'm starving. (lit: I have my stomach in my heels)
Je n'ai plus de jambes.	zher nay plew der zhomb I'm exhausted. (lit: I don't have any more legs)

I've been vaccinated for hepatitis.	Je me suis fait(e) vacciner contre l'hépatite. m/f zher mer swee fay/fet vak·see·nay kon·trer lay·pa·teet
I've been vaccinated for tetanus.	Je me suis fait(e) vacciner contre le tétanos. m/f zher mer swee fay/fet vak·see·nay kon·trer ler tay·ta·nos
I've been vaccinated for typhoid.	Je me suis fait(e) vacciner contre la typhoïde. m/f zher mer swee fay/fet vak·see·nay kon·trer la tee·fo·eed

Symptoms & Conditions

76a I'm sick.	Je suis malade. zher swee ma·lad
My friend is sick.	Mon ami(e) est malade. m/f mon a·mee ay ma·lad
76b It hurts here.	J'ai mal ici. zhay mal ee·see
I've been injured.	J'ai été blessé(e). m/f zhay ay·tay blay·say
I've been vomiting.	J'ai vomi. zhay vo·mee
I can't sleep.	Je n'arrive pas à dormir. zher na·reev pa a dor·meer
I have an infection.	J'ai une infection. zhay ewn un·fek·syon
I have a rash.	J'ai des démangeaisons. zhay day day·mon·zhe·zon

🔊 LISTEN FOR

Je voudrais prendre votre température.
zher voo·dray pron·drer vo·trer tom·pay·ra·tewr
I'd like to take your temperature.

Depuis quand êtes-vous dans cet état?
der·pwee kon et·voo don sayt ay·ta
How long have you been like this?

Cela vous est déjà arrivé?
ser·la voo zay day·zha a·ree·vay
Have you had this before?

Est-ce que vous buvez?
es·ker voo bew·vay
Do you drink?

Est-ce que vous fumez?
es·ker voo few·may
Do you smoke?

Est-ce que vous vous droguez?
es·ker voo voo dro·gay
Do you take drugs?

Êtes-vous allergique à quelque chose?
et·voo za·lair·zheek a kel·ker shoz
Are you allergic to anything?

Êtes-vous enceinte?
et·voo zon·sunt
Are you pregnant?

Vous avez une vie sexuelle?
voo za·vay ewn vee sek·swel
Are you sexually active?

Vous avez eu des rapports non protégés?
voo za·vay ew day ra·por non pro·tay·zhay
Have you had unprotected sex?

Est-ce que vous prenez des médicaments?
es·ker voo prer·nay day may·dee·ka·mon
Are you on any medication?

Il faut vous faire hospitaliser.
eel fo voo fair os·pee·ta·lee·zay
You need to be admitted to hospital.

SAFE TRAVEL

HEALTH

150

I feel ...		Je me sens ... zher mer son ...
anxious	inquiet/inquiète m/f	un·kyay/un·kyet
better	mieux	myer
weak	faible	fay·bler
worse	plus mal	plew mal

I feel ...		J'ai ... zhay ...
dizzy	des vertiges	day ver·teezh
hot and cold	chaud et froid	sho ay frwa
nauseous	des nausées	day no·zay
shivery	des frissons	day free·son

I have diarrhoea.	J'ai la diarrhée. zhay la dya·ray
I have a headache.	J'ai mal à la tête. zhay mal a la tet
I have a sore throat.	J'ai mal à la gorge. zhay mal a la gorzh
I've recently had ...	J'ai eu récemment ... zhay ew ray·sa·mon ...
I'm on medication for ...	Je prends des médicaments pour ... zher pron day may·dee·ka·mon poor ...
He/She is on medication for ...	Il/Elle prend des médicaments pour ... eel/el pron day may·dee·ka·mon poor ...

For more symptoms and conditions, see the **dictionary**.

Allergies

He/She's allergic to ...	Il/Elle est allergique ... eel/el ay ta·lair·zheek ...
77a **I'm allergic to antibiotics.**	Je suis allergique aux antibiotiques. zher swee a·lair·zheek o zon·tee·byo·teek
77b **I'm allergic to anti-inflammatories.**	Je suis allergique aux anti-inflammatoires. zher swee a·lair·zheek o zun·tee·un·fla·ma·twar
77c **I'm allergic to asprin.**	Je suis allergique à l'aspirine. zher swee a·lair·zheek a las·per·reen
77d **I'm allergic to codeine.**	Je suis allergique à la codéine. zher swee a·lair·zheek a la ko·day·een
77e **I'm allergic to penicillin.**	Je suis allergique à la pénicilline. zher swee a·lair·zheek a la pay·nee·see·leen

For food-related allergies, see **vegetarian & special meals** (p174).

Women's Health

I need a pregnancy test.	J'ai besoin d'un test de grossesse. zhay ber·zwun dun test der gro·ses
I haven't had my period for ... weeks.	Je n'ai pas eu mes règles depuis ... semaines. zher nay pa ew may re·gler der·pwee ... ser·men
I need contraception.	J'ai besoin d'un contraceptif. zhay ber·zwun dun kon·trer·sep·teef

I've noticed a lump here.	J'ai remarqué une grosseur ici.
	zhay rer·mar·kay ewn gro·ser ee·see
I need the morning-after pill.	J'ai besoin de la pilule du lendemain.
	zhay ber·zwun de la pee·lewl dew lon·der·mun

Parts of the Body

My ... hurts.	Mon/Ma/Mes ... me fait mal.
	m/f/pl
	mon/ma/may ... mer fay mal

78f
head
tête f
tet

78g
nose
nez m
nay

78h
mouth
bouche f
boosh

78i
chest
poitrine f
pwa·treen

78j
stomach
estomac m
es·to·ma

78k
leg
jambe f
zhomb

78a
eye
œil m
er·yer

78b
ear
oreille f
o·ray

78c
arm
bras m
bra

78d
hand
main f
mun

bum
fesses f pl
fess

78e
foot
pied m
pyay

I can't move my ...	Je n'arrive pas à bouger mon/ma ... **m/f** zher na·reev pa a boo·zhay mon/ma ...
I have a cramp in my ...	J'ai une crampe au/à la ... **m/f** zhay ewn kromp o/a la ...
My ... is swollen.	Mon/Ma ... est enflé(e). **m/f** mon/ma ... ay ton·flay

Dentist

I have a broken tooth.	J'ai une dent cassée. zhay ewn don ka·say
I have a toothache.	J'ai mal aux dents. zhay mal o don
I've lost a filling.	J'ai perdu un plombage. zhay pair·dew un plom·bazh
I don't want it extracted.	Je ne veux pas que vous l'arrachiez. zher ner ver pa ker voo la·rash·yay
My dentures are broken.	Mon dentier est cassé. mon don·tyay ay ka·say
Ouch!	Aïe! a·ee

🔊 **LISTEN FOR**

Ouvrez tout grand.	oo·vray too gron	Open wide.
Rinsez.	run·say	Rinse!
Ça ne fera pas de mal.	sa ne fer·ra pa der mal	This won't hurt a bit.
Ça pourrait faire un peu mal.	sa poo·ray fair un per mal	This might hurt a little.

SAFE TRAVEL HEALTH

🔊 LISTEN FOR

Avez-vous déjà pris ceci?	a·vay·voo day·zha pree ser·see Have you taken this before?
Deux fois par jour (avec nourriture).	der fwa par zhoor (a·vek noo·ree·tewr) Twice a day (with food).
Cela sera prêt dans (vingt minutes).	ser·la ser·ra pray don (vung mee·newt) It'll be ready to pick up in (20 minutes).
Traitement à suivre jusqu'au bout.	tret·mon a swee·vrer zhews·ko boo You must complete the course.

Chemist

I need something for ...	J'ai besoin d'un médicament pour ... zhay ber·zwun dun may·dee·ka·mom poor ...
Do I need a prescription for ...?	J'ai besoin d'une ordonnance pour ...? zhay ber·zwun dewn or·do·nons poor ...
How many times a day?	Combien de fois par jour? kom·byun der fwa par zhoor
Will it make me drowsy?	Est-ce que ça peut provoquer des somnolences? es ker sa per pro·vo·kay day som·no·lons

For pharmaceutical items, see the **dictionary**.

Food

FOOD EATING OUT

Eating Out

KEY PHRASES

Can you recommend a restaurant?	Est-ce que vous pouvez me conseiller un restaurant? pol	es ker voo poo·vay mer kon·say·yay un res·to·ron
I'd like a table for two, please.	Je voudrais une table pour deux personnes, s'il vous plaît. pol	zher voo·dray ewn ta·bler poor der pair·son seel voo play
Can I see the menu, please?	Est-ce que je peux voir la carte, s'il vous plaît? pol	es ker zher per vwar la kart seel voo play
I'd like ...	Je voudrais ...	zher voo·dray ...
I'd like the bill, please.	Je voudrais l'addition, s'il vous plaît. pol	zher voo·dray la·dee·syon seel voo play

Petit déjeuner per·tee day·zher·nay (breakfast) typically consists of bread and jam and a coffee or hot chocolate – pastries, yoghurt and cereals might also be eaten. *Déjeuner* day·zher·nay (lunch) is the main meal of the day and may involve a number of courses. *Dîner* dee·nay (dinner) is eaten around 8pm, and is a light version of lunch. Bread and wine feature at both lunch and dinner.

Basics

79a breakfast	le petit déjeuner m ler per·tee day·zher·nay
79b lunch	le déjeuner m ler day·zher·nay

79c dinner	le dîner m ler dee·nay
79d snack	le casse-croûte m ler kas·kroot
79e eat	manger mon·zhay
79f drink	boire bwar
daily special	suggestion du jour f sew·zhes·tyon dew zhoor
set menu	menu m mer·new
I'd like ...	Je voudrais ... zher voo·dray ...
I'm starving!	Je meurs de faim! zher mer der fum
Enjoy your meal!	Bon appétit! bon a·pay·tee

Finding a Place to Eat

80a Can you recommend a cafe?	Est-ce que vous pouvez me conseiller un café? pol es ker voo poo·vay mer kon·say·yay ung ka·fay
80b Can you recommend a restaurant?	Est-ce que vous pouvez me conseiller un restaurant? pol es ker voo poo·vay mer kon·say·yay un res·to·ron
Where would you go for a cheap meal?	Où est-ce qu'on trouve les restaurants bon marché? oo es kon troov lay res·to·ron bom mar·shay

158

FOOD EATING OUT

Where would you go for local specialities?	Où est-ce qu'on trouve les spécialités locales? oo es kon troov lay spay·sya·lee·tay lo·kal
Are you still serving food?	On peut toujours passer des commandes? om per too·zhoor pa·say day ko·mond
How long is the wait?	Il faut attendre combien de temps? eel fo a·ton·drer kom·byun der tom

At the Restaurant

I'd like to reserve a table for (eight) o'clock.	Je voudrais réserver une table pour (vingt) heures. zher voo·dray ray·zair·vay ewn ta·bler poor (vungt) er
I'd like to reserve a table for (two) people.	Je voudrais réserver une table pour (deux) personnes. zher voo·dray ray·zair·vay ewn ta·bler poor (der) pair·son
I'd like a table in the (non)smoking area, please.	Je voudrais une table dans un endroit pour (non-) fumeurs, s'il vous plaît. pol zher voo·dray ewn ta·bler don zun on·drwa poor (non·) few·mer seel voo play
81a I'd like a table for (two), please.	Je voudrais une table pour (deux) personnes, s'il vous plaît. zher voo·dray ewn ta·bler poor (der) pair·son seel voo play

✀	**For five, please.**	Pour cinq, s'il vous plaît. pol	poor sungk, seel voo play

Eating Out

Can I see the menu, please?

Est-ce que je peux voir la carte, s'il vous plaît? pol

es ker zher per vwar la kart seel voo play

What would you recommend for ...?

Que recommandez vous comme ...? pol

ker rer·ko·mon·day voo kom ...

 the main meal
plat principal
pla prun·see·pal

 drinks
boisson
bwa·son

dessert
dessert
day·sair

Can you bring me some ..., please?

Apportez-moi ..., s'il vous plaît. pol

a·por·tay·mwa ... seel voo play

I'd like the bill, please.

Je voudrais l'addition, s'il vous plaît. pol

zher voo·dray la·dee·syon seel voo play

🔊 **LISTEN FOR**

Nous sommes complets.	noo som kom·play We're fully booked.
Nous n'avons plus de tables.	noo na·von plew der ta·bler We have no tables.
Où voulez-vous vous asseoir?	oo voo·lay·voo voo zas·war Where would you like to sit?
C'est fermé.	say fair·may We're closed.

81b I'd like the drink list, please.
Je voudrais la liste des boissons, s'il vous plaît. **pol**
zher voo·dray la leest day bwa·son seel voo play

Can I see the menu, please?
Est-ce que je peux voir la carte, s'il vous plaît? **pol**
es ker zher per vwar la kart seel voo play

✂ **Menu, please.** | La carte, s'il vous plaît. **pol** | la kart seel voo play

---

81c What would you recommend?
Qu'est-ce que vous conseillez?
kes ker voo kon·say·yay

Can you tell me which traditional foods I should try?
Pouvez-vous me dire quelle nourriture traditionnelle je dois goûter?
poo·vay·voo me deer kel noo·ree·tewr tra·dee·syon·nel zhe dwa goo·tay

I'll have what they're having.
Je prendrai la même chose qu'eux.
zher pron·dray la mem shoz ker

What's in that dish?	Quels sont les ingrédients? kel son lay zun·gray·dyon
What's that called?	Ça s'appelle comment? sa sa·pel ko·mon
Do you have children's meals?	Est-ce que vous avez des repas enfants? pol es ker voo za·vay day rer·pa on·fon
Do you have a menu in English?	Est-ce que vous avez une carte en anglais? pol es ker voo za·vay ewn kart on ong·glay
Does it take long to prepare?	Est-ce que la préparation va prendre beaucoup de temps? es ker la pray·pa·ra·syon va pron·drer bo·koo der tom
Is service included in the bill?	Le service est compris? ler sair·vees ay kom·pree
Are these complimentary?	C'est gratuit ça? say gra·twee sa
Is it self-serve?	C'est self-service? say self·sair·vees
We're just having drinks.	C'est juste pour des boissons. say zhewst poor day bwa·son

✂	**Just drinks.**	Juste des boissons.	zhewst day bwa·son

I'd like a local speciality.	Je voudrais une spécialité locale. zher voo·dray ewn spay·sya·lee·tay lo·kal
I'd like a meal fit for a king.	Je voudrais un repas digne d'un roi. zher voo·dray un rer·pa dee·nyer dun rwa

FOOD EATING OUT

LISTEN FOR

Vous désirez?	voo day·zee·ray
	What can I get for you?
Quelle cuisson?	kel kwee·son
	How would you like it cooked?
Je vous conseille ...	zher voo kon·say ...
	I suggest ...
Voilà!	vwa·la
	Here you go!

Requests

I'd like it ...	J'aime ça ...
	zhem sa ...
I don't want it ...	Je ne veux pas ça ...
	zher ner ver pa sa ...

boiled	bouilli	boo·yee
fried	frit	free
grilled	grillé	gree·yay
medium	à point	a pwun
rare	saignant	say·nyon
reheated	réchauffé	ray·sho·fay
steamed	à la vapeur	a la va·per
well done	bien cuit	byun kwee
with the dress-ing on the side	avec la sauce à côté	a·vek la sos a ko·tay
without dressing/ sauce	sans sauce	son sos

For phrases to make other specific meal requests, see **vegetarian & special meals** (p174).

I'd like one slice (of pizza), please.	Je voudrais un morceau (de pizza), s'il vous plaît. pol zher voo·dray um mor·so (der peed·za) seel voo play
I'd like a sandwich, please.	Je voudrais un sandwich, s'il vous plaît. pol zher voo·dray un sond·weetsh seel voo play
I'd like that one, please.	Je voudrais ça, s'il vous plaît. pol zher voo·dray sa seel voo play
Please bring a (wine) glass.	Apportez-moi un verre (à vin), s'il vous plaît. pol a·por·tay·mwa un vair (a vun) seel voo play

For typical dishes, see the **menu decoder** (p178). For other food items see the **dictionary**.

spoon
cuillère f
kwee·yair

fork
fourchette f
foor·shet

plate
assiette f
a·syet

knife
couteau m
koo·to

wineglass
verre à vin m
vair a vun

glass
verre m
vair

table
table f
ta·bler

FOOD EATING OUT

Compliments & Complaints

I didn't order this.	Ce n'est pas ce que j'ai commandé. ser nay pa ser ker zhay ko·mon·day
We love the local cuisine.	Nous adorons la cuisine locale. noo za·do·ron la kwee·zeen lo·kal
That was delicious!	C'était délicieux! say·tay day·lee·syer
My compliments to the chef.	Mes compliments au chef. may kom·plee·mon o shef
I'm full.	Je n'ai plus faim. zher nay plew fum
This is burnt.	C'est brûlé. say brew·lay

| This is (too) cold. | C'est (trop) froid.
say (tro) frwa |
| This is superb. | C'est superbe.
say sew·pairb |

Paying the Bill

| 82a I'd like the bill, please. | Je voudrais l'addition,
s'il vous plaît. pol
zher voo·dray la·dee·syon
seel voo play |

| | Bill, please. | L'addition,
s'il vous plaît. pol | la·dee·syon
seel voo play |

| There's a mistake in the bill. | Il y a une erreur dans la note.
eel ya ewn ay·rer don la not |

Nonalcoholic Drinks

83a mineral water	de l'eau minérale der lo mee·nay·ral
83b (orange) juice	du jus (d'orange) m dew zhew (do·ronzh)
83c soft drink	une boisson non-alcoolisée f ewn bwa·son non·al·ko·lee·zay
83d I'd like a cup of coffee.	Je voudrais un café. zher voo·dray un ka·fay
83e I'd like a cup of tea.	Je voudrais un thé. zher voo·dray un tay
83f with milk	au lait o lay
83g without sugar	sans sucre son sew·krer

Alcoholic Drinks

beer	bière f	byair
brandy	cognac m	ko·nyak
Champagne	champagne m	shom·pan·yer
cocktail	cocktail m	kok·tel
84a a shot of (whiskey)	un petit verre de (whiskey)	um per·tee vair der (wees·kee)
84b a glass of red wine	un verre de vin rouge	un vair der vun roozh
84c a bottle of red wine	une bouteille de vin rouge	ewn boo·tay der vun roozh
84d a glass of white wine	un verre de vin blanc	un vair der vun blong
84e a bottle of red wine	une bouteille de vin blanc	ewn boo·tay der vun blong
a glass of ... wine	un verre de vin ...	un vair der vun ...

dessert	de dessert	der day·sair
rose	rosé	ro·zay
sparkling	mousseux	moo·ser
table	de table	der ta·bler

84f a glass of beer	un verre de bière	un vair der byair
a pint of beer	un demi de bière	un der·mee der byair
84g a bottle of beer	une bouteille de bière	ewn boo·tay der byair

In the Bar

Excuse me.	Excusez-moi. pol ek·skew·zay·mwa
I'm next.	C'est mon tour. say mon toor
85a Q What would you like?	Qu'est-ce que vous voulez? kes ker voo voo·lay
A I'll have (a gin).	Je prends (un gin). zher pron (un zheen)
Same again, please.	La même chose, s'il vous plaît. pol la mem shoz seel voo play
No ice, thanks.	Pas de glaçons, merci. pa der gla·son mair·see
85b I'll buy you a drink.	Je vous offre un verre. pol zher voo zo·frer un vair
It's my round.	C'est ma tournée. say ma toor·nay
Do you serve meals here?	Faites-vous les repas ici? pol fet·voo lay rer·pa ee·see

Drinking Up

85c Cheers!	Santé! son·tay

🔊 LISTEN FOR

Qu'est-ce que vous desirez prendre?	kes ker voo der·zee·ray pron·drer What'll it be?
Je pense que ça suffit.	zher pons ker sa sew·fee I think you've had enough.

FOOD EATING OUT

168

◀)) : LISTEN FOR

Au chef!	o shef	To the chef!
À tout le monde!	a too ler mond	Here's to everyone!
À la France!	a la frons	Here's to France!
Encore un coup!	ong·kor ung koo	Have another!

Thanks, but I don't feel like it.	Je n'en ai pas envie, merci. zher non ay pa on·vee mair·see
No thanks, I'm driving.	Non merci, je conduis. non mair·see zher kon·dwee
This is hitting the spot.	C'est justement ce qu'il me faut. say zhewst·mon ser keel mer fo
I'm tired, I'd better go home.	Je suis fatigué, je dois rentrer. zher swee fa·tee·gay zher dwa ron·tray
I'm feeling drunk.	Je suis ivre. zher swee zee·vrer
I feel fantastic!	Je me sens vachement bien! zher mer son vash·mon byun
I really, really love you.	Je t'aime vraiment beaucoup. zher tem vray·mon bo·koo
Can you call a taxi for me?	Pouvez-vous appeler un taxi pour moi? pol poo·vay·voo a·play un tak·see poor mwa
I don't think you should drive.	Je ne pense pas que vous êtes en état de conduire. pol zher ner pons pa ker voo zet on ay·ta der kon·dweer
I feel ill.	Je me sens malade. zher mer son ma·lad

Self-Catering

KEY PHRASES

What's the local speciality?	Quelle est la spécialité locale?	kel ay la spay·sya·lee·tay lo·kal
Where can I find the ... section?	Où est-ce qu'on trouve le rayon ...?	oo es kon troov ler ray·yon ...
What's that?	Qu'est-ce que c'est, ça?	kes ker say sa..

Buying Food

How much is ...?	C'est combien ...? say kom·byun ...
86a What's the local speciality?	Quelle est la spécialité locale? kel ay la spay·sya·lee·tay lo·kal
Do you sell locally produced food?	Est-ce que vous vendez de la nourriture produite localement? pol es ke voo von·day de la noo·ree·tewr pro·dweet lo·kal·mon
86b What's that?	Qu'est-ce que c'est, ça? kes ker say sa
Can I taste it?	Je peux goûter? zher per goo·tay
Do you have other kinds?	Est-ce que vous avez autre chose? pol es ker voo za·vay o·trer shoz

> **CULTURE TIP**
>
> **Cheese**
> There are around 400 kinds of cheese in France, from subtle cream cheeses to pungent, whiplash-inducing mould cheeses. Like wines, some cheeses are particular to certain regions and have been awarded an *appellation d'origine* a·pe·la·syon do·ree·zheen, which guarantees the cheese's origin. Cheeses can be broadly grouped into the following styles:
>
> | | |
> |---|---|
> | **goat's milk cheese** | fromage de chèvre
fro·mazh der she·vrer |
> | **hard cheese** | fromage à pâte dure
fro·mazh a pat dewr |
> | **sheep's milk cheese** | fromage de brebis
fro·mazh der brer·bee |
> | **soft cheese** | fromage à pâte molle
fro·mazh a pat mol |

Can I have a bag, please?	Puis-je avoir un sac, s'il vous plaît? pol pweezh a·vwar un sak seel voo play
87a **I'd like (200) grams.**	Je voudrais (deux cents) grammes. zher voo·dray (der son) gram
87b **I'd like (two) kilos.**	Je voudrais (deux) kilos. zher voo·dray (der) kee·lo
87c **I'd like (three) pieces.**	Je voudrais (trois) morceaux. zher voo·dray (trwa) mor·so
87d **I'd like (six) slices.**	Je voudrais (six) tranches. zher voo·dray (see) tronsh

Do you have anything cheaper?	Est-ce que vous avez quelque chose de moins cher? pol es ker voo za·vay kel·ker shoz der mwun shair
Where can I find the (frozen goods) section?	Où est-ce qu'on trouve le rayon (des surgelés)? oo es kon troov ler ray·yon (day sewr·zher·lay)
Where can I find the fruit and vegetable section?	Où est-ce qu'on trouve le rayon des fruits et legumes? oo es kon troov ler ray·yon day frwee ay lay·gewm
Where can I find the meat section?	Où est-ce qu'on trouve le rayon viande? oo es kon troov ler ray·yon vyond

Je peux goûter?
zher per goo·tay
Can I taste it?

© WILL SALTER / LONELY PLANET IMAGES

🔊 LISTEN FOR

Que puis-je faire pour vous?	ker pwee·zher fair poor voo Can I help you?
Vous désirez?	voo day·zee·ray What would you like?
Je n'en ai plus.	zher non ay plew I don't have any.
Il n'en reste plus.	eel non rest plew There's none left.
Encore quelque chose?	ong·kor kel·ker shoz Would you like anything else?
Ça, c'est (un camembert).	sa say (tung ka·mom·bair) That's (a Camembert).
Ça fait (cinq euros).	sa fay (sungk er·ro) That's (five euros).

Where is the health-food store?	Où se trouve la boutique bio? oo ser troov la boo·teek bee·yo
Do you sell organic produce?	Est-ce que vous vendez des produits biologiques? pol es ke voo von·day day pro·dwee byo·lo·zheek

For food items, see the **menu decoder** (p178) and the **dictionary**.

Cooking

cooked	cuit(e) m/f kwee(t)
dried	sec/sèche m/f sek/sesh
fresh	frais/fraîche m/f fray/fresh

frozen	surgelé(e) m/f sewr·zher·lay
raw	cru(e) m/f krew
smoked	fumé(e) m/f few·may
stale	rassis(e) m/f ra·see(z)
bottle opener	ouvre-bouteilles m oo·vrer·boo·tay
can opener	ouvre-boîtes m oo·vrer·bwat
chopping board	planche à découper f plonsh a day·koo·pay
corkscrew	tire-bouchon m teer·boo·shon
frying pan	poêle à frire f pwal a freer
saucepan	casserole f kas·rol
toaster	grille-pain m gree·pun

For more cooking implements, see the **dictionary**.

Vegetarian & Special Meals

KEY PHRASES

I'm a vegetarian.	Je suis végétarien(ne). m/f	zher swee vay·zhay·ta·ryun/ vay·zhay·ta·ryen
I don't eat/ drink ...	Je ne mange/ bois pas ...	zher ner monzh/ bwa pa ...
I'm allergic to ...	Je suis allergique à ...	zher swee a·lair·zheek a ...

Special Diets & Allergies

88a Is there a vegetarian restaurant near here?	Y a-t-il un restaurant végétarien par ici? ya·teel un res·to·ron vay·zhay·ta·ryen par ee·see
Do you have halal food?	Vous faites les repas halal? pol voo fet lay rer·pa a·lal
Do you have kosher food?	Vous faites les repas casher? pol voo fet lay rer·pa ka·shair
I'm a vegan.	Je suis végétalien(ne). m/f zher swee vay·zhay·ta·lyun/ vay·zhay·ta·lyen
I'm a vegetarian.	Je suis végétarien(ne). m/f zher swee vay·zhay·ta·ryun/ vay·zhay·ta·ryen
I'm on a special diet.	Je suis au régime. zher swee zo ray·zheem

I don't eat/drink ...	Je ne mange/bois pas ...	
	zher ner monzh/bwa pa ...	
I can't eat it for health reasons.	Je ne mange pas ça pour des raisons de santé.	
	zher ner monzh pa sa poor day ray·zon der son·tay	
I can't eat it for religious reasons.	Je ne mange pas ça à cause de ma religion.	
	zher ner monzh pa sa a koz der ma rer·lee·zhyon	
I can't eat it for philosophical reasons.	Je ne mange pas ça pour des raisons philosophiques.	
	zher ner monzh pa sa poor day ray·zon fee·lo·zo·feek	
89a I'm allergic to dairy produce.	Je suis allergique aux produits latiers.	
	zher swee a·lair·zheek o pro·dwee lay·tyay	
89b I'm allergic to MSG.	Je suis allergique au glutamate de sodium.	
	zher swee a·lair·zheek o glew·ta·mat der so·dyom	
89c I'm allergic to nuts.	Je suis allergique aux noix.	
	zher swee a·lair·zheek o nwa	
89d I'm allergic to seafood.	Je suis allergique aux fruits de mer.	
	zher swee a·lair·zheek o frwee der mair	
I'm allergic to ...	Je suis allergique ...	
	zher swee za·lair·zheek ...	

eggs	aux œufs	o zer
pork	au porc	o por
red meat	à la viande rouge	a la vyond roozh
shellfish	aux crustacés	o krew·sta·say
wheat flour	à la farine de blé	a la fa·reen der blay

🔊 LISTEN FOR

Vous pouvez manger ...?	voo poo·vay mon·zhay ... Can you eat ...?
C'est cuisiné avec de la viande.	say kee·zee·nay avek der la vyond It has meat in it.
Je vais demander au cuisinier/chef.	zher vay der·mon·day o kwee·zee·nyay/shef I'll check with the cook/chef.

Ordering Food

Is this ...?	C'est un produit ...? say tun pro·dwee ...

free of animal produce	qui n'est pas d'origine animale	kee nay pa do·ree·zheen a·nee·mal
free-range	de ferme	der fairm
genetically modified	qui contient des organismes génétiquement modifiés	kee kon·tyun day zor·ga·nees·mer zhay·nay·teek·mom mo·dee·fyay
gluten-free	sans gluten	son glew·ten
low in sugar	à faible teneur en sucre	a fe·bler ter·ner on sew·krer
low-fat	allégé	a·lay·zhay
organic	biologique	byo·lo·zheek
salt-free	sans sel	son sel

Can I order this without ... in it?	Je peux commander ça sans ...? zher per ko·mon·day sa son ...

LANGUAGE TIP

Translating 'Nuts'
There is no single word to translate 'nuts'. You have to say which kind of nut you mean, for example *noix* nwa, 'walnut'; *cacahuète* ka·ka·wet, 'peanut'; or *noisette* nwa·zet, 'hazelnut'.

Could you prepare a meal without butter?	Pouvez-vous préparer un repas sans beurre? poo·vay·voo pray·pa·ray un rer·pa son ber
90a Could you prepare a meal without eggs?	Pouvez-vous préparer un repas sans œufs? poo·vay·voo pray·pa·ray un rer·pa son zer
90b Could you prepare a meal without meat stock?	Pouvez-vous préparer un repas sans bouillon de viande? poo·vay·voo pray·pa·ray un rer·pa son boo·yon der vyond

A

Menu
~ DECODER ~
le glossaire gastronomique

This miniguide to French cuisine is designed to help you navigate menus. French nouns, and adjectives affected by gender have their gender indicated by ⓜ or ⓕ. If it's a plural noun, you'll also see pl.

~ A ~

à la a la served with • in the style of
abats ⓜ a-ba giblets
— de boucherie der boo-shree offal
abricot ⓜ ab-ree-ko apricot
addition ⓕ a-dee-syon bill • check
agneau ⓜ a-nyo lamb
— de lait ⓜ der lay baby lamb • spring lamb
aiguillette ⓕ ay-gwee-yet long & thin slice of meat, usually poultry breast, especially duck
ail ⓜ ai garlic
aile ⓕ ayl wing (bird or poultry)
aïoli ⓜ ay-o-lee garlic-flavoured mayonnaise sauce, served cold
alcool ⓜ al-kol alcohol
aligot ⓜ a-lee-go mashed potatoes, garlic & melted cheese (Auvergne)
alouette ⓕ al-wet lark
alsacienne (à la —) al-zas-yen (a la —) 'Alsatian style' – dish usually garnished with sauerkraut, pork, sausages or simmered with wine & mushrooms
amande ⓕ a-mond almond
— de mer der mair queen or bay scallop

américaine (à la —) a-may-ree-ken (a la —) 'American style' – generally a dish of fish or shellfish, particularly lobster, flamed in brandy & simmered in white wine & tomatoes
amuse-gueule ⓜ a-mewz-gerl cocktail snack or appetiser
ananas ⓜ a-na-nas pineapple
anchoïade ⓕ on-sho-yad dip of puréed anchovies mixed with garlic & olive oil (Provence)
anchois ⓜ on-shwa anchovy
àncienne ⓕ on-syen 'old style' – depending on the meat used, can be served in a cream sauce with mushrooms, vegetables, onions or shallots, and/or with wine & herbs
andouille ⓕ on-doo-yer smoked sausage made of pork tripe usually eaten cold
andouillette ⓕ on-doo-yet smaller version of *andouille*
aneth ⓜ a-net dill
anglaise (à la —) ong-glayz (a la —) 'English style' – usually boiled meat or vegetables • breaded & fried vegetables, meat, fish or poultry
anguille ⓕ ong-gee-yer eel
anis ⓜ a-nees anis • aniseed

appellation d'origine contrôlée (AOC) ⓕ a·pe·la·syon do·ree·zheen kon·tro·lay (a o say) refers to officially recognised produce with a guarantee of origin

artichaut ⓜ ar·tee·sho artichoke

asperge ⓕ a·spairzh asparagus

assiette ⓕ a·syet plate

— anglaise ong·glayz assorted cold meats & gherkins

— de charcuterie der shar·kew·tree assorted pork & other meat products, including sausages, hams, pates & *rillettes*

— variée va·ree·ay assorted vegetables and/or meat or fish products

assorti(e) ⓜ/ⓕ a·sor·tee assorted

au o served as in • in the style of

aubergine ⓕ o·bair·zheen eggplant

avocat ⓜ a·vo·ka avocado

~ B ~

baba au rhum ⓜ ba·ba o rom small sponge cake, often with raisins, soaked in a rum-flavoured syrup after baking

bacon ⓜ bay·kon bacon

— fumé few·may smoked bacon

— maigre may·grer lean bacon

baguette ⓕ ba·get long & crispy loaf of bread • chopstick

ballottine ⓕ ba·lo·teen boned meat, stuffed & poached

— de volaille der vo·lai poultry *ballottine* stuffed with forcemeat

banane ⓕ ba·nan banana

barbue ⓕ bar·bew brill or barbel, a carp-like fish

barquette ⓕ bar·ket small boat-shaped shell made of shortcrust pastry (sometimes puff pastry) with sweet or savoury fillings

basilic ⓜ ba·zee·leek basil

basquaise (à la —) bas·kayz (a la —) 'Basque style' – usually prepared with tomatoes & sweet or red peppers

bavarois ⓜ ba·va·rwa Bavarian – a cold mousse-like dessert of cream and/or fruit purée

bavaroise ⓕ ba·va·rwaz syrupy tea that can be set into ice cream

bavette ⓕ ba·vet 'bib apron' – flank steak

béarnaise ⓕ bay·ar·nayz white sauce made of wine or vinegar beaten with egg yolks & flavoured with herbs

bécasse ⓕ bay·kas woodcock, a game bird

Béchamel ⓕ bay·sha·mel milk-based sauce

belon ⓜ ber·lon round pinkish oyster

Bercy bair·see 'Bercy style' – butter, white wine & shallot sauce

betterave ⓕ be·trav beetroot

beurre ⓜ ber butter

— blanc blong white sauce made of a vinegar & white wine reduction blended with softened butter & shallots

— noir nwar 'black butter' – butter browned until nearly burned, sometimes flavoured with capers & parsley

— ravigote ra·vee·got butter with herbs

bien cuit(e) ⓜ/ⓕ byun kwee(t) well-done

bière ⓕ bee·yair beer

— blonde blond light-coloured or pale beer • lager

— en bouteille on boo·tay bottled beer

— brune brewn dark beer or stout

— lager la·ger lager

— pression pre·syon draught • draft beer • beer on tap

bifteck ⓜ beef·tek steak

bio(logique) byo(·lo·zheek) organic

biscuit ⓜ bees·kwee biscuit • cookie

bisque ⓕ beesk spicy shellfish soup or chowder, with cream & Cognac

B

blanc de blanc blong der blong white wine made of white grapes with white juice

blanc de volaille ⓜ blong der vo·lai boned breast of fowl, cooked without browning

blanquette de veau ⓕ blong·ket der vo veal stew in white sauce enriched with cream

blé ⓜ blay wheat

bleu ⓜ bler blue-veined cheese, often used to flavour dishes or sauces • nearly raw beef • fish boiled in vinegar bouillon

bœuf ⓜ berf beef

— **à la mode** a la mod larded chunks of beef, braised in wine, either served hot with carrots & onions, or cold in aspic

— **bourguignon** boor·geen·yon chunks of beef marinated in red wine, spices & herbs, stewed with mushrooms, onions & bacon

— **en daube** on dob chunks of beef & chopped ham flamed in Armagnac brandy & stewed with red wine, onions, garlic, vegetables & herbs

— **miroton** mee·ro·ton pre-cooked boiled beef slices, usually left over from *pot-au-feu*, gently stewed with onions

boisson ⓕ bwa·son drink • beverage

— **non alcoolisée** non al·ko·lee·zay soft drink

bombe glacée ⓕ bom·ber gla·say ice cream dessert – two different ice creams moulded together in a cone shape, decorated with candied (glazed) fruits, candied chestnuts & *Chantilly* cream

bonbon ⓜ bom·bon sweet • candy

bordelaise bor·der·layz red wine sauce with shallots, beef juices, thyme & sometimes boletus mushrooms

bouchée ⓕ boo·shay various types of cocktail snacks or small puffs with a variety of fillings, served hot or cold

boucherie ⓕ boo·shree butcher's shop

boudin ⓜ boo·dun smooth sausage, may be grilled or pan-fried

— **blanc** blong white veal, pork or chicken sausage

— **noir** nwar black pork blood sausage (see also *sanguette*)

bouillabaisse ⓕ bwee·ya·bes soup traditionally made of assorted fish stewed in a broth with garlic, orange peel, fennel, tomatoes & saffron. Modern versions include lobster & shrimps. The broth & the fish may be served separately, with croutons & *rouille*. (Marseilles)

bouillon ⓜ boo·yon broth • stock

boulangerie ⓕ boo·lon·zhree bakery

boulette ⓕ boo·let small meatball or croquette (often leftovers) sautéed, browned or poached in a broth

boulghour ⓜ bool·goor bulgur wheat

bouquet garni ⓜ boo·kay gar·nee mix of herbs tied together – usually parsley, bay leaf & thyme

bourguignonne (à la —) boor·gee·nyon (a la —) 'Burgundy style' – dishes may include button mushrooms, bacon & pearl onions or shallots, braised in red wine

bourride ⓕ boo·reed fish soup or stew using firm whitefish like monkfish

bouteille ⓕ boo·tay bottle

brandade de morue ⓕ bron·dad der mo·rew salt cod puréed with milk, olive oil, garlic & sometimes mashed potatoes

brebis ⓕ brer·bee ewe (female sheep)

brème ⓕ brem bream

brioche ⓕ bree·yosh small roll or cake made of yeast, flour, eggs & butter, sometimes flavoured with nuts, currants or candied fruits

MENU DECODER

broche ① brosh spit roast
brochet ⑩ bro·shay pike
brochette ① bro·shet grilled skewer of meat, fish or vegetables
brocoli ⑩ bro·ko·lee broccoli
brouillé(e) ⑩/① broo·yay scrambled
brûlot ⑩ brew·lo sugar flamed in brandy & added to coffee
brut ⑩ brewt extra dry (Champagne)
bûche de Noël ① bewsh der no·el traditionally served for Christmas – a rolled sponge cake filled & covered with butter-cream (usually chocolate, vanilla or coffee flavoured) or ice cream

~ C ~

cabillaud ⑩ ka·bee·yo cod
cacahuète ① ka·ka·wet peanut
cacao ⑩ ka·ka·o cocoa
café ⑩ ka·fay cafe • coffee
caille ① kay·yer quail
caillette ① kay·yet rissole • meatball
calmar ⑩ kal·mar squid
canard ⑩ ka·nar duck
— à la rouennaise a la roo·en·nayz stuffed duck in a red-wine sauce
— à l'orange a lo·ronzh duck braised with Cognac & Cointreau, served with oranges & an orange-based sauce
cannelé ⑩ ka·ner·lay brioche-like pastry made with cornflour, often spelled *canallé* (Bordeaux)
cannelle ① ka·nel cinnamon
câpre ① kap·rer caper
carbonnade ① kar·bo·nad selection of chargrilled meats (often pork)
— de bœuf der berf stew of beef slices, onions & herbs, simmered in beer (Northern France)
carotte ① ka·rot carrot
carpe ① karp carp

carré ⑩ ka·ray loin • rib
— d'agneau da·nyo rack of lamb
— de porc (au chou) der por (o shoo) loin of pork (with cabbage)
carte ① kart menu
— des vins day vun wine list
cassate ① ka·sat ice cream combining different flavours, often studded with candied fruits
casse-croûte ⑩ kas·kroot snack
cassis ⑩ ka·sees blackcurrant (liqueur)
cassoulet ⑩ ka·soo·lay casserole or stew with beans & meat (southwest France)
céleri ⑩ sayl·ree celery
cendre son·drer baked in the embers
cépage ⑩ say·pazh grape or vine variety
cèpe ① sep wild mushroom of the boletus family known for its full flavour & meaty texture
céréale ① say·ray·al cereal • grain
cerf ⑩ ser venison • stag deer
cerise ① ser·reez cherry
cervelas ⑩ sair·ver·la fat pork sausage cured with garlic & eaten hot
cervelle ① sair·vel brain
champignon ⑩ shom·pee·nyon mushroom
— de Paris der pa·ree button mushroom
chanterelle ① shon·trel boletus mushroom – same as *girolle*
Chantilly ① shon·tee·yee sweetened whipped cream flavoured with vanilla
chapon ⑩ sha·pon capon • castrated cock
charbonnade ① shar·bo·nad chargrilled meat
charcuterie ① shar·kew·tree variety of pork products that are cured, smoked or processed, including sausages, hams, *pâtés* & *rillettes* • the shop where these products are sold

charlotte ① shar·lot dessert of bread slices or sponge fingers, lining a deep, round mould, filled with fruits, whipped cream or a fruit mousse

chasselas ① sha·sla type of white grape

chasseur sha·ser 'hunter' – sauce of white wine with mushrooms, shallots & bacon cubes

châtaigne ① sha·tayn·yer chestnut

chateaubriand ⓜ sha·to·bree·yon thick fillet or rump steak

chaud(e) ⓜ/① sho(d) hot • warm

chaud-froid ⓜ sho·frwa 'hot-cold' – a piece of poached or roasted meat, poultry or fish that, while cooling, is coated with a white creamy sauce that solidifies

chaudrée ① sho·dray Atlantic fish stew

chef de cuisine ⓜ shef der kwee·zeen chef

cheval ⓜ she·val horse • horse meat

chèvre ① she·vrer goat • goat's milk cheese

chevreuil ⓜ sher·vrer·yer venison

chicorée ① shee·ko·ray chicory • endive

chipolata ① shee·po·la·ta chipolata • a small sausage

chocolat ⓜ sho·ko·la chocolate

— chaud sho hot chocolate

chou ⓜ shoo cabbage

— de Bruxelles der brew·sel Brussels sprout

— rouge roozh red cabbage

choucroute ① shoo·kroot sauerkraut

chou-fleur ⓜ shoo·fler cauliflower

ciboule ① see·bool spring onion • shallot

cidre ⓜ see·drer cider

citron ⓜ see·tron lemon

— pressé ⓜ see·tron pray·say freshly squeezed lemon juice

citronnade ① see·tro·nad lemon squash • lemonade

citrouille ① see·troo·yer pumpkin

civelle ① see·vel small eel or alevin, generally served fried

civet ⓜ see·vay stew usually containing game marinated in red wine

clam ⓜ klam clam

cochon ⓜ ko·shon pig

— de lait der lay suckling pig

cocktail ⓜ kok·tel cold starter of shellfish & raw vegetables or fruits

cœur ⓜ ker heart

— de filet der fee·lay tenderloin steak

coing ⓜ kwung quince

commande ① ko·mond order

compote ① kom·pot stewed fruit

compris(e) ⓜ/① kom·pree(z) included

concombre ⓜ kong·kom·brer cucumber

confiserie ① kon·feez·ree confectionery (sweets in general) • sweet shop or candy store

confit ⓜ kon·fee preserved meat, usually duck, goose or pork. The meat is cooked in fat until it is tender, then potted & covered with the fat to preserve it.

confiture ① kon·fee·tewr jam

congolais ⓜ kong·go·lay small coconut meringue cake

consommation ① kon·so·ma·syon consumption • the general term for food & drink ordered in a cafe

consommé ⓜ kon·so·may clarified meat, poultry or fish-based broth used as a base for sauces & soups

— à la printanière a la prun·tan·yair *consommé* with spring vegetables

contre-filet ⓜ kon·trer·fee·lay beef sirloin roast

coq ⓜ kok cockerel • rooster

— de bruyère der brew·yair grouse

coque ① kok cockle

coquelet ⓜ ko·klay young cockerel

coquillage ⓜ ko·kee·yazh shellfish

coquille Saint-Jacques ① ko·kee·yer sun·zhak scallop

corbeille de fruits ① kor·bay·yer der frwee basket of assorted fruits

cornichon Ⓜ kor·nee·shon gherkin

côte ① kot chop containing eye fillet

côtelette ① kot·let cutlet • chop

coulis Ⓜ koo·lee fruit or vegetable purée, usually used as a sauce

courge ① koorzh gourd • marrow

courgette ① koor·zhet zucchini • baby marrow

couvert Ⓜ koo·vair number of people in a group at a restaurant • cover charge

— gratuit gra·twee no cover charge

— vin et service compris vun ay sair·vees kom·pree price includes wine, service & cover charges

crabe Ⓜ krab crab

crème Ⓜ krem cream • a dessert with cream • a cream-based soup

— anglaise ong·glayz custard

— crue krew raw or unpasteurised cream

— fouettée fwe·tay whipped cream

— fraîche fresh naturally thickened cream, has a slightly sour tang

— glacée gla·say ice cream

crêpe ① krep large, paper-thin pancake served with various fillings

— flambée flom·bay pancake flamed with brandy or other liqueur

— Suzette sew·zet pancake with tangerine or orange sauce & brandy

cresson Ⓜ kray·son watercress

crevette grise/rose ① krer·vet greez/roz small shrimp

croissant Ⓜ krwa·son flaky crescent-shaped roll, usually served for breakfast

croquant Ⓜ kro·kon butter cookie or biscuit

croque-madame Ⓜ krok·ma·dam grilled or pan-fried ham & cheese sandwich, topped with a fried egg

croquembouche Ⓜ kro·kom·boosh grand dessert of cream puffs dipped in caramel & assembled into a large pyramid shape

croque-monsieur Ⓜ krok·mers·yer grilled or pan-fried ham & cheese sandwich

croustade ① kroo·stad puff pastry shell filled with stewed fish, seafood, meat, poultry, mushrooms or vegetables

croûte ① kroot crust • a puff pastry case filled with various savoury foods

croûte (en —) kroot (on —) 'in crust' – food cooked enclosed in pastry

croûton Ⓜ kroo·ton small piece of bread toasted or fried until crisp, used to garnish salads or soups

cru Ⓜ krew growth • referring to a particular vineyard & its wine

cru(e) Ⓜ/① krew raw

crudités ① pl krew·dee·tay selection of raw vegetables served sliced, grated or diced with dressing as an entrée

crustacé Ⓜ krew·sta·say shellfish

cuire kweer to cook

cuisine ① kwee·zeen cooking • kitchen

— bourgeoise boor·zhwaz French home cooking of the highest quality

— campagnarde kom·pan·yard country or provincial cooking, using the finest ingredients & most refined techniques to prepare traditional rural dishes

cuisse ① kwees thigh • leg

cuisses de grenouille kwees der grer·noo·yer frogs' legs

cuit(e) Ⓜ/① kwee(t) cooked

— au four o foor baked

cul de veau Ⓜ kew der vo veal fillet or rump steak

cuvée ① kew·vay blend of wine from various vineyards when making Champagne • vintage

D

~ D ~

darne ⓜ darn slice of a large raw fish, such as hake, salmon or tuna

datte ⓕ dat date

daube ⓕ dob beef, poultry or game stewed in a rich wine-laden broth

déjeuner ⓜ day·zher·nay lunch

demi der·mee half • beer glass size, about a pint

— -glace ⓕ ·glas rich brown stock & gravy

— -sec ⓜ ·sek slightly sweet (of wine)

— -sel ·sel slightly salty

dieppoise (à la —) ⓕ dyep·waz (a la —) 'Dieppe style' – soup generally consisting of fish, shrimp, mussels, mushrooms, vegetables, herbs & cream, cooked in cider

digestif ⓜ dee·zhe·steef digestive • drink served after a meal

dijonnaise (à la —) dee·zho·nez (a la —) 'Dijon style' – dishes containing mustard or served with a mustard-based sauce (Burgundy)

dinde/dindon ⓜ/ⓕ dund/dun·don turkey

diplomate ⓜ dee·plo·mat trifle – sponge fingers steeped in milk or liqueur, put into a mould & filled with custard & candied fruits

dodine de canard ⓕ do·deen der ka·nar boned duck stuffed with forcemeat, rolled, cooked & served with a spicy sauce

domaine ⓜ do·mayn vineyard • used on a wine label, it indicates a wine of exceptional quality

dos ⓜ do back • meatiest portion of fish

doux/douce ⓜ/ⓕ doo(s) mild • sweet • soft • without salt (butter)

duxelles ⓕ dewk·sel finely chopped mushrooms sautéed in butter with shallots or onions, used as a seasoning or a sauce

~ E ~

eau ⓕ o water

— de source der soors spring water

— du robinet dew ro·bee·nay tap water

— minérale mee·nay·ral mineral water

eau-de-vie ⓕ o·der·vee 'water of life' – clear fruit or nut brandy

écrevisse ⓕ ay·krer·vees crayfish

— à la nage a la nazh crayfish simmered in white wine, usually served with bread & butter as an entrée

émincé ⓜ ay·mun·say thinly sliced meat

endive ⓕ on·deev chicory • endive

— à la bruxelloise a la brew·sel·waz chicory/endive leaves rolled in a slice of ham & covered with cheese sauce

entrecôte ⓕ on·trer·kot rib steak

— chasseur sha·ser pan-broiled steak with a brown sauce made of white wine, mushrooms & tomatoes

— marchand de vin mar·shon der vun steak poached in red wine, shallots & onions

entrée ⓕ on·tray the course before the *plat principal* (main course)

entremets ⓜ on·trer·may cream-based sweet or dessert

épaule ⓕ ay·pol shoulder

épinard ⓜ ay·pee·nar spinach

escabèche ⓕ es·ka·besh highly seasoned marinade used to flavour & preserve small fish

escalope ⓕ es·ka·lop thin boneless slice of meat, usually from the top round

— viennoise vyen·waz breaded veal *escalope* or cutlet

escargot ⓜ es·kar·go snail

espadon ⓜ es·pa·don swordfish

espagnole (à la —) es·pan·yol (a la —) 'Spanish style' – generally including tomatoes, pimentos, capsicum, onion, garlic & rice

F

estomac ⓜ es·to·ma stomach

estouffade ⓕ es·too·fad meat, usually beef or pork, stewed in wine with carrots & herbs (southern France)

estragon ⓜ es·tra·gon tarragon

étouffé(e) ⓜ/ⓕ ay·too·fay food steamed or braised in a tightly sealed vessel with minimal liquid

extra-sec ⓜ ek·stra·sek very dry (of wine)

~ **F** ~

faisan ⓜ fer·zon pheasant

fait(e) maison ⓜ/ⓕ fe(t) may·zon homemade, of the house

farce ⓕ fars forcemeat • stuffing

farci(e) ⓜ/ⓕ far·see stuffed

faux-filet ⓜ fo·fee·lay beef sirloin

fenouil ⓜ fer·noo·yer fennel

feuilletage ⓜ fer·yer·tazh puff pastry

feuilleté ⓜ fer·yer·tay puff pastry usually filled with fruit, cheese, mushrooms, meat, seafood or poultry

fève ⓕ fev broad or lima bean

ficelle ⓕ fee·sel long thin *baguette* • a tender cut of meat, often beef or duck poached in rich broth

figue ⓕ feeg fig

filet ⓜ fee·lay fillet of meat or fish

financière fee·non·syair food served with a rich dressing of pike dumplings, truffles, mushrooms & Madeira wine

fines herbes ⓕ pl feen zairb mixture of chopped fresh herbs consisting of tarragon, parsley, chervil & chives

flageolet ⓜ fla·zho·lay kidney bean

flamande (à la —) fla·mond (a la —) 'Flemish style' – usually food with braised carrots, cabbage, turnips & sometimes bacon, potatoes or sausage, sometimes simmered in beer

flambé(e) ⓜ/ⓕ flom·bay dish with liqueur spooned or poured over it & ignited

flamiche ⓕ fla·meesh tart filled with leeks, eggs & cream, & sometimes pumpkin & Maroilles cheese (Picardy)

flan ⓜ flon open-top tart with various fillings • dessert made of baked custard flavoured with caramel

— parisien pa·ree·zyun tart filled with a vanilla cream

florentine (à la —) flo·ron·teen (a la —) 'Florence style' – commonly dishes containing spinach & sometimes a cream sauce

flûte ⓕ flewt long bread roll, similar to baguette

foie ⓜ fwa liver

— gras gra fatted goose or duck liver. The birds are force-fed to speed the fattening process.

fondue ⓕ fon·dew usually a pot of melted cheeses, or hot oil or broth, that diners dip meat or bread in

— bourguignonne boor·geen·yon bite-size pieces of beef cooked in boiling oil & dipped in a variety of sauces

— chocolat sho·ko·la fruits & pieces of cake dipped in hot melted chocolate

— savoyarde sa·vwa·yard bread dipped in hot melted cheeses flavoured with white wine, garlic & cherry brandy (Savoy)

forestière fo·re·styair generally food sautéed with mushrooms & bacon, or with a Cognac-based sauce

four ⓜ foor oven

fourchette ⓕ foor·shet fork

frais/fraîche ⓜ/ⓕ fray/fresh fresh

fraise ⓕ frez strawberry

framboise ⓕ from·bwaz raspberry • raspberry liqueur

frappé ⓜ fra·pay syrup/liquid poured over crushed ice

G

frappé(e) ⓜ/ⓕ fra·pay chilled • iced
friand ⓜ free·yon pastry stuffed with minced sausage meat, ham & cheese, or almond cream
friandise ⓕ free·on·deez titbit • delicacy • sweets or candy
fricadelle ⓕ free·ka·del small fried mincemeat patty or meatball
fricandeau ⓜ free·kon·do veal fillet simmered in white wine, vegetables herbs & spices • a pork pate
fricassée ⓕ free·ka·say lamb, veal or poultry served in a thick creamy sauce, often with mushrooms & onions • quickly pan-fried foods, sometimes with wild mushrooms
frit(e) ⓜ/ⓕ free(t) fried
frites ⓕ pl freet chips • French fries
friture ⓕ free·tewr deep-fried food, often fish like whitebait
froid(e) ⓜ/ⓕ frwa(d) cold
fromage ⓜ fro·mazh cheese
— blanc blong cream cheese
— de tête der tet brawn • head cheese (usually pork)
— frais fray fermented dairy product similar to curds or cottage cheese
fromagerie ⓕ fro·ma·zhree cheese shop
fruit ⓜ frwee fruit
— confit kon·fee candied or glazed fruit
— de mer der mair seafood
— glacé gla·say candied or glazed fruit
fumé(e) ⓜ/ⓕ few·may smoked
fumet ⓜ few·may aromatic broth used in soups & sauces

~ G ~

galantine ⓕ ga·lon·teen pressed cold meat, usually poultry, stuffed with forcemeat, served cold as an entrée
galette ⓕ ga·let crêpe made with buckwheat flour • flat plain cake of

brioche-type dough or puff pastry, with a variety of fillings • small short butter cookies
— sarrasin sa·ra·zun buckwheat flour *crêpe*
gamba ⓕ gom·ba king prawn
garbure ⓕ gar·bewr thick cabbage soup with salted pork, potatoes, vegetables, spices, herbs & sometimes *confit d'oie*. May be covered with bread slices & cheese, then browned in the oven.
garni(e) ⓜ/ⓕ gar·nee garnished
gâteau ⓜ ga·to cake
gaufre ⓕ go·frer waffle
gelée ⓕ zher·lay aspic or fruit jelly
genièvre ⓕ zher·nye·vrer juniper
génoise ⓕ zhay·nwaz very rich sponge cake, eaten as is or used as the foundation for other cake preparations
gésier ⓜ zhay·zyay poultry entrails
gibelotte de lapin ⓕ zhee·blot der la·pun rabbit stewed in wine sauce with bacon, potatoes, mushrooms, garlic, onion & herbs
gibier ⓜ zheeb·yay game
— en saison on say·zon game in season
gigot ⓜ zhee·go leg, generally of lamb or mutton
gigue ⓕ zheeg haunch
gingembre ⓜ zhun·zhom·brer ginger
girolle ⓕ zhee·rol boletus mushroom – same as chanterelle mushroom
glace ⓕ glas ice • ice cream
glacé(e) ⓜ/ⓕ gla·say glazed • iced
glaçon ⓜ gla·son ice cube
graisse ⓕ gres grease • fat • suet
grand cru ⓜ gron krew wine of exceptional quality
grand vin ⓜ gron vun wine of exceptional quality
grand(e) ⓜ/ⓕ gron(d) large • big

granité ⓜ gra·nee·tay granular-textured fruit-flavoured water-ice or sorbet

gras-double ⓜ gra·doo·bler tripe – may be cooked in water, moulded in a rectangular block, or cut in strips & braised with tomatoes or onions

grecque (à la —) grek (a la —) 'Greek style' – foods prepared with olive oil, onions, lemon, & sometimes with tomato, peppers or fennel added

grenadin ⓜ grer·na·dun veal (or sometimes poultry) fillet, wrapped in a thin slice of bacon

grenouille ⓕ grer·noo·yer frog

grillade ⓕ gree·yad mixed grill

grillé(e) ⓜ/ⓕ gree·yay grilled

grillons ⓜ gree·yon chunks of fatty pork or duck cooked until crisp

griotte ⓕ gree·yot morello cherry

grive ⓕ greev thrush

groseille ⓕ gro·zay·yer (red) currant

— à maquereau a ma·kro gooseberry

~ H ~

haché(e) ⓜ/ⓕ a·shay minced · chopped

hareng ⓜ a·rung herring

— fumé few·may smoked herring · kipper

haricot ⓜ a·ree·ko bean

— blanc blong white haricot or kidney bean

— rouge roozh red kidney bean

— vert vair green bean · French or string bean

haute cuisine ⓕ ot kwee·zeen 'high cuisine' – classic French style of cooking originating in the spectacular feasts of French kings. It's typified by super-rich, elaborately prepared & beautifully presented multicourse meals.

herbe ⓕ airb herb

hollandaise o·lon·dez emulsified oil & egg-yolk sauce, flavoured with fresh lemon juice

homard ⓜ o·mar Atlantic lobster

— à l'armoricaine/à l'américaine a lar·mo·ree·ken/a la·may·ree·ken lobster simmered in white wine, tomatoes, shallots, garlic, pepper, flamed in Cognac or whisky & served with a lobster coral (roe) sauce

— Newburg nyoo·boorg lobster cut into sections, cooked in Madeira wine & served with creamy sauce

— Thermidor ter·mee·dor sautéed lobster, served in its shell with a white wine & *Béchamel* sauce flavoured with shallots, herbs & mustard, sprinkled with cheese & browned

hors-d'œuvre ⓜ or·der·vrer appetiser

huile ⓕ weel oil

huître ⓕ wee·trer oyster

~ I ~

île flottante ⓕ eel flo·tont dessert of egg whites floating on a custard surface, coated with caramel sauce

indienne (à la —) un·dyen (a la —) 'Indian style' – generally a dish flavoured with curry

infusion ⓕ un·few·zyon herbal tea

~ J ~

jalousie ⓕ zha·loo·zee latticed flaky pastry filled with almond paste & jam

jambon ⓜ zhom·bon ham

— chaud sho baked ham

— cru krew raw ham

— de Bayonne der bay·yon fine raw, slightly salty ham (Basque)

— de canard der ka·nar cured or smoked duck breast

jardinière (à la —) zhar·dee·nyair (a la —) 'gardener's style' – dish of cooked vegetables

jarret ⓜ zha·ray knuckle or shank
joue ⓕ zhoo cheek
julienne ⓕ zhew·lyen usually vegetables, sometimes ham or chicken breast, cut in long, fine strips, cooked in butter or served raw
jus ⓜ zhew juice • gravy

~ **K** ~

kascher ka·shair kosher
kir ⓜ keer white wine sweetened with *cassis*
— **royal** rwa·yal Champagne with *cassis*
kirsch ⓜ keersh cherry *eau-de-vie* or brandy
kriek ⓕ kreek Belgian beer flavoured with cherries
kugelhopf ⓜ kew·gerl·hopf chocolate, almond & sultana cake (Alsace)

~ **L** ~

lait ⓜ lay milk
— **cru** krew raw or unpasteurised milk used to make certain cheeses
— **écrémé** ay·kray·may skimmed milk
laitance ⓕ lay·tons soft roe
laitue ⓕ lay·tew lettuce
langouste ⓕ long·goost spiny lobster • rock lobster (Mediterranean)
langoustine ⓕ long·goo·steen scampi • Dublin Bay prawn • langoustine
langue ⓕ long tongue
lapin ⓜ la·pun rabbit
— **de garenne** der ga·ren wild rabbit
lard ⓜ lar bacon
— **fumé** few·may smoked bacon
— **maigre** may·grer lean bacon
lardon ⓜ lar·don bacon cube
légume ⓜ lay·gewm vegetable
légumes jardinière ⓜ pl lay·gewm zhar·dee·nyair diced fresh vegetables (usually carrots, turnips, beans &

cauliflower) with butter, chervil & cream
lentille ⓕ lon·tee·yer lentil
lièvre ⓕ lye·vrer hare
— **en civet** on see·vay jugged hare (hare stew)
limande ⓕ lee·mond lemon sole • dab
limonade ⓕ lee·mo·nad lemonade
longe ⓕ lonzh loin
— **de veau farcie** der vo far·see stuffed loin of veal
lorraine (à la —) lo·ren (a la —) 'Lorraine style' – generally a dish garnished with red cabbage & potato croquettes, or bacon slices & Gruyère cheese
lyonnaise (à la —) lee·o·nez (a la —) 'Lyon style' – dish generally including onions cooked golden brown, seasoned with wine, garlic & parsley

~ **M** ~

madeleine ⓕ mad·len small shell-shaped cake, generally flavoured with lemon but also almonds or cinnamon.
madère (à la —) ma·dair (a la —) 'Madeira style' – dishes served with a sauce flavoured with sweet Madeira (Portuguese fortified wine)
magret ⓜ ma·gray breast meat from a fattened mallard or Barbary duck specially raised for *foie gras* (see *jambon de canard*)
maigre may·grer lean, or without meat
maïs ⓜ ma·ees corn/maize
maison (de la —) may·zon (der la —) speciality of the restaurant
mange-tout ⓜ monzh·too snow pea
maquereau ⓜ ma·kro mackerel
marc ⓜ mar drink made from distilled grape skins & pulp left over after being pressed for wine

marcassin ⓜ mar·ka·sun young boar

marchand de vin mar·shon der vun wine merchant • 'wine merchant style' – dish cooked with (red) wine

marengo ⓜ ma·rung·go stewed chicken or veal that is served over toast & garnished with crayfish or shrimps

marinade ⓕ ma·ree·nad marinade – a highly flavoured liquid; may include wine or vinegar, oil, aromatic vegetables & herbs, that meat, fish or vegetables are steeped in to be flavoured & tenderised

mariné(e) ⓜ/ⓕ ma·ree·nay marinated

marinière (à la —) ma·ree·nyair (a la —) 'mariner's style' – usually mussels or other seafood, simmered in white wine with onions, parsley, thyme & bay leaves

marmelade ⓕ mar·mer·lad thick purée of fresh fruits stewed in sugar or *compote*

marron ⓜ ma·ron chestnut (see also *châtaigne*)

massepain ⓜ mas·pun marzipan – almond paste

matelote ⓕ mat·lot fish stew (often eel) with wine, onions, shallots, garlic & sometimes mushrooms

mayonnaise ⓕ ma·yo·nez mayonnaise

melon ⓜ mer·lon melon

menthe ⓕ mont mint

menu ⓜ mer·new generally means a set meal at a fixed price (*menu à prix fixe*)

— de dégustation der day·gew·sta·syon tasting menu – special menu giving a small sample of several dishes

merguez ⓕ mair·gez spicy red sausage made from beef or mutton, originally from North Africa

merveille ⓕ mair·vay·yer fried pastry shapes, sprinkled with sugar

meunière mer·nyair lightly sautéed in butter, usually with lemon juice & chopped parsley

meurette ⓕ mer·ret red wine sauce

michette ⓕ mee·shet savoury bread stuffed with cheese, olives, onions & anchovies (Nice)

miel ⓜ myel honey

mignon ⓜ meen·yon small piece of tenderloin of beef, pork or veal

mijoté(e) ⓜ/ⓕ mee·zho·tay simmered

millas ⓜ mee·las cornflour & goose fat cake eaten with a meat course

— de Bordeaux der bor·do custard & cherry tart

mille-feuille ⓜ meel·fer·yer '1000 leaves' – flaky pastry layered with custard or thick cream filling

mirabelle ⓕ mee·ra·bel small yellow plum, used in tarts as well as liqueurs & plum brandy (Alsace, Lorraine)

miroton ⓜ mee·ro·ton slices of pre-cooked beef, usually leftovers, simmered with onions, often served as stew

mode (à la —) mod (a la —) 'of the fashion' – often means made according to a local recipe (see also *bœuf à la mode*)

moelle ⓕ mwal bone marrow

mont-blanc ⓜ mon blong canned chestnut purée with or without a meringue base, topped with *crème Chantilly*

morceau ⓜ mor·so morsel or piece

morille ⓕ mo·ree·yer morel mushroom, a wild mushroom, with a honeycomb cap & hollow stem

Mornay (sauce —) ⓕ mor·nay Bechamel sauce with Gruyère cheese, sometimes enriched with egg yolks

morue ⓕ mo·rew cod

moule ⓕ mool mussel

N

mousseline ⓕ moos·leen fine purée or forcemeat lightened with whipped cream • a variation of hollandaise sauce made with whipped cream
mousseron ⓜ moos·ron blewit – fleshy wild mushroom
mousseux ⓜ moo·ser sparkling • sparkling wine
moutarde ⓕ moo·tard mustard
mouton ⓜ moo·ton mutton
mulet ⓜ mu·lay mullet
mûre ⓕ mewr blackberry
muscat ⓜ mew·ska type of grape • a sweet dessert wine
museau ⓜ mew·zo muzzle or snout • pork brawn or head cheese
myrtille ⓕ meer·tee·yer bilberry or European blueberry

~ N ~

nature na·tewr plain
navarin ⓜ na·va·run mutton or lamb stew with vegetables & herbs
navet ⓜ na·vay turnip
neige ⓕ nezh 'snow' – stiff beaten egg white
noir(e) ⓜ/ⓕ nwar black
noisette ⓕ nwa·zet hazelnut • a round, boneless cut of lamb or venison
noix ⓕ nwa nut • walnut
— de coco der ko·ko coconut
— du Brésil bray·zeel brazil nut
normande (à la —) nor·mond (a la —) 'Norman style' – usually a dish of meat, shellfish or vegetables, served with cream
note ⓕ not bill or check (restaurant)
nouilles ⓕ noo·yer noodles
nouvelle cuisine ⓕ noo·vel kwee·zeen food prepared & presented to emphasise the inherent textures & colours of the ingredients – features rather small portions served with light sauces

~ O ~

œuf ⓜ erf egg
— à la coque a la kok soft-boiled egg
— brouillé broo·yay scrambled egg
— dur dewr hard-boiled egg
— frit free fried egg
oie ⓕ wa goose
oignon ⓜ on·yon onion
olive ⓕ o·leev olive
omelette ⓕ om·let omelette
onglet ⓜ ong·glay prime cut of beef
orange ⓕ o·ronzh orange
— pressée pray·say freshly squeezed orange juice
oreille ⓕ o·ray·yer ear
orge ⓕ orzh barley
os ⓜ os bone
— à moelle a mwal marrow-bone

~ P ~

pain ⓜ pun bread
palmier ⓜ pal·myay sweet pastry shaped like a heart or a palm leaf
palourde ⓕ pa·loord medium-sized clam
pamplemousse ⓜ pom·pler·moos grapefruit
panaché ⓜ pa·na·shay shandy (beer & lemonade)
panais ⓜ pa·nay parsnip
pan-bagnat ⓜ pun ban·ya small round bread loaves, split or hollowed out, soaked with olive oil & filled with onions, vegetables, anchovies & black olives (Nice)
pané(e) ⓜ/ⓕ pa·nay coated in breadcrumbs • breaded
panisse ⓕ pa·nees pancake or patty of chickpea flour, fried & served with certain meat dishes (Provence)
papillote ⓕ pa·pee·yot dish cooked encased in greaseproof paper or foil
parfait ⓜ par·fay ice cream dessert, often served in a tall glass, sometimes with custard, fruit, nuts & liqueur

Paris-Brest ⓜ pa·ree·brest ring-shaped cake of choux pastry, filled with butter-cream, decorated with flaked almonds & icing sugar

Parmentier ⓜ par·mon·tyay any dish containing potatoes

pastèque ⓕ pas·tek watermelon

pastis ⓜ pa·stees an aniseed-flavoured drink, drunk as an aperitif & always mixed with water

patate douce ⓕ pa·tat doos sweet potato

pâté ⓜ pa·tay pate – thick paste, often pork. Sometimes called terrine.

— de foie gras der fwa gra goose or duck liver paste

— maison may·zon pate made according the restaurant's own recipe

pâtes ⓕ pl pat pasta • noodles

pâtisserie ⓕ pa·tees·ree pastries, cakes & other sweetmeats • the place where they are sold

pavé ⓜ pa·vay thickly-cut steak

paysanne (à la —) pay·zan (a la —) 'peasant style' – dish containing various vegetables & wine, or assorted chopped vegetables, usually used to garnish a soup or an omelette

pêche ⓕ pesh peach

perche ⓕ persh perch

perdrix ⓕ per·dree partridge

périgourdine (à la —) pay·ree·goor·deen (a la —) 'Périgourd style' – dish containing truffles & sometimes *foie gras*

persil ⓜ pair·seel parsley

persillade ⓕ pair·see·yad mixture of chopped parsley & garlic, added to recipes at the end of cooking

pet-de-nonne ⓜ pay·der·non 'nun's fart' – small deep-fried fritter or choux pastry, served hot with sugar or with fruit coulis

pied ⓜ pyay foot • trotter

pigeon ⓜ pee·zhon pigeon

pignon ⓜ pee·nyon pine nut/kernel

piment ⓜ pee·mon pimento, small red pepper • allspice

pintade ⓕ pun·tad guinea fowl

pistache ⓕ pees·tash pistachio nut

pistache (en —) pee·stash (on —) dish prepared with garlic

pistou ⓜ pee·stoo pesto – basil & garlic paste

plat ⓜ pla plate • dish

— du jour dew zhoor speciality of the day

— principal prun·see·pal main course or dish

plateau de fromage ⓜ pla·to der fro·mazh cheese board or platter

pleurote ⓜ pler·rot pleurotus – mild white mushroom with tender flesh

pluvier ⓜ plew·vyay plover (small game bird)

poché(e) ⓜ/ⓕ po·shay poached

poêlé(e) ⓜ/ⓕ pwa·lay pan-fried

point (à —) pwun (a —) medium meat, usually still pink

poire ⓕ pwar pear

poiré ⓜ pwa·ray perry (pear cider)

poireau ⓜ pwa·ro leek

pois ⓜ pwa pea

— cassé ka·say split pea

— chiche sheesh chickpea

poisson ⓜ pwa·son fish

— de mer der mair saltwater fish

— d'eau douce do doos freshwater fish

poissonnerie ⓕ pwa·son·ree fish shop

poitrine ⓕ pwa·treen chest (meat from the chest area)

poivre ⓜ pwa·vrer pepper

poivron ⓜ pwa·vron capsicum or sweet pepper

pomme ⓕ pom apple

pomme chips pom sheeps crisps or potato chips

pomme de terre ⓕ pom der tair potato

pomme duchesse pom dew·shes deep-fried fritter of mashed potato, butter & egg yolk

porc ⓜ por pig • pork

porto ⓜ por·to port

potage ⓜ po·tazh usually a thickened soup of puréed vegetable base

pot-au-feu ⓜ po·to·fer beef, root vegetable & herb stockpot. Traditionally, the stock is served as an entrée & the meat & vegetables are served as a main course.

potée ⓕ po·tay meat (usually pork) & vegetables cooked in an earthenware pot

potimarron ⓜ po·tee·ma·ron gourd – variety of squash

potiron ⓜ po·tee·ron pumpkin

pouding ⓜ poo·deeng pudding

poularde ⓕ poo·lard pullet or fattened chicken

poulet ⓜ poo·lay chicken

— au pot o po whole chicken filled with giblets, ham & bread, stewed with vegetables

— chasseur sha·ser chicken sautéed in white wine with mushrooms, shallots & bacon

poulpe ⓕ poolp octopus

poussin ⓜ poo·sun very young chicken

praire ⓕ prair clam

praline ⓕ pra·leen almonds, sometimes flavoured with coffee or chocolate & a sugar coating

premier cru prer·myay krew high-quality wines from specific vineyards

pré-salé ⓜ pray·sa·lay lamb pastured in the salty meadows of the Atlantic or the English Channel

primeur ⓜ pree·mer spring or early vegetable or fruit

printanière prun·ta·nyair dish often prepared or served with fresh spring vegetables

produits de la mer ⓜ pl pro·dwee der la mair seafood

profiterole ⓜ pro·fee·trol small ball of choux pastry with savoury or sweet fillings

provençale (à la —) pro·von·sal (a la —) 'Provence style' – dish usually cooked with olive oil, tomatoes, garlic, onions, olives, sweet peppers & various herbs

prune ⓕ prewn plum

pruneau ⓜ prew·no prune

puits d'amour ⓜ pwee da·moor small puff pastry shell filled with custard or jam & sprinkled with sugar

~ Q ~

quenelle ⓕ ker·nel oval-shaped dumpling of fish or meat, forcemeat, egg & flour, often served poached

— de brochet der bro·shay pike dumpling

queue ⓕ ker tail

quiche ⓕ keesh open-top tart with meat, fish or vegetable filling, baked with beaten eggs & cream

~ R ~

raclette ⓕ ra·klet hot melted cheese scraped from a block of cheese placed in front of a vertical grill, served with potatoes & gherkins (Savoy)

radis ⓜ ra·dee radish

ragoût ⓜ ra·goo stew of meat, poultry or fish and/or vegetables

raie ⓕ ray skate • ray

raisin ⓜ ray·zun grape

rascasse ⓕ ras·kas scorpion fish – grotesque but delicious fish essential in *bouillabaisse* (Mediterranean)

ratatouille ⓕ ra·ta·too·ee vegetable 'stew' – tomatoes, zucchini, eggplant, sweet peppers & onions, flavoured with garlic, herbs & olive oil, served with lemon juice

reine (à la —) ren (a la —) 'queen's style' – a dish with poultry

religieuse ⓕ rer·lee·zhyerz double-decker choux pastry puff, filled with coffee or chocolate-flavoured custard & coated with icing

rémoulade ⓕ re·moo·lad classic sauce made by combining mayonnaise with mustard, capers, chopped gherkins, herbs & anchovies, served chilled with grated celery, or as an accompaniment to cold meat or seafood

rillettes ⓕ pl ree·yet coarsely shredded, potted meat (usually pork), eaten as a spread on toast or bread

rillons ⓜ ree·yon chunks of fatty pork or duck cooked until crisp

ris de veau ⓜ ree der vo sweetbreads

rissole ⓕ ree·sol fried or baked pastry turnover, filled with a savoury filling of meat, poultry or vegetables

riz ⓜ ree rice

rognon ⓜ ron·yon kidney

romarin ⓜ ro·ma·run rosemary

rosbif ⓜ ros·beef roast beef

rosette de Lyon ⓕ ro·zet der lee·on large pork sausage (like salami)

rôti ⓜ ro·tee roast

rouget ⓜ roo·zhay mullet

rouille ⓕ roo·ee thick *aïoli* sauce

roulade ⓕ roo·lad slice of meat or fish rolled around stuffing • a rolled-up vegetable souffle

roulé(e) ⓜ/ⓕ roo·lay rolled

~ S ~

sabayon ⓜ sa·ba·yon creamy dessert of beaten eggs, sugar & wine or liqueur, flavoured with lemon juice

sablé ⓜ sa·blay rich shortbread biscuit

safran ⓜ sa·fron saffron

saignant(e) ⓜ/ⓕ sen·yon(t) rare (meat)

saisi(e) ⓜ/ⓕ say·zee seared

salade ⓕ sa·lad salad • lettuce

— composée kom·po·zay mixed salad

— verte vairt green salad

salé(e) ⓜ/ⓕ sa·lay salted

salmis ⓜ sal·mee game or poultry partially roasted, then simmered in wine

sang ⓜ song blood

sanglier (sauvage) ⓜ song·glee·yay (so·vazh) (wild) boar

sanguette ⓕ song·get *boudin* sausage (often flat) made from rabbit, duck or goose blood (Périgord)

sauce ⓕ sos sauce • gravy

saucisse ⓕ so·sees sausage

— de Francfort der frongk·for frankfurt

— de Strasbourg der straz·boor knackwurst

— de Toulouse der too·looz mild pork sausage

saucisson ⓜ so·see·son large sausage usually air-dried & eaten cold

— à l'ail lai garlic sausage

— de Lyon der lee·on long air-dried pork sausage, flavoured with garlic & pepper, or a boiling sausage similar to *saucisson à l'ail*

— sec sek air-dried sausage (like salami)

saumon ⓜ so·mon salmon

sauté(e) ⓜ/ⓕ so·tay sautéed

sauvage so·vazh wild

savarin ⓜ sa·va·run ring-shaped sponge cake soaked with a rum syrup & filled with custard or whipped cream & fresh or poached fruits

savoie ⓕ sav·wa light, airy cake made with beaten egg whites

sec/sèche ⓜ/ⓕ sek/sesh dry

séché(e) ⓜ/ⓕ say·shay dried

seiche ⓕ sesh cuttlefish

sel ⓜ sel salt

semoule ⓕ ser·mool semolina

T

service ⓜ sair·vees service (charge)
— compris kom·pree service included (often abbreviated as 's.c.' at the bottom of the bill) – service charge is built into the price of each dish
— en sus on sews service charge is calculated after the food & drink ordered is added up
serviette ⓕ sair·vyet serviette • napkin
sésame ⓜ say·zam sesame
sirop ⓜ see·ro fruit syrup or cordial served mixed with water, soda or with carbonated mineral water
soja ⓜ so·zha soya bean
solette ⓕ so·let baby sole
sorbet ⓜ sor·bay sorbet
soubise ⓕ soo·beez dish served with creamed onion purée & rice
soufflé ⓜ soof·lay soufflé
soupe ⓕ soop soup
spéciale ⓕ spay·syal top-quality oyster
spécialité (de la maison) ⓕ spay·sya·lee·tay (der la may·zon) speciality of the house
steak ⓜ stek steak
— tartare tar·tar steak tartare – raw minced beef served with raw onion, egg yolk, capers & parsley
sucre ⓜ sew·krer sugar
sucré(e) ⓜ/ⓕ sew·kray sweetened
suprême de volaille ⓕ sew·prem der vo·lai boned chicken breast with creamy sauce
sur commande sewr ko·mond to your special order

~ **T** ~

table d'hôte ⓕ ta·bler dot meal at a set price & hour
taboulé ⓜ ta·boo·lay tabouli – common salad of couscous with parsley & mint, tomatoes & onions, seasoned with olive oil & lemon juice

tapenade ⓕ ta·per·nad savoury spread or dip of puréed olives, anchovies, capers, olive oil & lemon, eaten with bread or hard-boiled eggs
tarte ⓕ tart flan • tart
— aux fraises o frez strawberry tart
— Tatin ta·tun type of tart with pastry baked on top of fruit (usually apples)
tartiflette ⓕ tar·tee·flet dish of potatoes, Reblochon cheese & sometimes bacon (Savoy)
tartine ⓕ tar·teen slice of bread with any topping or garnish, such as butter, jam, honey, cream cheese
tendron ⓜ ton·dron cut of meat from the end of ribs to the breastbone
terrine ⓕ tay·reen preparation of meat, poultry, fish or game, baked in a ceramic dish called a *terrine*, & served cold
tête ⓕ tet head
thé ⓜ tay tea
— au citron o see·tron tea with lemon
— au lait o lay tea with milk
— nature na·tewr plain tea (no milk)
thon ⓜ ton tuna
timbale ⓕ tum·bal meat, fish, or seafood stew cooked in a pastry case • rice or pasta with vegetables, cooked in a round or cup-shaped mould, served with sauce
tisane ⓕ tee·zan herbal tea
— de camomille der ka·mo·mee·yer camomile tea
— de menthe der mont mint tea
— de tilleul der tee·yerl tea made with dried linden blossoms
tomate ⓕ to·mat tomato
topinambour ⓜ to·pee·nom·boor Jerusalem artichoke
tournedos ⓜ toor·ner·do thick round slice of beef fillet
— Rossini ro·see·nee *tournedos* garnished with *foie gras* & truffles, served with Madeira wine sauce

V

tourte ① toort sweet or savoury pie
tourteau ⓜ toor·to large crab
tourtière ① toor·tyair sweet or
savoury pie
tout compris too kom·pree all-
inclusive (price)
traiteur ⓜ tray·ter caterer or
delicatessen selling prepared dishes
tranche ① tronsh slice
tranché ⓜ tron·shay sliced
tripes ① pl treep tripe
— **à la mode de Caen** a la mod der
kon tripe simmered with cider, leeks
& carrots
troquet ⓜ tro·kay bistro • tavern •
cafe • small restaurant
truffe ① trewf truffle
— **en chocolat** on sho·ko·la melted
chocolate enriched with butter,
cream & egg yolks, rolled into small
balls & covered with cocoa
truite ① trweet trout
— **au bleu** o bler trout poached in a
court-bouillon broth of vinegar, white
wine, vegetables & herbs
tuile ① tweel 'tile' – fragile, wing-like
almond biscuit

~ V ~

vache ① vash cow
vanille ① va·nee·yer vanilla
vapeur ① va·per steam
vapeur (à la —) va·per (a la —)
steamed
varié(e) ⓜ/① var·yay assorted
veau ⓜ vo veal
velouté ⓜ ver·loo·tay rich, creamy
soup, usually prepared with
vegetables, shellfish or fish purée
venaison ① ver·nay·zon venison
verdure ① vair·dewr green
vegetables
viande ① vyond meat
— **froide** frwad cold meat
— **hachée** ha·shay minced meat

— **séchée** say·shay dried beef served
in paper-thin slices as *hors d'œuvre*
viennoiserie ① vyen·wa·zree baked
goods like *croissants* & *brioches*
vin ⓜ vun wine
— **blanc** blong white wine
— **de pays** der pay·yee reasonable
quality & generally drinkable wine
— **de table** der ta·bler table wine –
very cheap lower-quality wine
— **doux** doo sweet, dessert wine
— **mousseux** moo·ser sparkling wine
— **ordinaire** or·dee·nair table wine
— **rouge** roozh red wine
— **sec** sek dry wine
vinaigre ⓜ vee·nay·grer vinegar
volaille ① vo·lai poultry • fowl
vol-au-vent ⓜ vo·lo·von round
puff-pastry cases filled with a mixture
of sauce & meat, poultry, seafood or
vegetables

~ W ~

waterzoï ⓜ wa·ter·zoy chicken, or
sometimes fish, poached with shredded vegetables (especially leeks) &
served with a sauce of broth, cream
& egg yolks (northern France)

~ Y ~

yaourt ⓜ ya·oort yoghurt
— **à boire** a bwar yoghurt drink
— **brassé** bra·say thick creamy
yoghurt
— **maigre** may·grer low-fat yoghurt

Dictionary
ENGLISH *to* FRENCH
anglais–français

Nouns have their gender indicated by ⓜ or ⓕ. You'll also see sg and pl for singular and plural nouns. Where a word that could be either a noun or a verb has no gender indicated, it's a verb.

A

a/an un(e) ⓜ/ⓕ un/ewn
a little un peu ⓜ um per
a lot (of) beaucoup (de) bo·koo (der)
aboard à bord a bor
abortion avortement ⓜ a·vor·ter·mon
about environ on·vee·ron
above au-dessus o·der·sew
abroad à l'étranger a lay·tron·zhay
accept accepter ak·sep·tay
accident accident ⓜ ak·see·don
accommodation logement ⓜ lozh·mon
account compte ⓜ kont
ache douleur ⓕ doo·ler
achievement réussite ⓕ ray·ew·seet
acid (drug) acide ⓜ a·seed
across de l'autre côté de der lo·trer ko·tay der
act jouer zhoo·ay
activist militant/militante ⓜ/ⓕ mee·lee·ton(t)
actor acteur/actrice ⓜ/ⓕ ak·ter/ ak·trees
acupuncture acupuncture ⓕ a·kew·pongk·tewr
adaptor adaptateur ⓜ a·dap·ta·ter
addicted (to drugs) drogué dro·gay
addiction dépendance ⓕ day·pon·dons
additional supplémentaire sew·play·mon·tair
address adresse ⓕ a·dres
administration administration ⓕ ad·mee·nee·stra·syon
admire admirer ad·mee·ray
admission (price) prix d'entrée ⓜ pree don·tray
admit admettre ad·me·trer
adult adulte ⓜ&ⓕ a·dewlt
advertisement publicité ⓕ pewb·lee·see·tay
advice conseil ⓜ kon·say
aerobics aérobic ⓕ a·ay·ro·beek
aerogram aérogramme ⓜ a·ay·ro·gram
aeroplane avion ⓜ a·vyon
affair liaison ⓕ lyay·zon
Africa Afrique ⓕ a·freek
after après a·pray
afternoon après-midi ⓜ a·pray·mee·dee
aftershave après-rasage ⓜ a·pray·ra·zazh
again encore ong·kor
against contre kon·trer
age âge ⓜ azh

A

aggressive agressif/agressive ⓜ/ⓕ
a·gray·seef/a·gray·seev

agree être d'accord e·trer da·kor

agriculture agriculture ⓕ
a·gree·kewl·tewr

ahead en avant on a·von

AIDS SIDA ⓜ see·da

air air ⓜ air

air-conditioned climatisé
kee·ma·tee·zay

airline ligne aérienne ⓕ lee·nyer
a·ay·ryen

airmail par avion par a·vyon

airplane avion ⓜ a·vyon

airport aéroport ⓜ a·ay·ro·por

airport tax taxe d'aéroport ⓕ taks
da·ay·ro·por

aisle (on plane) couloir ⓜ koo·lwar

alarm clock réveil ⓜ ray·vay

alcohol alcool ⓜ al·kol

alive vivant(e) ⓜ/ⓕ vee·von(t)

all tout too

allergy allergie ⓕ a·lair·zhee

allow permettre pair·me·trer

almost presque pres·ker

alone tout(e) seul(e) ⓜ/ⓕ too(t) serl

already déjà day·zha

also aussi o·see

altar autel ⓜ o·tel

alternative alternative ⓕ
al·tair·na·teev

altitude altitude ⓕ al·tee·tewd

always toujours too·zhoor

amateur amateur ⓜ a·ma·ter

amazing stupéfiant(e) ⓜ/ⓕ
stew·pay·fyon(t)

ambassador ambassadeur/
ambassadrice ⓜ/ⓕ om·ba·sa·der/
om·ba·sa·drees

ambulance ambulance ⓕ
om·bew·lons

among parmi par·mee

amount (money) somme ⓕ som

ancient antique on·teek

and et ay

angry fâché(e) ⓜ/ⓕ fa·shay

animal animal ⓜ a·nee·mal

ankle cheville ⓕ sher·vee·yer

annual annuel(le) ⓜ/ⓕ a·nwel

another un/une autre ⓜ/ⓕ un/ewn
o·trer

answer réponse ⓕ ray·pons

answer répondre ray·pon·drer

ant fourmi ⓕ foor·mee

antibiotics antibiotiques ⓜ
on·tee·byo·teek

antinuclear anti-nucléaire
on·tee·new·klay·air

antique antiquité ⓕ on·tee·kee·tay

antiseptic antiseptique ⓜ
on·tee·sep·teek

any n'importe quel/quelle ⓜ/ⓕ
num·port kel

anyone n'importe qui num·port kee

anything n'importe quoi num·port
kwa

anywhere n'importe où num·port oo

apartment appartement ⓜ
a·par·ter·mon

appendix appendice a·pun·dees

appointment rendez-vous ⓜ
ron·day·voo

approximately à peu près a per pray

April avril ⓜ a·vreel

archaeology archéologie ⓕ
ar·kay·o·lo·zhee

architect architecte(e) ⓜ/ⓕ
ar·shee·tekt

architecture architecture
ar·shee·tek·tewr

argue se disputer ser dees·pew·tay

argument débat ⓜ day·ba

arm bras ⓜ bra

armchair fauteuil ⓜ fo·ter·yee

aromatherapy aromathérapie ⓕ
a·ro·ma·tay·ra·pee

around autour o·toor

arrest arrêter a·ray·tay

arrivals arrivées ⓕ a·ree·vay

arrive arriver a·ree·vay

art art ⓜ ar

art gallery galerie ⓕ gal·ree

artist artiste ⓜ/ⓕ ar·teest

as comme kom

B

ashtray cendrier ⓜ son·dree·yay
Asia Asie ⓕ a·zee
ask (a question) poser po·zay
ask for (something) demander der·mon·day
aspirin aspirine ⓕ as·pee·reen
ass (bum) cul ⓜ kew
asthma asthme ⓜ as·mer
at à a
athletics athlétisme ⓜ at·lay·tees·mer
atmosphere atmosphère ⓕ at·mos·fair
attached attaché(e) ⓜ/ⓕ a·ta·shay
auction vente aux enchères ⓕ vont o zon·shair
August août ⓜ oot
aunt tante ⓕ tont
Australia Australie ⓕ o·stra·lee
Austria Autriche ⓕ o·treesh
automatic automatique o·to·ma·teek
automatic teller machine (ATM) guichet ⓜ automatique de banque (GAB) gee·shay o·to·ma·teek der bonk
autumn automne ⓜ o·ton
avenue avenue ⓕ av·new
awful affreux/affreuse ⓜ/ⓕ a·frer/a·frerz

B

B&W (film) noir et blanc nwar ay blong
baby bébé ⓜ bay·bay
baby food bouillie ⓕ boo·yee
baby powder talc ⓜ talk
back (body) dos ⓜ do
backpack sac à dos ⓜ sak a do
bad mauvais(e) ⓜ/ⓕ mo·vay(z)
bag sac ⓜ sak
baggage bagages ⓜ ba·gazh
baggage allowance franchise ⓕ fron·sheez
baggage claim retrait des bagages ⓜ rer·tray day ba·gazh
bakery boulangerie ⓕ boo·lon·zhree
balance (account) solde ⓜ sold
balcony balcon ⓜ bal·kon

ball (tennis/football) balle/ballon ⓕ/ⓜ bal/ba·lon
ballet ballet ⓜ ba·lay
band (music) bande ⓕ bond
bandage pansement ⓜ pons·mon
Band-Aid sparadrap ⓜ spa·ra·dra
bank banque ⓕ bonk
bank account compte bancaire ⓜ kont bong·kair
bank draft traite bancaire ⓕ tret bong·kair
banknote billet de banque ⓜ bee·yay der bonk
baptism baptême ⓜ ba·tem
bar bar ⓜ bar
bar work travail dans un bar ⓜ tra·vai don zun bar
baseball baseball ⓜ bez·bol
basic fondamental fon·da·mon·tal
basket panier ⓜ pan·yay
basketball basket(ball) ⓜ bas·ket(·bol)
bastard salaud ⓜ sa·lo
bath baignoire ⓕ be·nywar
bath (have a) (prendre un) bain (pron·drer un) bun
bathing suit maillot de bain ⓜ may·yo der bun
bathroom salle de bain ⓕ sal der bun
battery pile ⓕ peel
battery (car) batterie ⓕ bat·ree
be être e·trer
beach plage ⓕ plazh
beautiful beau/belle ⓜ/ⓕ bo/bel
beauty salon salon de beauté ⓜ sa·lon der bo·tay
because parce que pars ker
become devenir derv·neer
bed lit ⓜ lee
bed linen draps ⓜ dra
bedding literie ⓕ leet·ree
bedroom chambre à coucher ⓕ shom·brer a koo·shay
bee abeille ⓕ a·bay
beer bière ⓕ byair
before avant a·von
begin commencer ko·mon·say

behind derrière dair·yair

Belgium Belgique ① bel·zheek

belief croyance ① krwa·yons

believe croire krwar

below sous soo

beside à côté de a ko·tay der

best le/la meilleur(e) ⓜ/① ler/la may·yer

bet pari ⓜ pa·ree

bet parier par·yay

better meilleur(e) ⓜ/① may·yer

between entre on·trer

bib bavoir ⓜ ba·vwar

bible bible ① bee·bler

bicycle vélo ⓜ vay·lo

big grand(e) ⓜ/① gron(d)

bigger plus grand(e) ⓜ/① plew gron(d)

biggest le/la plus grand(e) ⓜ/① ler/la plew gron(d)

bike vélo ⓜ vay·lo

bike chain chaîne de bicyclette ① shen der bee·see·klet

bike path piste cyclable ① peest see·kla·bler

bill (restaurant) addition ① a·dee·syon

bird oiseau ⓜ wa·zo

birth certificate acte de naissance ⓜ akt der nay·sons

birthday anniversaire ⓜ a·nee·vair·sair

bitch salope ① sa·lop

bite mordre mor·drer

bite (dog) morsure ① mor·sewr

bite (insect) piqûre ① pee·kewr

bitter amer/amère ⓜ/① a·mair

black noir(e) ⓜ/① nwar

blanket couverture ① koo·vair·tewr

blessing grâce ① gras

blind aveugle a·ver·gler

blister ampoule ① om·pool

blocked bloqué(e) ⓜ/① blo·kay

blood sang ⓜ son

blood group groupe sanguin ⓜ groop song·gun

blood pressure tension artérielle ① ton·syon ar·tay·ryel

blood test analyse de sang ① a·na·leez der son

blue bleu(e) ⓜ/① bler

board (a plane, ship) monter à bord de mon·tay a bor der

boarding house pension ① pon·syon

boarding pass carte d'embarquement ① kart dom·bar·ker·mon

boat bateau ⓜ ba·to

body corps ⓜ kor

bone os ⓜ os

book livre ⓜ leev·rer

book (make a booking) réserver ray·zair·vay

booked up complet/complète ⓜ/① kom·play/kom·plet

bookshop librairie ① lee·bray·ree

boot (footwear) botte ① bot

border frontière ① fron·tyair

bored (be) s'ennuyer son·nwee·yay

boring ennuyeux/ennuyeuse ⓜ/① on·nwee·yer/on·nwee·yerz

born né(e) ⓜ/① nay

borrow emprunter om·prun·tay

botanic garden jardin botanique ⓜ zhar·dun bo·ta·neek

both tous les deux too lay der

bottle bouteille ① boo·tay

bottle opener ouvre-bouteille ⓜ oo·vrer·boo·tay

boulevard boulevard ⓜ bool·var

bowl bol ⓜ bol

box boîte ① bwat

boxer shorts boxer-short ⓜ bok·sair·short

boxing boxe ① boks

boy garçon ⓜ gar·son

boyfriend petit ami ⓜ per·tee ta·mee

bra soutien-gorge ⓜ soo·tyung·gorzh

Braille braille ⓜ bra·yer

brakes freins ⓜ frun

brave courageux/courageuse ⓜ/① koo·ra·zher/koo·ra·zherz

bread pain ⓜ pun

break casser ka·say

C

break down tomber en panne
tom·bay on pan
breakfast petit déjeuner ⓜ per·tee
day·zher·nay
breast sein ⓜ sun
breathe respirer res·pee·ray
brewery brasserie ⓕ bra·ser·ree
bribe pot-de-vin ⓜ po·der·vun
bribe suborner sew·bor·nay
bridge pont ⓜ pon
briefcase serviette ⓕ sair·vyet
brilliant génial(e) ⓜ/ⓕ zhay·nyal
bring (a person) amener am·nay
bring (a thing) apporter a·por·tay
brochure brochure ⓕ bro·shewr
broken cassé(e) ⓜ/ⓕ ka·say
broken down (tombé) en panne
(tom·bay) on pan
bronchitis bronchite ⓕ bron·sheet
brother frère ⓜ frair
brown brun/brune ⓜ/ⓕ brun/brewn
bruise bleu ⓜ bler
brush brosse ⓕ bros
bucket seau ⓜ so
Buddhist bouddhiste boo·deest
budget budget ⓜ bew·dzay
buffet buffet ⓜ bew·fay
bug (insect) insecte ⓜ un·sekt
build construire kon·strweer
building bâtiment ⓜ ba·tee·mon
burn brûlure ⓕ brew·lewr
burn brûler brew·lay
bus (city) (auto)bus ⓜ (o·to)bews
bus (intercity) (auto)car ⓜ (o·to)kar
bus station gare routière ⓕ gar
roo·tyair
bus stop arrêt d'autobus ⓜ a·ray
do·to·bews
business affaires ⓕ a·fair
business class classe affaires ⓕ
klas a·fair
business man/woman homme/
femme d'affaires ⓜ/ⓕ om/fam da·fair
business trip voyage d'affaires ⓜ
vwa·yazh da·fair
busker musicien(ne) des rues ⓜ/ⓕ
mew·zee·syun/mew·zee·syen day rew

busy occupé(e) ⓜ/ⓕ o·kew·pay
but mais may
butcher's shop boucherie ⓕ
boosh·ree
butterfly papillon ⓜ pa·pee·yon
button bouton ⓜ boo·ton
buy acheter ash·tay
by par par

C

cable câble ⓜ ka·bler
cable car téléphérique ⓜ
tay·lay·fay·reek
cafe café ⓜ ka·fay
cake shop pâtisserie ⓕ pa·tees·ree
calculator calculatrice ⓕ
kal·kew·la·trees
calendar calendrier ⓜ ka·lon·dree·yay
call appeler a·play
camera appareil photo ⓜ a·pa·ray
fo·to
camp camp ⓜ kon
camping ground camping ⓜ
kom·peeng
camping store magasin pour
équipement de camping ⓜ
ma·ga·zun poor ay·keep·mon der
kom·peeng
campsite terrain de camping ⓜ
tay·run der kom·peeng
can (be able) pouvoir poo·vwar
can (have permission) pouvoir
poo·vwar
can (tin) boîte ⓕ bwat
can opener ouvre-boîte ⓜ
oo·vrer·bwat
Canada Canada ⓜ ka·na·da
cancel annuler a·new·lay
cancer cancer ⓜ kon·sair
candle bougie ⓕ boo·zhee
capitalism capitalisme ⓜ
ka·pee·ta·lees·mer
car voiture ⓕ vwa·tewr
car hire location de voitures ⓕ
lo·ka·syon der vwa·tewr
car owner's title carte grise ⓕ kart
greez

car registration immatriculation
ee·ma·tree·kew·la·syon
caravan caravane ⓕ ka·ra·van
care for (someone) soigner swa·nyay
career carrière ⓕ kar·ryair
careful soigneux/soigneuse ⓜ/ⓕ
swa·nyer/swa·nyerz
caring aimant(e) ⓜ/ⓕ ay·mon(t)
carpark parking ⓜ par·keeng
carpenter menuisier ⓜ
mer·nwee·zyay
carry porter por·tay
carton (for ice cream) boîte ⓕ bwat
carton (for yoghurt) pot ⓜ po
cartoon dessin animé ⓜ day·sun
a·nee·may
cash argent ⓜ ar·zhon
cash (a cheque) encaisser ong·kay·say
cash register caisse (enregistreuse) ⓕ
kes (on·rer·zhee·strerz)
cashier caissier/caissière ⓜ/ⓕ
kay·syay/kay·syair
cassette cassette ⓕ ka·set
castle château ⓜ sha·to
casual work travail intermittent ⓜ
tra·vai un·tair·mee·ton
cat chat ⓜ sha
catch attraper a·tra·pay
cathedral cathédrale ⓕ ka·tay·dral
Catholic catholique ka·to·leek
cause cause ⓕ koz
caution prudence ⓕ prew·dons
cave grotte ⓕ grot
CD CD ⓜ say·day
celebration fête ⓕ fet
cemetery cimetière ⓜ seem·tyair
cent cent ⓜ sent
centimetre centimètre ⓜ
son·tee·me·trer
centre centre ⓜ son·trer
ceramic céramique ⓕ say·ra·meek
certain certain(e) ⓜ/ⓕ sair·tun/·ten
certificate certificat ⓜ sair·tee·fee·ka
chain chaîne ⓕ shen
chair chaise ⓕ shez
chairlift (skiing) télésiège ⓜ
tay·lay·syezh

Champagne champagne ⓜ
shom·pa·nyer
championship championnat ⓜ
shom·pyo·na
chance hasard ⓜ a·zar
change changer shon·zhay
change (coins) monnaie ⓕ mo·nay
change (money) échanger
ay·shon·zhay
changing room (in shop) cabine
d'essayage ⓕ ka·been day·say·yazh
channel chaîne ⓕ shen
charming charmant(e) ⓜ/ⓕ
shar·mon(t)
chat bavarder ba·var·day
chat up draguer dra·gay
cheap bon marché ⓜ bon mar·shay
cheat tricheur/tricheuse ⓜ/ⓕ
tree·sher/tree·sherz
check vérifier vay·ree·fyay
check (banking) chèque ⓜ shek
check (bill) addition ⓕ la·dee·syon
check-in (desk) enregistrement
on·rer·zhee·strer·mon
checkpoint contrôle ⓜ kon·trol
cheese fromage fro·mazh
chef chef de cuisine ⓜ shef der
kwee·zeen
chemist pharmacie ⓕ far·ma·see
chemist (person) pharmacien(ne)
ⓜ/ⓕ far·ma·syun/far·ma·syen
cheque (banking) chèque ⓜ shek
chess échecs ⓜ ay·shek
chess board échiquier ⓜ
ay·shee·kyay
chest poitrine ⓕ pwa·treen
chicken poulet ⓜ poo·lay
child enfant ⓜ&ⓕ on·fon
child seat siège pour enfant ⓜ syezh
poor on·fon
childminding garderie ⓕ gard·ree
children enfants ⓜ&ⓕ pl on·fon
chiropractor chiropracteur ⓜ
kee·ro·prak·ter
chocolate chocolat ⓜ sho·ko·la
choice choix ⓜ shwa
choose choisir shwa·zeer

C

C

Christian chrétien(ne) ⓜ/ⓕ kray·tyun/kray·tyen
Christian name prénom ⓜ pray·non
Christmas Noël ⓜ no·el
Christmas Day jour de Noël ⓜ zhoor der no·el
Christmas Eve veille de Noël ⓕ vay der no·el
church église ⓕ ay·gleez
cigar cigare ⓜ see·gar
cigarette cigarette ⓕ see·ga·ret
cigarette lighter briquet ⓜ bree·kay
cinema cinéma ⓜ see·nay·ma
circle cercle ⓜ sair·kler
circus cirque ⓜ seerk
citizen citoyen(ne) ⓜ/ⓕ see·twa·yun/see·twa·yen
citizenship citoyenneté ⓕ see·twa·yen·tay
city ville ⓕ veel
city centre centre-ville ⓜ son·trer·veel
city hall mairie ⓕ may·ree
civil rights droits civils ⓜ pl drwa see·veel
class classe ⓕ klas
classical classique kla·seek
clean propre pro·prer
clean nettoyer net·wa·yay
cleaning nettoyage ⓜ net·wa·yazh
clear clair(e) ⓜ/ⓕ klair
client client(e) ⓜ/ⓕ klee·on(t)
cliff falaise ⓕ fa·lez
climb monter mon·tay
cloak cape ⓕ kap
cloakroom vestiaire ⓜ vays·tyair
clock pendule ⓕ pon·dewl
close proche prosh
close fermer fair·may
closed fermé(e) ⓜ/ⓕ fair·may
clothes line corde à linge ⓕ kord a lunzh
clothing vêtements ⓜ vet·mon
clothing store magasin de vêtements ⓜ ma·ga·zun der vet·mon
cloud nuage ⓜ nwazh
cloudy nuageux/nuageuse ⓜ/ⓕ nwa·zher/nwa·zherz

clutch embrayage om·bray·yazh
coach entraîneur ⓜ on·tray·ner
coast côte ⓕ kot
coat manteau ⓜ mon·to
cocaine cocaïne ⓕ ko·ka·een
cockroach cafard ⓜ ka·far
cocktail cocktail ⓜ kok·tel
coffee café ⓜ ka·fay
coins pièces ⓕ pyes
cold froid(e) ⓜ/ⓕ frwa(d)
colleague collègue ⓜ/ⓕ ko·leg
collect (stamps etc) collectionner ko·lek·syo·nay
collect call appel en PCV ⓜ a·pel on pay·say·vay
collection accumulation ⓕ a·kew·mew·la·syon
college institut universitaire ⓜ un·stee·tew ew·nee·vair·see·tair
college (vocational) école professionnelle ⓕ ay·kol pro·fay·syo·nel
colour couleur ⓕ koo·ler
comb peigne ⓜ pe·nyer
combination combinaison ⓕ kom·bee·nay·zon
come venir ver·neer
comedy comédie ⓕ ko·may·dee
comfortable confortable kon·for·ta·bler
comic (magazine) bande dessinée ⓕ bond day·see·nay
commission commission ⓕ ko·mee·syon
common commun(e) ⓜ/ⓕ ko·mun/ko·mewn
communism communisme ⓜ ko·mew·nees·mer
communist communiste ko·mew·neest
community communauté ⓕ ko·mew·no·tay
companion compagnon/compagne ⓜ/ⓕ kom·pa·nyon/kom·pa·nyer
company entreprise ⓕ on·trer·preez
compass boussole ⓕ boo·sol
competition compétition ⓕ kom·pay·tees·yon

C

complain se plaindre ser plun·drer
complaint plainte ① plunt
complimentary (free) gratuit(e)
 ⓜ/① gra·twee(t)
computer ordinateur ⓜ or·dee·na·ter
computer game jeu électronique ⓜ
 zher ay·lek·tro·neek
concert concert ⓜ kon·sair
concussion commotion cérébrale ①
 ko·mo·syon say·ray·bral
conditioner (hair) après-shampooing
 ⓜ a·pray·shom·pwung
condom préservatif ⓜ
 pray·zair·va·teef
conductor (bus) receveur ⓜ
 rer·ser·ver
conference (big) congrès ⓜ
 kong·gray
conference (small) colloque ⓜ
 ko·lok
confession (religious) confession ①
 kon·fay·syon
confirm (a booking) confirmer
 kon·feer·may
congratulations félicitations
 fay·lee·see·ta·syon
connection rapport ⓜ ra·por
conservative conservateur/
 conservatrice ⓜ/① kon·sair·va·ter/
 kon·sair·va·trees
constipation constipation ①
 kon·stee·pa·syon
consulate consulat ⓜ kon·so·la
contact lenses verres de contact ⓜ
 vair der kon·takt
contraceptive contraceptif ⓜ
 kon·trer·sep·teef
contract contrat ⓜ kon·tra
convenience store supérette de
 quartier ① sew·pay·ret der kar·tyay
convent couvent ⓜ koo·von
conversation conversation ①
 kon·vair·sa·syon
cook cuisinier/cuisinière ⓜ/①
 kwee·zee·nyay/kwee·zee·nyair
cook cuire kweer
cool frais/fraîche ⓜ/① fray/fresh

cooperate coopérer ko·o·pay·ray
cop flic ⓜ fleek
corkscrew tire-bouchon ⓜ
 teer·boo·shon
corner coin ⓜ kwun
correct correct(e) ⓜ/① ko·rekt
corrupt corrompu(e) ⓜ/①
 ko·rom·pew
cost coût ⓜ koo
cotton coton ⓜ ko·ton
cotton balls ouate de coton ① wat
 der ko·ton
cough toux ① too
cough medicine sirop contre la
 toux ⓜ see·ro kon·trer la too
count compter kon·tay
counter (at bar) comptoir ⓜ
 kon·twar
country pays ⓜ pay·ee
countryside campagne ①
 kom·pa·nyer
coupon coupon ⓜ koo·pon
court (legal) tribunal ⓜ tree·bew·nal
court (tennis) court ⓜ koor
cover charge couvert ⓜ koo·vair
cow vache ① vash
crafts artisanat ⓜ ar·tee·za·na
crash accident ⓜ ak·see·don
crazy fou/folle ⓜ/① foo/fol
cream crème ① krem
creche crèche ① kresh
credit crédit ⓜ kray·dee
credit card carte de crédit ① kart der
 kray·dee
creek crique ① kreek
crime délit ⓜ day·lee
crop (gathered) récolte ① ray·kolt
crop (grown) culture ① kewl·tewr
cross traverser tra·vair·say
cross (angry) fâché(e) ⓜ/① fa·shay
cross (religious) croix ① krwa
crowd foule ① fool
crowded bondé(e) ⓜ/① bon·day
cry pleurer pler·ray
cup tasse ① tas
cupboard placard ⓜ pla·kar
current actuel(le) ⓜ/① ak·twel**

D

currency exchange taux de change Ⓜ to der shonzh
current (electricity) courant Ⓜ koo·ron
current affairs actualité ak·twa·lee·tay
custom coutume Ⓕ koo·tewm
customer client(e) Ⓜ/Ⓕ klee·on(t)
customs douane Ⓕ dwan
cut couper koo·pay
cute mignon/mignonne Ⓜ/Ⓕ mee·nyon/mee·nyon
cutlery couverts Ⓜ koo·vair
CV CV Ⓜ say·vay
cycle faire du vélo fair dew vay·lo
cycling cyclisme Ⓜ see·lee·smer
cyclist cycliste Ⓜ/Ⓕ see·kleest

D

dad papa Ⓜ pa·pa
daily quotidien(ne) Ⓜ/Ⓕ ko·tee·dyun/ko·tee·dyen
damage dégâts Ⓜ day·ga
dance danser don·say
dancing danse Ⓕ dons
dangerous dangereux/dangereuse Ⓜ/Ⓕ don·zhrer/don·zhrerz
dark obscur(e) Ⓜ/Ⓕ ob·skewr
dark (of colour) foncé(e) Ⓜ/Ⓕ fon·say
date (appointment) rendez-vous Ⓜ ron·day·voo
date (day) date Ⓕ dat
date (go out with) sortir avec sor·teer a·vek
date of birth date de naissance Ⓕ dat der nay·sons
daughter fille Ⓕ fee·yer
dawn aube ob
day jour Ⓜ zhoor
day after tomorrow après-demain a·pray·der·mun
day before yesterday avant-hier a·von·tyair
dead mort(e) Ⓜ/Ⓕ mor(t)
deaf sourd(e) Ⓜ/Ⓕ soor(d)
deal (cards) donner do·nay
death mort Ⓕ mor

December décembre Ⓜ day·som·brer
decide se décider ser day·see·day
decision décision Ⓕ day·see·zyon
deep profond(e) Ⓜ/Ⓕ pro·fon(d)
definite bien déterminé byun day·tair·mee·nay
deforestation déboisement Ⓜ day·bwaz·mon
degree diplôme Ⓜ dee·plom
delay retard Ⓜ rer·tard
delicatessen charcuterie Ⓕ shar·kew·tree
deliver livrer leev·ray
demand exiger eg·zee·zhay
democracy démocratie Ⓕ day·mo·kra·see
demonstration manifestation Ⓕ ma·nee·fay·sta·syon
Denmark Danemark Ⓜ dan·mark
dental floss fil dentaire Ⓜ feel don·tair
dentist dentiste Ⓜ don·teest
deny nier nee·ay
deodorant déodorant Ⓜ day·o·do·ron
depart (leave) partir par·teer
department store grand magasin Ⓜ gron ma·ga·zun
departure départ Ⓜ day·par
deposit dépôt Ⓜ day·po
descendent descendant(e) Ⓜ/Ⓕ day·son·don(t)
desert désert Ⓜ day·zair
design concevoir kon·ser·vwar
dessert dessert Ⓜ day·sair
destination destination Ⓕ des·tee·na·syon
destroy détruire day·trweer
detail détail Ⓜ day·tai
development développement Ⓜ day·vlop·mon
diabetes diabète Ⓜ dya·bet
dial tone tonalité Ⓕ to·na·lee·tay
diaper couche Ⓕ koosh
diaphragm diaphragme Ⓜ dya·frag·mer
diarrhoea diarrhée Ⓕ dya·ray

diary agenda ⓜ a·zhun·da
dice dés ⓜ day
dictionary dictionnaire ⓜ
deek·syo·nair
die mourir moo·reer
diesel gas-oil ⓜ gaz·wal
diet régime ⓜ ray·zheem
different différent(e) ⓜ/ⓕ
dee·fay·ron(t)
difficult difficile dee·fee·seel
digital camera appareil photo
numérique ⓜ a·pa·ray fo·to
new·may·reek
dining car wagon-restaurant ⓜ
va·gon·res·to·ron
dinner dîner ⓜ dee·nay
diploma diplôme ⓜ dee·plom
direct direct(e) ⓜ/ⓕ dee·rekt
direct (a film) réaliser ray·a·lee·zay
direct-dial composition directe ⓕ
kom·po·zees·yon dee·rekt
direction direction ⓕ dee·rek·syon
director (film) réalisateur/
réalisatrice ⓜ/ⓕ ray·a·lee·za·ter/
ray·a·lee·za·trees
dirty sale sal
disabled handicapé(e) ⓜ/ⓕ
on·dee·ka·pay
disappointed déçu(e) ⓜ/ⓕ day·sew
disaster désastre ⓜ day·zas·trer
discount remise ⓕ rer·meez
discover découvrir day·koov·reer
discrimination discrimination ⓕ
dee·skree·mee·na·syon
discuss discuter dee·skew·tay
disease maladie ⓕ ma·la·dee
dish plat ⓜ pla
dishonest malhonnête mal·o·net
disinfectant désinfectant ⓜ
day·zun·fek·ton
disk (CD-ROM) disque ⓜ deesk
disposable camera appareil photo
jetable ⓜ a·pa·ray fo·to zhay·ta·bler
distance distance ⓕ dees·tons
distributor concessionnaire ⓜ
kon·say·syo·nair
disturb déranger day·ron·zhay

dive plonger plon·zhay
diving plongée sous-marine ⓕ
plon·zhay soo·ma·reen
diving equipment équipement de
plongée ⓜ ay·keep·mon der plon·zhay
divorced divorcé(e) ⓜ/ⓕ dee·vor·say
dizzy (be dizzy) avoir la tête qui
tourne a·vwar la tet kee toorn
do faire fair
doctor médecin ⓜ mayd·sun
dog ⓜ chien shyun
dole allocation de chômage ⓕ
a·lo·ka·syon der sho·mazh
doll poupée ⓕ poo·pay
door porte ⓕ port
dope (drugs) drogue ⓕ drog
dose dose ⓕ doz
double double doo·bler
double bed grand lit ⓜ gron lee
double room chambre pour deux
personnes ⓕ shom·brer poor der
pair·son
down en bas on ba
dozen douzaine ⓕ doo·zen
drama (theatre) théâtre ⓜ tay·a·trer
draw (picture) dessiner day·see·nay
dream rêver ray·vay
dress robe ⓕ rob
dress (oneself) s'habiller sa·bee·yay
drink boisson ⓕ bwa·son
drink boire bwar
drink (alcoholic) verre ⓜ vair
drive conduire kon·dweer
driver's licence permis de conduire
ⓜ pair·mee der kon·dweer
drop laisser tomber lay·say tom·bay
drug drogue ⓕ drog
drug addiction toxicomanie ⓕ
tok·see·ko·ma·nee
drug dealer trafiquant de drogue ⓜ
tra·fee·kon der drog
drugs drogue ⓕ drog
drum tambour ⓜ tom·boor
drums batterie ⓕ ba·tree
drunk ivre ee·vrer
dry sec/sèche ⓜ/ⓕ sek/sesh
dry (clothes) sécher say·shay

E

duck canard ⓜ ka·nar
dummy (pacifier) tétine ⓕ tay·teen
during pendant pon·don
dust poussière ⓕ poo·syair
duty devoir ⓜ der·vwar

E

each chaque shak
ear oreille ⓕ o·ray
early tôt to
earn gagner ga·nyay
earrings boucles d'oreille ⓕ boo·kler
do·ray
Earth Terre ⓕ tair
earth (ground) terre ⓕ tair
earthquake tremblement de terre ⓜ
trom·bler·mon der tair
east est ⓜ est
Easter Pâques pak
easy facile fa·seel
eat manger mon·zhay
economy économie ⓕ ay·ko·no·mee
economy class classe touriste ⓕ
klas too·reest
ecstasy (drug) ecstasy ⓜ ek·sta·zee
eczema eczéma ⓜ eg·zay·ma
edge bord ⓜ bor
editor rédacteur/rédactrice ⓜ/ⓕ
ray·dak·ter/ray·dak·trees
education éducation ⓕ
ay·dew·ka·syon
effect effet ⓜ ay·fay
eight huit weet
elderly âgé(e) ⓜ/ⓕ a·zhay
election élection ⓕ ay·lek·syon
electrical store magasin qui
vend des appareils électriques ⓜ
ma·ga·zunkee von day za·pa·ray
ay·lek·treek
electricity électricité ⓕ
ay·lek·tree·see·tay
elevator ascenseur ⓜ a·son·ser
email e-mail ⓜ ay·mel
embarrass gêner zhay·nay
embarrassed gêné(e) ⓜ/ⓕ zhay·nay
embarrassing gênant(e) ⓜ/ⓕ
zhay·non(t)

embassy ambassade ⓕ om·ba·sad
embroidery broderie ⓕ bro·dree
emergency cas urgent ⓜ ka
ewr·zhon
emotional (person) facilement ému
fa·seel·mon ay·mew
employee employé/employée ⓜ/ⓕ
om·plwa·yay/om·plwa·yay
employer employeur ⓜ om·plwa·yer
empty vide veed
end bout ⓜ boo
end finir fee·neer
endangered species espèce
menacée de disparition ⓕ es·pes
mer·na·say der dees·pa·rees·yon
energy énergie ⓕ ay·nair·zhee
engaged fiancé(e) ⓜ/ⓕ fyon·say
engagement fiançailles ⓕ fyon·sai
engine moteur ⓜ mo·ter
engineer ingénieur ⓜ un·zhay·nyer
engineering ingénierie
un·zhay·nee·ree
England Angleterre ⓕ ong·gler·tair
English anglais(e) ⓜ/ⓕ ong·glay(z)
enjoy (oneself) s'amuser
sa·mew·zay
enough assez a·say
enter entrer on·tray
entertainment guide programme
des spectacles ⓜ pro·gram day
spek·tak·ler
enthusiastic enthousiaste
on·tooz·yast
entry entrée ⓕ on·tray
envelope enveloppe ⓕ on·vlop
environment environnement ⓜ
on·vee·ron·mon
epilepsy épilepsie ⓕ ay·pee·lep·see
equal égale ay·gal
equal opportunity égalité des
chances ⓕ ay·ga·lee·tay day shons
equality égalité ⓕ ay·ga·lee·tay
equipment équipement ⓜ
ay·keep·mon
escalator escalier roulant ⓜ
es·ka·lyay roo·lon
escape échapper ay·sha·pay

estate agency agence immobilière ⓕ
a·zhons ee·mo·bee·lyair
euro euro ⓜ er·ro
Europe Europe ⓕ er·rop
euthanasia euthanasie ⓕ
er·ta·na·zee
evening soir ⓜ swar
event événement ⓜ ay·ven·mon
every chaque shak
every day tous les jours too lay
zhoor
everyone tout le monde too ler mond
everything tout too
exactly exactement eg·zak·ter·mon
exam examen ⓜ eg·za·mun
example exemple ⓜ eg·zom·pler
excellent excellent(e) ⓜ/ⓕ ek·say·lon
except sauf sof
excess (baggage) excédent
ek·say·don
exchange échange ⓜ ay·shonzh
exchange échanger ay·shon·zhay
exchange rate taux de change ⓜ to
der shonzh
excluded pas compris pa kom·pree
exercise exercice ⓜ eg·zair·sees
exhaust (car) pot d'échappement ⓜ
po day·shap·mon
exhausted épuisé(e) ⓜ/ⓕ
ay·pwee·zay
exhibition exposition ⓕ
ek·spo·zee·syon
exit sortie ⓕ sor·tee
expensive cher/chère ⓜ/ⓕ shair
experience expérience ⓕ
eks·pair·yons
explain expliquer eks·plee·kay
exploitation exploitation ⓕ
eks·plwa·ta·syon
export exporter eks·por·tay
express (mail) exprès eks·pres
express mail (by) par exprès par
eks·pres
extension (visa) prolongation ⓕ
pro·long·ga·syon
extra supplémentaire
sew·play·mon·tair

extraordinary extraordinaire
eks·tra·or·dee·nair
eye œil ⓜ er·yee
eyes yeux ⓜ yer

F

fabric tissu ⓜ tee·sew
face visage ⓜ vee·zazh
face cloth gant de toilette ⓜ gon
der twa·let
fact fait ⓜ fet
factory usine ⓕ ew·zeen
factory worker ouvrier/ouvrière
d'usine ⓜ/ⓕ oo·vree·yay/oo·vree·yair
dew·zeen
failure échec ⓜ ay·shek
faith foi ⓕ fwa
fall tomber tom·bay
fall (autumn) automne ⓜ o·ton
false faux/fausse ⓜ/ⓕ fo/fos
family famille ⓕ fa·mee·yer
family name nom de famille ⓜ non
der fa·mee·yer
famous célèbre say·leb·rer
fan (of person) fan ⓜ/ⓕ fan
fan (machine) ventilateur ⓜ
von·tee·la·ter
fanbelt courroie de ventilateur ⓕ
koor·wa der von·tee·la·ter
far lointain(e) ⓜ/ⓕ lwun·tun/lwun·ten
fare tarif ⓜ ta·reef
farm ferme ⓕ ferm
farmer agriculteur/agricultrice ⓜ/ⓕ
a·gree·kewl·ter/a·gree·kewl·trees
fascist fasciste fa·sheest
fashion mode ⓕ mod
fast rapide ra·peed
fat gras/grasse ⓜ/ⓕ gra/gras
fate destin ⓜ des·tun
father père ⓜ pair
father-in-law beau-père ⓜ bo·pair
faucet robinet ⓜ ro·bee·nay
fault (someone's) faute ⓕ fot
faulty défectueux/défectueuse ⓜ/ⓕ
day·fek·twer/day·fek·twerz
fax machine fax ⓜ faks
fear peur ⓕ per

F

February février ⓜ fayv·ree·yay
feed nourrir noo·reer
feel (touch) toucher too·shay
feeling (emotion) sentiment ⓜ son·tee·mon
feeling (physical) sensation ⓕ son·sa·syon
female femelle fer·mel
fence barrière ⓕ bar·yair
fencing escrime ⓕ es·kreem
ferry bac ⓜ bak
festival fête ⓕ fet
fever fièvre ⓕ fyev·rer
few peu per
fiancé fiancé ⓜ fyon·say
fiancée fiancée ⓕ fyon·say
fiction fiction ⓕ feek·syon
field champ ⓜ shom
fight bagarre ⓕ ba·gar
fill remplir rom·pleer
film (cinema) film ⓜ feelm
film (for camera) pellicule ⓕ pay·lee·kewl
film speed sensibilité de la pellicule ⓕ son·see·bee·lee·tay der la pay·lee·kewl
find trouver troo·vay
fine (penalty) amende ⓕ a·mond
finger doigt ⓜ dwa
finish finir fee·neer
fire feu ⓜ fer
firewood bois de chauffage ⓜ bwa der sho·fazh
first premier/première ⓜ/ⓕ prer·myay/prer·myair
first class première classe ⓕ prer·myair klas
first-aid kit trousse à pharmacie ⓕ troos a far·ma·see
fish poisson ⓜ pwa·son
fish shop poissonnerie ⓕ pwa·son·ree
fishing pêche ⓕ pesh
five cinq sungk
flag drapeau ⓜ dra·po
flannel (washing) gant de toilette ⓜ gon der twa·let

flashlight lampe de poche ⓕ lomp der posh
flat plat(e) ⓜ/ⓕ pla(t)
flavour goût ⓜ goo
flea puce ⓕ pews
fleamarket marché aux puces ⓜ mar·shay o pews
flight vol ⓜ vol
flood inondation ⓕ ee·non·da·syon
flooding inondation ⓕ ee·non·da·syon
floor plancher ⓜ plon·shay
floor (storey) étage ⓜ ay·tazh
florist fleuriste ⓜ&ⓕ fler·reest
flower fleur ⓕ fler
flu grippe ⓕ greep
fly mouche ⓕ moosh
fly voler vo·lay
foggy brumeux/brumeuse ⓜ/ⓕ brew·mer/brew·merz
follow suivre swee·vrer
food nourriture ⓕ noo·ree·tewr
food supplies provisions ⓕ pl pro·vee·zyon
foot pied ⓜ pyay
football (soccer) football ⓜ foot·bol
footpath sentier ⓜ son·tyay
for pour poor
forecast prévision ⓕ pray·vee·zyon
forecast prévoir pray·vwar
foreign étranger/étrangère ⓜ/ⓕ ay·tron·zhay/ay·tron·zhair
forest forêt ⓕ fo·ray
forever pour toujours poor too·zhoor
forget oublier oo·blee·yay
forgive pardonner par·do·nay
fork fourchette ⓕ foor·shet
fortnight quinze jours ⓜ pl kunz zhoor
fortune (money) fortune ⓕ for·tewn
fortune teller diseuse de bonne aventure ⓕ dee·zerz der bon a·von·tewr
foul (football) faute ⓕ fot
four quatre ka·trer
foyer (of cinema) hall ⓜ ol
fragile fragile fra·zheel
France France ⓕ frons
free (at liberty) libre lee·brer

free (available) disponible
dees·po·nee·bler
free (gratis) gratuit(e) ⓜ/ⓕ
gra·twee(t)
freedom liberté ⓕ lee·bair·tay
freeze geler zher·lay
frequent fréquent(e) ⓜ/ⓕ fray·kon(t)
fresh frais/fraîche ⓜ/ⓕ fray/fresh
Friday vendredi von·drer·dee
fridge réfrigérateur ⓜ
ray·free·zhay·ra·ter
friend ami/amie ⓜ/ⓕ a·mee
friendly amical(e) ⓜ/ⓕ a·mee·kal
friendship amitié ⓕ a·mee·tyay
frog grenouille ⓕ grer·noo·yer
from de der
frost gel ⓜ zhel
frozen gelé(e) ⓜ/ⓕ zher·lay
fruit fruit ⓜ frwee
fruit picking cueillette de fruits ⓕ
ker·yet der frwee
fry faire frire fair freer
frying pan poêle ⓕ pwal
full plein(e) ⓜ/ⓕ plun/plen
full-time à plein temps a plun ton
fun (have fun) s'amuser sa·mew·zay
funeral enterrement ⓜ on·tair·mon
funny drôle ⓜ&ⓕ drol
furnished meublé(e) ⓜ/ⓕ mer·blay
furniture meubles ⓜ pl mer·bler
future avenir av·neer

G

game jeu ⓜ zher
game (football) match ⓜ matsh
garage garage ⓜ ga·razh
garbage ordures ⓕ pl or·dewr
garbage can poubelle ⓕ poo·bel
garden jardin ⓜ zhar·dun
gardening jardinage ⓜ zhar·dee·nazh
gas (for cooking) gaz ⓜ gaz
gas (petrol) essence ⓕ ay·sons
gas cartridge cartouche de gaz ⓕ
kar·toosh der gaz
gastroenteritis gastro-entérite ⓕ
gastro·on·tay·reet
gate barrière ⓕ bar·yair

gay homosexuel(le) ⓜ/ⓕ
o·mo·sek·swel
general général(e) ⓜ/ⓕ zhay·nay·ral
generous généreux/généreuse ⓜ/ⓕ
zhay·nay·rer/zhay·nay·rerz
Germany Allemagne ⓕ al·ma·nyer
get off (a train, etc) descendre
day·son·drer
gift cadeau ⓜ ka·do
gig concert ⓜ kon·sair
girl fille ⓕ fee·yer
girlfriend petite amie ⓕ per·teet a·mee
give donner do·nay
glandular fever mononucléose
infectieuse ⓕ mo·no·new·klay·oz
un·fek·syerz
glass verre ⓜ vair
glasses (spectacles) lunettes ⓕ pl
lew·net
gloves gants ⓜ pl gon
glue colle ⓕ kol
go aller a·lay
go down (stairs, etc) descendre
day·son·drer
go out sortir sor·teer
go out with sortir avec sor·teer a·vek
go shopping faire les courses fair
lay koors
go to bed se coucher ser koo·shay
go window-shopping faire du lèche-
vitrines fair dew lesh·vee·treen
goal but ⓜ bewt
goalkeeper gardien ⓜ de but
gar·dyun der bewt
goat chèvre ⓕ shev·rer
god dieu ⓜ dyer
goggles (skiing) lunettes ⓕ pl lew·net
gold or ⓜ or
golf course terrain de golf ⓜ tay·run
der golf
good bon/bonne ⓜ/ⓕ bon/bon
goodbye au revoir o rer·vwar
government gouvernement ⓜ
goo·vair·ner·mon
gram gramme ⓜ gram
grandchild petit-fils/petite-fille ⓜ/ⓕ
per·tee fees/per·teet fee·yer

H

grandfather grand-père ⓜ
grom-pair
grandmother grand-mère ⓕ
grom-mair
grandparents grands-parents ⓜ pl
grom-pa-ron
grass (lawn) gazon ⓜ ga-zon
grass (marijuana) herbe ⓕ airb
grateful reconnaissant(e) ⓜ/ⓕ
rer-ko-nay-son(t)
grave tombe ⓕ tomb
gray gris(e) ⓜ/ⓕ gree(z)
great (fantastic) génial(e) ⓜ/ⓕ
zhay-nyal
greedy (food) gourmand(e) ⓜ/ⓕ
goor-mon(d)
greedy (money) avide a-veed
green vert(e) ⓜ/ⓕ vair(t)
greengrocer marchand de légumes
ⓜ mar-shon der lay-gewm
grey gris(e) ⓜ/ⓕ gree(z)
grocery épicerie ⓕ ay-pee-sree
grow pousser poo-say
G-string cache-sexe ⓜ kash-seks
guaranteed garanti(e) ⓜ/ⓕ
ga-ron-tee
guess deviner der-vee-nay
guesthouse pension (de famille) ⓕ
pon-syon (der fa-mee-yer)
guide (person) guide ⓜ geed
guide dog chien d'aveugle ⓜ shyun
da-ver-gler
guidebook guide ⓜ geed
guided tour visite guidée ⓕ vee-zeet
gee-day
guilty coupable koo-pa-bler
guitar guitare ⓕ gee-tar
gun pistolet ⓜ pees-to-lay
gym (place) gymnase ⓜ zheem-naz
gymnastics gymnastique ⓕ
zheem-na-steek
gynaecologist gynécologue ⓜ/ⓕ
zhee-nay-ko-log

H

habit habitude ⓕ a-bee-tewd
hair cheveux ⓜ shver

hairbrush brosse à cheveux ⓕ bros
a shver
haircut coupe ⓕ koop
hairdresser coiffeur/coiffeuse ⓜ/ⓕ
kwa-fer/kwa-ferz
Halal halal a-lal
half moitié ⓕ mwa-tyay
half a litre demi-litre ⓜ
der-mee-lee-trer
hallucinate avoir des
hallucinations a-vwar day
za-lew-see-na-syon
ham jambon ⓜ zhom-bon
hammer marteau ⓜ mar-to
hammock hamac ⓜ a-mak
hand main ⓕ mun
handbag sac à main ⓜ sak a mun
handicrafts objets artisanaux ⓜ pl
ob-zhay ar-tee-za-no
handkerchief mouchoir ⓜ moo-shwar
handlebars guidon ⓜ gee-don
handmade fait/faite à la main ⓜ/ⓕ
fay/fet a la mun
handsome beau/belle ⓜ/ⓕ bo/bel
happy heureux/heureuse ⓜ/ⓕ
er-rer/er-rerz
harassment harcèlement ⓜ ar-sel-mon
harbour port ⓜ por
hard (not easy) difficile dee-fee-seel
hard (not soft) dur(e) ⓜ/ⓕ dewr
hardware store quincaillerie ⓕ
kung-kay-ree
hare lièvre ⓜ lyev-rer
hash teush ⓜ tersh
hat chapeau ⓜ sha-po
hate détester day-tes-tay
have avoir a-vwar
have a cold être enrhumé e-trer
on-rew-may
have fun s'amuser sa-mew-zay
hay fever rhume des foins ⓜ rewm
day fwun
he il eel
head tête ⓕ tet
headache mal à la tête ⓜ mal a la tet
headlights phares ⓜ pl far
health santé ⓕ son-tay

hear entendre on·ton·drer
hearing aid appareil acoustique ⓜ a·pa·ray a·koos·teek
heart cœur ⓜ ker
heart condition maladie de cœur ⓕ ma·la·dee der ker
heat chaleur ⓕ sha·ler
heated chauffé(e) ⓜ/ⓕ sho·fay
heater appareil de chauffage ⓜ a·pa·ray der sho·fazh
heavy lourd(e) ⓜ/ⓕ loor(d)
height hauteur ⓕ o·ter
helmet casque ⓜ kask
help aider ay·day
help aide ⓕ ed
hepatitis hépatite ⓕ ay·pa·teet
her son/sa/ses ⓜ/ⓕ/pl son/sa/say
herbalist herboriste ⓜ/ⓕ air·bo·reest
herbs fines herbes ⓕ feen zairb
here ici ee·see
heroin héroïne ⓕ ay·ro·een
high haut(e) ⓜ/ⓕ o(t)
high school établissement d'enseignement secondaire ⓜ ay·ta·blees·mon don·say·nyer·mon zgon·dair
highway autoroute ⓕ o·to·root
hike faire la randonnée fair la ron·do·nay
hiking randonnée ⓕ ron·do·nay
hiking boots chaussures de marche ⓕ pl sho·sewr der marsh
hiking route itinéraire de randonnée ⓜ ee·tee·nay·rair der ron·do·nay
hill colline ⓕ ko·leen
Hindu hindou(e) ⓜ/ⓕ un·doo
hire louer loo·ay
his son/sa/ses ⓜ/ⓕ/pl son/sa/say
historical historique ees·to·reek
history histoire ⓕ ees·twar
hitchhike faire du stop fair dew stop
HIV VIH (virus immunodéficitaire humain) ⓜ vay·ee·ash (vee·rewsee·mew·no·day·fee·see·tair ew·mun)
HIV positive séropositif/séropositive ⓜ/ⓕ say·ro·po·zee·teef/say·ro·po·zee·teev
hobby passe-temps ⓜ pas·ton

hockey hockey ⓜ o·kay
hole trou ⓜ troo
holidays vacances ⓕ pl va·kons
home à la maison a la may·zon
homeless sans-abri son·za·bree
homemaker femme au foyer ⓕ fam o fwa·yay
homesick nostalgique nos·tal·zheek
homework devoirs ⓜ der·vwar
homosexual homosexuel(le) ⓜ/ⓕ o·mo·sek·swel
honest honnête o·net
honeymoon lune de miel ⓕ lewn der myel
hope espoir ⓜ es·pwar
hope espérer es·pay·ray
horoscope horoscope ⓜ o·ro·skop
horse cheval ⓜ shval
horse riding équitation ⓕ ay·kee·ta·syon
hospital hôpital ⓜ o·pee·tal
hospitality hospitalité ⓕ os·pee·ta·lee·tay
hot chaud(e) ⓜ/ⓕ sho(d)
hotel hôtel ⓜ o·tel
hour heure ⓕ er
house maison ⓕ may·zon
housework ménage ⓜ may·nazh
how comment ko·mon
hug serrer dans ses bras say·ray don say bra
huge énorme ay·norm
human humain ⓜ ew·mun
human rights droits de l'homme ⓜ pl drwa der lom
humanities lettres classiques ⓕ pl le·trer kla·seek
humour humour ⓜ ew·moor
hundred cent son
hungry (to be) avoir faim a·vwar fum
hunting chasse ⓕ shas
hurt blessé(e) ⓜ/ⓕ blay·say
husband mari ⓜ ma·ree

I

I je zher
ice glace ⓕ glas

I

ice cream glace ① glas
ice hockey hockey sur glace ⓜ o·kay sewr glas
idea idée ① ee·day
identification pièce d'identité ① pyes dee·don·tee·tay
identification card (ID) carte d'identité ① kart dee·don·tee·tay
idiot idiot(e) ⓜ/① ee·dyo(t)
if si see
ignorant ignorant(e) ⓜ/① ee·nyo·ron(t)
ill malade ma·lad
illegal illégal(e) ⓜ/① ee·lay·gal
imagination imagination ① ee·ma·zhee·na·syon
immediately/right now immédiatement ee·may·dyat·mon
immigration immigration ① ee·mee·gra·syon
impolite impoli(e) ⓜ/① um·po·lee
import importer um·por·tay
important important(e) ⓜ/① um·por·ton(t)
impossible impossible um·po·see·bler
improve améliorer a·may·lyo·ray
in dans don
in a hurry pressé(e) ⓜ/① pray·say
in front of devant der·von
included compris(e) ⓜ/① kom·pree(z)
income revenus ⓜ pl rerv·new
income tax impôt sur le revenu ⓜ um·po sewr ler rerv·new
inconvenient inopportun(e) ⓜ/① ee·no·por·tun/ee·no·por·tewn
independent indépendant(e) ⓜ/① un·day·pon·don(t)
India Inde ① und
indicator (on car) clignotant ⓜ klee·nyo·ton
indigestion indigestion ① un·dee·zhes·tyon
individual individu ⓜ un·dee·vee·dew
industrial industriel/industrielle ⓜ/① un·dews·tree·el

industry industrie ① un·dews·tree
infection infection ① un·fek·syon
inflammation inflammation ① un·fla·ma·syon
influence influence ① un·flew·ons
influenza grippe ① greep
information renseignements ⓜ plron·sen·yer·mon
ingredient ingrédient ⓜ ung·gray·dyon
inject injecter un·zhek·tay
injection piqûre ① pee·kewr
injured blessé(e) ⓜ/① blay·say
injury blessure ① blay·sewr
innocent innocent(e) ⓜ/① ee·no·son(t)
insect insecte ⓜ un·sekt
inside dedans der·don
insurance assurance ① a·sew·rons
insure assurer a·sew·ray
intelligent intelligent(e) ⓜ/① un·tay·lee·zhon(t)
interesting intéressant(e) ⓜ/① un·tay·ray·son(t)
intermission entracte ⓜ on·trakt
international international(e) ⓜ/① un·tair·na·syo·nal
Internet Internet ⓜ un·tair·net
Internet cafe cybercafé ⓜ see·bair·ka·fay
interpreter interprète ⓜ/① un·tair·pret
intersection carrefour ⓜ kar·foor
interview entrevue ① on·trer·vew
intimate intime un·teem
into dans don
introduce (people) présenter pray·zon·tay
invite inviter un·vee·tay
Ireland Irlande ① eer·lond
iron (clothes) repasser rer·pa·say
iron (for clothes) fer à repasser ⓜ fair a rer·pa·say
island île ① eel
IT informatique ① un·for·ma·teek
Italy Italie ① ee·ta·lee
itch démangeaison ① day·mon·zhay·zon

itemised détaillé(e) ⓜ/ⓕ day·ta·yay
itinerary itinéraire ⓜ ee·tee·nay·rair
IUD stérilet ⓜ stay·ree·lay

J

jacket veste ⓕ vest
jail prison ⓕ pree·zon
January janvier ⓜ zhon·vyay
Japan Japon ⓜ zha·pon
jar (jam) pot ⓜ po
jaw mâchoire ⓕ ma·shwar
jealous jaloux/jalouse ⓜ/ⓕ zha·loo/zha·looz
jeans jean ⓜ zheen
jeep jeep ⓕ zheep
jet lag fatigue due au décalage horaire ⓕ fa·teeg dew o day·ka·lazh o·rair
jewellery bijoux ⓜ pl bee·zhoo
Jewish juif/juive ⓜ/ⓕ zhweef/zhweev
job travail ⓜ tra·vai
jockey jockey ⓜ zho·kay
jogging jogging ⓜ zho·geeng
join joindre zhwun·drer
joke plaisanterie ⓕ play·zon·tree
journalist journaliste ⓜ/ⓕ zhoor·na·leest
journey voyage ⓜ vwa·yazh
joy joie ⓕ zhwa
judge juge ⓜ zhewzh
July juillet ⓜ zhwee·yay
jump sauter so·tay
jumper (sweater) pull ⓜ pewl
jumper leads câbles de démarrage ⓜ pl ka·bler der day·ma·razh
June juin ⓜ zhwun
justice justice ⓕ zhew·stees

K

kerb bord du trottoir ⓜ bor dew tro·twar
key clé ⓕ klay
keyboard clavier ⓜ kla·vyay
kick (person) donner un coup de pied à do·nay ung koo der pyay a

kick (football) donner un coup de pied dans do·nay ung koo der pyay don
kid (child) gamin/gamine ⓜ/ⓕ ga·mun/ga·meen
kill tuer tew·way
kilo kilo ⓜ kee·lo
kilogram kilogramme ⓜ kee·lo·gram
kilometre kilomètre ⓜ kee·lo·may·trer
kind (nice) gentil/gentile ⓜ/ⓕ zhon·tee
kind (type) genre ⓜ zhon·rer
kindergarten jardin d'enfants ⓜ zhar·dun don·fon
king roi ⓜ rwa
kingdom royaume ⓜ rwa·yom
kiosk kiosque ⓜ kyosk
kiss baiser ⓜ bay·zay
kiss embrasser om·bra·say
kitchen cuisine ⓕ kwee·zeen
kitten chaton ⓜ sha·ton
knee genou ⓜ zhnoo
kneel se mettre à genoux ser may·trer a zher·noo
knife couteau ⓜ koo·to
knitting tricot ⓜ tree·ko
know savoir sa·vwar
know (be familiar with) connaître ko·nay·trer
kosher casher/kascher ka·shair

L

labourer manoeuvre ⓜ ma·ner·vrer
lace dentelle ⓕ don·tel
lake lac ⓜ lak
lamp lampe ⓕ lomp
land terre ⓕ tair
landlady propriétaire ⓕ prop·ryay·tair
landlord propriétaire ⓜ prop·ryay·tair
lane (city) ruelle ⓕ rwel
lane (country) chemin ⓜ shmun
language langue ⓕ long
laptop ordinateur portable ⓜ or·dee·na·ter por·ta·bler
large grand(e) ⓜ/ⓕ gron(d)
last (previous) dernier/dernière ⓜ/ⓕ dair·nyay/dair·nyair

late en retard on rer·tar
later plus tard plew·tar
laugh rire reer
launderette laverie ⓕ lav·ree
laundry (clothes) linge ⓜ lunzh
laundry (place) blanchisserie ⓕ
blon·shees·ree
law loi ⓕ lwa
law (study, professsion) droit ⓜ drwa
lawyer avocat(e) ⓜ/ⓕ a·vo·ka(t)
laxative laxatif ⓜ lak·sa·teef
lazy paresseux/paresseuse ⓜ/ⓕ
pa·ray·ser/pa·ray·serz
leader chef ⓜ shef
leaf feuille ⓕ fer·yee
learn apprendre a·pron·drer
lease bail ⓜ ba·yer
lease louer à bail loo·way a ba·yer
least moins ⓜ mwun
leather cuir ⓜ kweer
leave partir par·teer
leave (something) laisser lay·say
lecturer professeur (à l'université) ⓜ
pro·fay·ser (a lew·nee·vair·see·tay)
ledge rebord ⓜ rer·bor
left (direction) à gauche a gosh
left luggage (office) consigne ⓕ
kon·see·nyer
left-wing de gauche der gosh
leg jambe ⓕ zhomb
legal légal(e) ⓜ/ⓕ lay·gal
legislation législation ⓕ
lay·zhee·sla·syon
length longueur ⓕ long·ger
lens objectif ⓜ ob·zhek·teef
lesbian lesbienne ⓕ les·byen
less moins mwun
less moins de mwun der
letter lettre ⓕ lay·trer
level niveau ⓜ nee·vo
liar menteur/menteuse ⓜ/ⓕ
mon·ter/mon·terz
library bibliothèque ⓕ bee·blee·o·tek
lice poux ⓜ pl poo
license plate number plaque
d'immatriculation ⓕ plak
dee·ma·tree·kew·la·syon

lie mensonge ⓜ mon·sonzh
lie (not stand) s'allonger sa·lon·zhay
lie (tell lies) mentir mon·teer
life vie ⓕ vee
life jacket gilet de sauvetage ⓜ
zhee·lay der sov·tazh
lift (arm) lever ler·vay
lift (elevator) ascenseur ⓜ a·son·ser
lift (something heavy) soulever
sool·vay
light lumière ⓕ lew·myair
light (on vehicle) phare ⓜ far
light (not heavy) léger/légère ⓜ/ⓕ
lay·zhay/lay·zhair
light (of colour) clair(e) ⓜ/ⓕ klair
light bulb ampoule ⓕ om·pool
light meter posemètre ⓜ poz·may·trer
lighter briquet ⓜ bree·kay
lights (on car) phares ⓜ pl far
like (as) comme kom
like (love) aimer ay·may
line ligne ⓕ lee·nyer
linen (material) lin ⓜ lun
linen (sheets etc) linge ⓜ lunzh
lingerie lingerie ⓕ lun·zhree
lip lèvre ⓕ lay·vrer
lip balm pommade pour les lèvres ⓕ
po·mad poor lay lay·vrer
lipstick rouge à lèvres ⓜ roozh a
lay·vrer
liquor store magasin de vins et
spiritueux ⓜ ma·ga·zun der vun ay
spee·ree·twer
listen (to) écouter ay·koo·tay
little petit(e) ⓜ/ⓕ per·tee(t)
little bit peu ⓜ per
live vivre vee·vrer
live (in a place) habiter a·bee·tay
liver foie ⓕ fwa
lizard lézard ⓜ lay·zar
local local(e) ⓜ/ⓕ lo·kal
lock fermer à clé fair·may a klay
lock serrure ⓕ say·rewr
locked fermé(e) à clé ⓜ/ⓕ fair·may
a klay
long long/longue ⓜ/ⓕ long
long-distance (flight) long-courrier
long·koo·ryay

look regarder rer·gar·day
look after s'occuper de so·kew·pay der
look at regarder rer·gar·day
look for chercher shair·shay
look out faire attention fair a·ton·syon
loose (clothes) ample om·pler
loose change petite monnaie ⓕ
per·teet mo·nay
lorry camion ⓜ ka·myon
lose perdre pair·drer
loser perdant(e) ⓜ/ⓕ pair·don(t)
loss perte ⓕ pairt
lost perdu(e) ⓜ/ⓕ pair·dew
lost property office bureau des
objets trouvés ⓜ bew·ro day zob·zhay
troo·vay
loud fort(e) ⓜ/ⓕ for(t)
love amour a·moor
love aimer ay·may
lover amant(e) ⓜ/ⓕ a·mon(t)
low bas/basse ⓜ/ⓕ ba(s)
loyal loyal(e) ⓜ/ⓕ lwa·yal
lubricant lubrifiant ⓜ lew·bree·fyon
luck chance ⓕ shons
lucky (to be) avoir de la chance
a·vwar der la shons
luggage bagages ⓜ pl ba·gazh
luggage lockers consigne automatique ⓕ kon·see·nyer o·to·ma·teek
luggage tag étiquette ⓕ ay·tee·ket
lump grosseur ⓕ gro·ser
lunch déjeuner ⓜ day·zher·nay
lung poumon ⓜ poo·mon
luxury luxe ⓜ lewks
luxury de luxe der lewks

M

machine machine ⓕ ma·sheen
mad (angry) fâché(e) ⓜ/ⓕ fa·shay
mad (crazy) fou/folle ⓜ/ⓕ foo/fol
made of (cotton, wood etc) en on
magazine magazine ⓜ ma·ga·zeen
magician magicien/magicienne ⓜ/ⓕ
ma·zhee·syun/ma·zhees·yen
mail (letters) courrier ⓜ koo·ryay
mail (postal system) poste ⓕ post

mailbox boîte aux lettres ⓕ bwat o
lay·trer
main principal(e) ⓜ/ⓕ prun·see·pal
main road grande route ⓕ grond root
main square place centrale ⓕ plas
son·tral
majority majorité ⓕ ma·zho·ree·tay
make faire fair
make-up maquillage ⓜ ma·kee·yazh
mammogram mammographie ⓕ
ma·mo·gra·fee
man homme ⓜ om
manage (business) diriger
dee·ree·zhay
manager directeur/directrice ⓜ/ⓕ
dee·rek·ter/dee·rek·trees
manager (restaurant, hotel)
gérant(e) ⓜ/ⓕ zhay·ron(t)
manner façon ⓕ fa·son
manual ⓜ/ⓕ manuel ma·nwel
manual worker ouvrier/ouvrière
ⓜ/ⓕ oo·vree·yay/oo·vree·yair
many beaucoup de bo·koo der
map (of country) carte ⓕ kart
map (of town) plan ⓜ plon
March mars ⓜ mars
marihuana marihuana ⓕ
ma·ree·wa·na
marital status situation familiale ⓕ
see·twa·syon fa·mee·lyal
market marché ⓜ mar·shay
marriage mariage ⓜ ma·ryazh
married marié(e) ⓜ/ⓕ ma·ryay
marry épouser ay·poo·zay
martial arts arts martiaux ⓜ pl
ar mar·syo
mass (Catholic) messe ⓕ mes
massage massage ⓜ ma·sazh
massage masser ma·say
masseur/masseuse masseur/
masseuse ⓜ/ⓕ ma·ser/ma·serz
mat petit tapis ⓜ per·tee ta·pee
match (sports) match ⓜ matsh
matches (for lighting) allumettes ⓕ
pl a·lew·met
material matériel ⓜ ma·tay·ryel

M

mattress matelas ⓜ mat·la
May mai ⓜ may
maybe peut-être per·tay·trer
mayor maire ⓜ mair
me moi mwa
meal repas ⓜ rer·pa
measles rougeole ⓕ roo·zhol
meat viande ⓕ vyond
mechanic mécanicien/
mécanicienne ⓜ/ⓕ may·ka·nee·syun/
may·ka·nee·syen
media médias ⓜ pl may·dya
medicine médecine ⓕ med·seen
medicine (medication) médicament
ⓜ may·dee·ka·mon
meditation méditation ⓕ
may·dee·ta·syon
meet rencontrer ron·kon·tray
member membre ⓜ mom·brer
memory (ability to remember)
mémoire ⓕ may·mwar
memory (recollection) souvenir ⓜ
soov·neer
menstruation menstruation ⓕ
mon·strew·a·syon
menu carte kart
message message ⓜ may·sazh
messy en désordre on day·zor·drer
metal métal ⓜ may·tal
metre mètre ⓜ may·trer
metro station station de métro ⓕ
sta·syon der may·tro
microwave (oven) four à micro-ondes
ⓜ foor a mee·kro·ond
midday/noon midi mee·dee
midnight minuit mee·nwee
migraine migraine ⓕ mee·gren
military militaire mee·lee·tair
military service service militaire ⓜ
sair·vees mee·lee·tair
milk lait ⓜ lay
millennium millénaire ⓜ mee·lay·nair
millimetre millimètre ⓜ
mee·lee·may·trer
million million ⓜ mee·lyon
mind esprit ⓜ ay·spree
mineral water eau minérale ⓕ
o mee·nay·ral

minority minorité ⓕ mee·no·ree·tay
minute minute ⓕ mee·newt
mirror miroir ⓜ mee·rwar
miscarriage (to have a) faire une
fausse couche fair ewn fos koosh
miss manquer mong·kay
mistake erreur ⓕ ay·rer
mix mélanger may·lon·zhay
mix up (confuse) confondre
kon·fon·drer
mobile phone téléphone portable ⓜ
tay·lay·fon por·ta·bler
modem modem ⓜ mo·dem
modern moderne mo·dairn
moisturiser crème hydratante ⓕ
krem ee·dra·tont
mom maman ⓕ ma·mon
monarchy monarchie ⓕ mo·nar·shee
monastery monastère ⓜ mo·na·stair
Monday lundi ⓜ lun·dee
money argent ⓜ ar·zhon
monkey singe ⓜ sunzh
month mois ⓜ mwa
monument monument ⓜ
mo·new·mon
more plus de plews der
more plus plew
morning matin ⓜ ma·tun
morning sickness nausées
plmatinales ⓕ no·zay ma·tee·nal
mosque mosquée ⓕ mo·skay
mosquito moustique ⓜ moo·steek
mosquito coil allume-feu anti-
moustiques ⓜ a·lewm·fer
on·tee·moo·steek
mosquito net moustiquaire ⓕ
moo·stee·kair
most plus ⓜ plews
motel motel ⓜ mo·tel
mother mère ⓕ mair
mother-in-law belle-mère ⓕ bel·mair
motorboat canot automobile ⓜ
ka·no o·to·mo·beel
motorcycle moto ⓕ mo·to
motorway (tollway) autoroute ⓕ
o·to·root
mountain montagne ⓕ mon·ta·nyer

mountain bike vélo tout terrain (VTT) m vay·lo too tay·run (vay·tay·tay)
mountain path chemin de montagne m shmun der mon·ta·nyer
mountain range chaîne de montagnes f shen der mon·ta·nyer
mountaineering alpinisme m al·pee·nee·smer
mouse souris f soo·ree
mouth bouche f boosh
move bouger boo·zhay
movie film m feelm
Miss Mademoiselle mad·mwa·zel
Mr Monsieur mer·syer
Mrs/Ms Madame ma·dam
mud boue f boo
mum maman f ma·mon
muscle muscle m mews·kler
museum musée m mew·zay
music musique f mew·zeek
music shop disquaire m dee·skair
musician musicien/musicienne m/f mew·zees·yun/mew·zees·yen
Muslim musulman(e) m/f mew·zewl·mon/mew·zewl·man
my mon/ma/mes m/f/pl mon/ma/may

N

nail clippers coupe-ongles m koop·ong·gler
name nom m nom
napkin serviette f sair·vyet
nappy couche f koosh
narcotic stupéfiant m stew·pay·fyon
national park parc national m park na·syo·nal
nationality nationalité f na·syo·na·lee·tay
nature nature f na·tewr
naturopath naturopathe m/f na·tew·ro·pat
nausea nausée f no·zay
near près de pray der
nearby tout près too pray
nearest le/la plus proche m/f ler/la plew prosh

necessary nécessaire nay·say·sair
necklace collier m ko·lyay
need avoir besoin de a·vwar ber·zwun de
needle aiguille f ay·gwee·yer
neither ni nee
net filet m fee·lay
Netherlands Pays-Bas m pl pay·ee·ba
network réseau m ray·zo
never jamais zha·may
new nouveau/nouvelle m/f noo·vo/noo·vel
New Year's Day jour de l'An m zhoor der lon
New Year's Eve Saint-Sylvestre f sun·seel·ves·trer
New Zealand Nouvelle-Zélande f noo·vel·zay·lond
news les nouvelles lay noo·vel
news (on TV etc) les actualités lay zak·twa·lee·tay
newsagent marchand de journaux m mar·shon der zhoor·no
newspaper journal m zhoor·nal
next (month) prochain(e) m/f pro·shun/pro·shen
next to ... à côté de ... a ko·tay der
nice (kind) gentil/gentille m/f zhon·tee/zhon·tee·yer
nice (pleasant) agréable a·gray·a·bler
nickname surnom m sewr·nom
night nuit f nwee
night out soirée f swa·ray
nightclub boîte f bwat
nine neuf nerf
no non non
no vacancy complet kom·play
noisy bruyant(e) m/f brew·yon(t)
nondirect non-direct non·dee·rekt
none aucun(e) m/f o·kun/o·kewn
nonsmoking non-fumeur non·few·mer
noon midi mee·dee
north nord m nor
northern hemisphere hémisphère nord m ay·mees·fair nor
nose nez m nay

N

O

not bad pas mal pa mal
not yet pas encore pa zong·kor
notebook carnet ⓜ kar·nay
nothing rien ryun
novel roman ⓜ ro·mon
now maintenant mun·ter·non
nuclear energy énergie nucléaire ⓕ ay·nair·zhee new·klay·air
nuclear power puissance nucléaire ⓕ pwee·sons new·klay·air
nuclear test essai nucléaire ⓜ ay·say new·klay·air
nuclear waste déchets nucléaires ⓜ day·shay new·klay·air
number numéro ⓜ new·may·ro
nun religieuse ⓕ rer·lee·zhyerz
nurse infirmier/infirmière ⓜ/ⓕ un·feer·myay/un·feer·myair

O

obtain obtenir op·ter·neer
obvious évident(e) ⓜ/ⓕ ay·vee·don(t)
occupation occupation ⓕ o·kew·pa·syon
ocean océan ⓜ o·say·on
off (meat) mauvais(e) ⓜ/ⓕ mo·vay(z)
offence délit ⓜ day·lee
office bureau ⓜ bew·ro
office worker employé(e) de bureau ⓜ/ⓕ om·plwa·yay der bew·ro
officer officier ⓜ o·fees·yay
officer (police) agent de police ⓜ a·zhon der po·lees
offside (sport) hors jeu or·zher
often souvent soo·von
oil huile ⓕ weel
oil (petrol) pétrole ⓜ pay·trol
old vieux/vieille ⓜ/ⓕ vyer/vyay
Olympic Games Les Jeux Olympiques lay zher zo·lum·peek
on sur sewr
on strike en grève ong grev
on the corner au coin o kwun
on time à l'heure a ler
once une fois ewn fwa
one un(e) ⓜ/ⓕ un/ewn

one-way (ticket) (billet) simple (bee·yay) sum·pler
only seul(e) ⓜ/ⓕ serl
open ouvert(e) ⓜ/ⓕ oo·vair(t)
open ouvrir oo·vreer
opening hours heures d'ouverture ⓕ pl lay zer doo·vair·tewr
opera opéra ⓜ o·pay·ra
operation opération ⓕ o·pay·ra·syon
operator opérateur/opératrice ⓜ/ⓕ o·pay·ra·ter/o·pay·ra·trees
opinion avis ⓜ a·vee
opponent adversaire ⓜ/ⓕ ad·vair·sair
opportunity occasion ⓕ o·ka·zyon
opposite en face de on fas der
or ou oo
orange (colour) orange o·ronzh
order ordre ⓜ or·drer
order ordonner or·do·nay
ordinary ordinaire or·dee·nair
organisation organisation ⓕ or·ga·nee·za·syon
organise organiser or·ga·nee·zay
orgasm orgasme ⓜ or·gas·mer
original original(e) ⓜ/ⓕ o·ree·zhee·nal
other autre o·trer
our notre no·trer
out of order hors service or sair·vees
outside dehors der·or
oven four ⓜ foor
over (above) par-dessus par·der·sew
over (finished) fini(e) ⓜ/ⓕ fee·nee
overdose overdose ⓕ o·vair·doz
overnight pendant la nuit pon·don la nwee
overseas outre-mer oo·trer·mair
owe devoir de·vwar
owner propriétaire ⓜ/ⓕ pro·pree·ay·tair
ox bœuf ⓜ berf
oxygen oxygène ⓜ ok·see·zhen
ozone layer couche d'ozone ⓕ koosh do·zon

P

pacemaker pacemaker ⓜ pes·may·ker

pacifier (dummy) tétine ⓕ tay·teen

package paquet ⓜ pa·kay

packet (general) paquet ⓜ pa·kay

padlock cadenas ⓜ kad·na

page page ⓕ pazh

pain douleur ⓕ doo·ler

painful douloureux/douloureuse ⓜ/ⓕ doo·loo·rer/doo·loo·rerz

painkiller analgésique ⓜ a·nal·zhay·zeek

painter peintre ⓜ pun·trer

painting (a work) tableau ⓜ ta·blo

painting (the art) peinture ⓕ pun·tewr

pair (couple) paire ⓕ pair

palace palais ⓜ pa·lay

pan casserole ⓕ kas·rol

panties slip ⓜ sleep

pants pantalon ⓜ pon·ta·lon

pants (underpants) slip ⓜ sleep

panty liners protège-slips ⓜ pl pro·tezh·sleep

pantyhose collant ⓜ ko·lon

pap smear frottis ⓜ fro·tee

paper papier ⓜ pa·pyay

paperwork paperasserie ⓕ pa·pras·ree

parade (ceremony) parade ⓕ pa·rad

paraplegic paraplégique pa·ra·play·zheek

parcel colis ⓜ ko·lee

parents parents ⓜ pl pa·ron

park parc ⓜ park

park (a car) garer (une voiture) ga·ray (ewn vwa·tewr)

part partie ⓕ par·tee

participate participer par·tee·see·pay

particular particulier/particulière ⓜ/ⓕ par·tee·kew·lyay/par·tee·kew·lyair

part-time à temps partiel a tom par·syel

party (night out) soirée ⓕ swa·ray

party (politics) parti ⓜ par·tee

pass passer pa·say

pass (football) passe ⓕ pas

passenger voyageur/voyageuse ⓜ/ⓕ vwa·ya·zher/vwa·ya·zherz

passport passeport ⓜ pas·por

passport number numéro de passeport ⓜ new·may·ro der pas·por

past passé ⓜ pa·say

path chemin ⓜ shmun

pay payer pay·yay

payment paiement ⓜ pay·mon

peace paix ⓕ pay

peak cime ⓕ seem

pedal pédale ⓕ pay·dal

pedestrian piéton ⓜ pyay·ton

pen (ballpoint) stylo ⓜ stee·lo

pencil crayon ⓜ kray·yon

penicillin pénicilline ⓕ pay·nee·see·leen

penis pénis ⓜ pay·nees

penknife canif ⓜ ka·neef

pensioner retraité(e) ⓜ/ⓕ rer·tray·tay

people gens ⓜ pl zhon

per (day) par par

percent pour cent poor son

perfect parfait(e) ⓜ/ⓕ par·fay(t)

performance spectacle ⓜ spek·ta·kler

perfume parfum ⓜ par·fum

period pain règles douloureuses ⓕ pl ray·gler doo·loo·rerz

permanent permanent(e) ⓜ/ⓕ pair·ma·non(t)

permission permission ⓕ pair·mee·syon

permit permis ⓜ pair·mee

permit permettre pair·may·trer

person personne ⓕ pair·son

personal personnel(le) ⓜ/ⓕ pair·so·nel

personality personnalité ⓕ pair·so·na·lee·tay

pet animal familier ⓜ a·nee·mal fa·mee·lyay

petition pétition ⓕ pay·tees·yon

petrol essence ⓕ ay·sons

P

petrol station station-service ⓕ sta·syon·sair·vees

pharmacy pharmacie ⓕ far·ma·see

phone book annuaire ⓜ an·wair

phone box cabine téléphonique ⓕ ka·been tay·lay·fo·neek

phone card télécarte ⓕ tay·lay·kart

photo photo ⓕ fo·to

photographer photographe ⓜ/ⓕ fo·to·graf

photography photographie ⓕ fo·to·gra·fee

phrase expression ⓕ ek·spray·syon

phrasebook recueil d'expressions ⓜ rer·ker·yer dek·spray·syon

physiotherapist kinésithérapeute ⓜ&ⓕ kee·nay·zee·tay·ra·pert

physiotherapy kinésithérapie ⓕ kee·nay·zee·tay·ra·pee

pick (choose) choisir shwa·zeer

pick up (something) ramasser ra·ma·say

picnic pique-nique ⓜ peek·neek

picture image ⓕ ee·mazh

piece morceau ⓜ mor·so

pig cochon ⓜ ko·shon

pill pilule ⓕ pee·lewl

pillow oreiller ⓜ o·ray·yay

pillowcase taie d'oreiller ⓕ tay do·ray·yay

pin épingle ⓕ ay·pung·gler

pink rose roz

pipe pipe ⓕ peep

place lieu ⓜ lyer

place of birth lieu de naissance ⓜ lyer der nay·sons

plane avion ⓜ a·vyon

planet planète ⓕ pla·net

plastic plastique ⓜ plas·teek

plate assiette ⓕ a·syet

platform quai ⓜ kay

play (cards etc) jouer zhoo·ay

play (football etc) jouer au zhoo·ay o

play (guitar etc) jouer de zhoo·ay der

play (theatre) pièce de théâtre ⓕ pyes der tay·a·trer

playground terrain de jeux ⓜ tay·run der zher

plenty abondance ⓕ a·bon·dons

plenty beaucoup de bo·koo der

plug (bath) bonde ⓕ bond

plug (electricity) prise ⓕ preez

pocket poche ⓕ posh

poetry poésie ⓕ po·ay·zee

point pointe ⓕ pwunt

point indiquer un·dee·kay

poisonous venimeux/venimeuse ⓜ/ⓕ ver·nee·mer/ver·nee·merz

police police ⓕ po·lees

police car voiture de police ⓕ vwa·tewr der po·lees

police officer (in city) policier ⓜ po·lee·syay

police officer (in country) gendarme ⓜ zhon·darm

police station commissariat ⓜ ko·mee·sar·ya

policy politique ⓕ po·lee·teek

politician homme/femme politique ⓜ/ⓕ om/fam po·lee·teek

politics politique ⓕ po·lee·teek

pollen pollen ⓜ po·len

pollution pollution ⓕ po·lew·syon

pond étang ⓜ ay·tong

pool (game) billard américain ⓜ bee·yar a·may·ree·kun

pool (swimming) piscine ⓕ pee·seen

poor pauvre po·vrer

popular populaire po·pew·lair

port port ⓜ por

positive positif/positive ⓜ/ⓕ po·zee·teef/po·zee·teev

possible possible po·see·bler

post code code postal ⓜ kod pos·tal

post office bureau de poste ⓜ bew·ro der post

postage tarifs postaux ⓜ pl ta·reef pos·to

postcard carte postale ⓕ kart pos·tal

postman facteur ⓜ fak·ter

pot (ceramics) pot ⓜ po

pottery poterie ⓕ po·tree

pound (money, weight) livre ⓕ leev·rer

poverty pauvreté ⓕ po·vrer·tay

power pouvoir ⓜ poo·vwar
practical pratique pra·teek
practise pratiquer pra·tee·kay
prayer prière ⓕ pree·yair
prefer préférer pray·fay·ray
pregnancy test kit test de grossesse
ⓜ test der gro·ses
pregnant enceinte on·sunt
premenstrual tension
syndrome prémenstruel ⓜ sun·drom
pray·mon·strwel
prepare préparer pray·pa·ray
prescription ordonnance ⓕ
or·do·nons
present (gift) cadeau ⓜ ka·do
present (time) présent ⓜ pray·zon
president président ⓜ pray·zee·don
pressure pression ⓕ pray·syon
pretend faire semblant fair som·blon
pretty joli(e) ⓜ/ⓕ zho·lee
prevent empêcher om·pay·shay
previous précédent(e) ⓜ/ⓕ
pray·say·don(t)
price prix ⓜ pree
priest prêtre ⓜ pray·trer
prime minister premier ministre ⓜ
prer·myay mee·nee·strer
printer (computer) imprimante ⓕ
um·pree·mont
prison prison ⓕ pree·zon
prisoner prisonnier/prisonnière ⓜ/ⓕ
pree·zo·nyay/pree·zo·nyair
private privé(e) ⓜ/ⓕ pree·vay
private hospital clinique privée ⓕ
klee·neek pree·vay
probable probable pro·ba·bler
problem problème ⓜ pro·blem
produce produire pro·dweer
professional professionnel(le) ⓜ/ⓕ
pro·fay·syo·nel
profit bénéfice ⓜ bay·nay·fees
programme programme ⓜ pro·gram
projector projecteur ⓜ pro·zhek·ter
promise promesse ⓕ pro·mes
promise promettre pro·may·trer
promote promouvoir pro·moo·vwar
prostitute prostituée ⓕ pro·stee·tway
protect protéger pro·tay·zhay

protected (species) protégé(e) ⓜ/ⓕ
pro·tay·zhay
protection protection ⓕ pro·tek·syon
protest manif(estation) ⓕ
ma·neef(ay·sta·syon)
protest manifester ma·nee·fay·stay
provisions provisions ⓕ pl
pro·vee·zyon
psychotherapy psychothérapie ⓕ
psee·ko·tay·ra·pee
pub (bar) bar ⓜ bar
public public ⓜ pewb·leek
public telephone téléphone public ⓜ
tay·lay·fon pewb·leek
public toilet toilettes ⓕ pl twa·let
pull tirer tee·ray
pump pompe ⓕ pomp
puncture crevaison ⓕ krer·vay·zon
punish punir pew·neer
puppy chiot ⓜ shyo
pure pur(e) ⓜ/ⓕ pewr
purple violet(te) ⓜ/ⓕ vyo·lay(·let)
purpose objet ⓜ ob·zhay
purse porte-monnaie ⓕ port·mo·nay
push pousser poo·say
pushchair poussette ⓕ poo·set
put mettre may·trer

Q

qualification qualification ⓕ
ka·lee·fee·ka·syon
quality qualité ⓕ ka·lee·tay
quantity quantité ⓕ kon·tee·tay
quarantine quarantaine ⓕ ka·ron·ten
quarrel dispute ⓕ dees·pewt
quarter quart ⓜ kar
queen reine ⓕ ren
question question ⓕ kay·styon
queue queue ⓕ ker
quick rapide ra·peed
quiet tranquille trong·keel
quit quitter kee·tay

R

rabbit lapin ⓜ la·pun
race race ⓕ ras

R

race (sport) course ① koors
racetrack champ de courses ⓜ shon der koors
racism racisme ⓜ ra·sees·mer
racquet raquette ① ra·ket
radiator radiateur ⓜ ra·dya·ter
radical radical(e) ⓜ/① ra·dee·kal
radio radio ① ra·dyo
rail garde-fou ⓜ gard·foo
railway chemin de fer ⓜ shmun der fair
railway station gare ① gar
rain pluie ① plwee
rain pleuvoir pler·vwar
raincoat imperméable um·pair·may·abler
raise (lift) soulever sool·vay
rape violer vyo·lay
rare rare rar
rash rougeur ① roo·zher
rat rat ⓜ ra
rave rave ① raiv
raw cru(e) ⓜ/① krew
razor rasoir ⓜ ra·zwar
razor blade lame de rasoir ① lam der ra·zwar
reach atteindre a·tun·drer
read lire leer
ready prêt(e) ⓜ/① pray/pret
real vrai(e) ⓜ/① vray
real estate agent agent immobilier ⓜ a·zhon ee·mo·bee·lyay
realise se rendre compte de ser ron·drer kont der
realistic réaliste ray·a·leest
reality réalité ① ray·a·lee·tay
really vraiment vray·mon
rear (seat etc) arrière a·ryair
reason raison ① ray·zon
receipt reçu ⓜ rer·sew
receive recevoir rer·ser·vwar
recently récemment ray·sa·mon
recognise reconnaître rer·ko·nay·trer
recommend recommander rer·ko·mon·day
record enregistrer on·rer·zhees·tray
record (music) disque ⓜ deesk

recording enregistrement ⓜ on·rer·zhees·trer·mon
recyclable recyclable rer·see·kla·bler
recycle recycler rer·see·klay
recycling recyclage ⓜ rer·see·klazh
red rouge roozh
reduce réduire ray·dweer
referee arbitre ⓜ ar·bee·trer
reference référence ① ray·fay·rons
reflexology réflexologie ① ray·flek·so·lo·zhee
refrigerator réfrigérateur ⓜ ray·free·zhay·ra·ter
refugee réfugié(e) ⓜ/① ray·few·zhyay
refund remboursement ⓜ rom·boor·ser·mon
refuse refuser rer·few·zay
region région ① ray·zhyon
registered mail/post (by) en recommandé on rer·ko·mon·day
regular normal(e) ⓜ/① nor·mal
relationship relation ① rer·la·syon
relax (rest) se reposer ser rer·po·zay
relevant pertinent(e) ⓜ/① pair·tee·non(t)
religion religion ① rer·lee·zhyon
religious religieux/religieuse ⓜ/① rer·lee·zhyer/rer·lee·zhyerz
remember se souvenir ser soo·ver·neer
remote éloigné(e) ⓜ/① ay·lwa·nyay
remote control télécommande ① tay·lay·ko·mond
rent louer loo·ay
repair réparer ray·pa·ray
reply répondre ray·pon·drer
represent représenter rer·pray·zon·tay
republic république ① ray·pewb·leek
research recherches ① pl rer·shairsh
reservation réservation ① ray·zair·va·syon
response réponse ① ray·pons
rest repos ⓜ rer·po
restaurant restaurant ⓜ res·to·ron

resumé CV ⓜ say·vay
retired retraité(e) ⓜ/ⓕ rer·tray·tay
return revenir rerv·neer
return (ticket) aller retour ⓜ a·lay rer·toor
review (article) critique ⓕ kree·teek
revolution révolution ⓕ ray·vo·lew·syon
rhythm rythme ⓜ reet·mer
rice riz ⓜ ree
rich (wealthy) riche reesh
ride promenade ⓕ prom·nad
ride (horse) monter à (cheval) mon·tay a (shval)
right (direction) à droite a drwat
right (entitlement) droite ⓜ drwa
right (to be right) avoir raison a·vwar ray·zon
right-wing de droite der drwat
ring (of phone) sonner so·nay
ring (on finger) bague ⓕ bag
ring (shape) anneau ⓜ a·no
ring road (boulevard) périphérique (BP) ⓜ (bool·var) pay·ree·fay·reek (bay pay)
rip-off arnaque ⓕ ar·nak
risk risque ⓜ reesk
river rivière ⓕ ree·vyair
road route ⓕ root
road map carte routière ⓕ kart roo·tyair
rob (person) voler vo·lay
robbery vol ⓜ vol
rock rocher ⓜ ro·shay
rock climbing varappe ⓕ va·rap
rock group groupe de rock ⓜ groop der rok
rock music rock ⓜ rok
rollerblading roller ⓜ ro·lair
romantic romantique ro·mon·teek
roof toit ⓜ twa
room chambre ⓕ shom·brer
room number numéro de chambre ⓜ new·may·ro der shom·brer
rooster coq ⓜ kok
rope corde ⓕ kord
round rond(e) ⓜ/ⓕ ron(d)

roundabout (traffic) rond-point ⓜ rom·pwun
route itinéraire ⓕ ee·tee·nay·rair
rowing aviron ⓜ a·vee·ron
rubbish ordures ⓕ or·dewr
rubbish bin poubelle ⓕ poo·bel
rubbish dump décharge ⓕ day·sharzh
rude impoli(e) ⓜ/ⓕ um·po·lee
rug tapis ⓜ ta·pee
rugby rugby ⓜ rewg·bee
ruins ruines ⓕ pl rween
rules règles ⓕ ray·gler
run courir koo·reer
run out of manquer de mong·kay der

S

Sabbath sabbat ⓜ sa·ba
sad triste treest
saddle selle ⓕ sel
safe sans danger son don·zhay
safe coffre-fort ⓜ kof·rer·for
safe sex rapports sexuels protégés ⓜ pl ra·por seks·wel pro·tay·zhay
safety sécurité ⓕ say·kew·ree·tay
sail voile ⓕ vwal
sailing voile ⓕ vwal
saint saint(e) ⓜ/ⓕ sun(t)
salary salaire ⓜ sa·lair
sale vente ⓕ vont
sales tax taxe à la vente ⓕ taks a la vont
salt sel ⓜ sel
same même mem
sand sable ⓜ sa·bler
sandals sandales ⓕ son·dal
sanitary napkin serviette hygiénique ⓕ sair·vyet ee·zhyay·neek
satisfied satisfait(e) ⓜ/ⓕ sa·tees·fay/sa·tees·fet
Saturday samedi ⓜ sam·dee
sauna sauna ⓜ so·na
save sauver so·vay
say dire deer
scared effrayé(e) ⓜ/ⓕ ay·fray·yay
scarf écharpe ⓕ ay·sharp
scenery paysage ⓜ pay·yee·zazh
school école ⓕ ay·kol

science science ⓕ syons
science fiction science-fiction ⓕ
syons·feek·syon
scientist scientifique ⓜ/ⓕ
syon·tee·feek
scissors ciseaux ⓜ pl see·zo
score score ⓜ skor
scoreboard tableau d'affichage ⓜ
ta·blo da·fee·shazh
Scotland Ecosse ⓕ ay·kos
screen écran ⓜ ay·kron
script scénario ⓜ say·na·ryo
sculpture sculpture ⓕ skewl·tewr
sea mer ⓕ mair
seashell coquillage ⓜ ko·kee·yazh
seasick (to be) avoir le mal de mer
a·vwar ler mal der mair
seaside bord de la mer ⓜ bor der
la mair
season saison ⓕ say·zon
seat (place) place ⓕ plas
seatbelt ceinture de sécurité ⓕ
sun·tewr der say·kew·ree·tay
second second(e) ⓜ/ⓕ skon/skond
second class de seconde classe der
skond klas
second (clock) seconde ⓕ skond
secondhand d'occasion do·ka·zyon
secret secret ⓜ ser·kray
secretary secrétaire ⓜ/ⓕ
ser·kray·tair
security sécurité ⓕ say·kew·ree·tay
see voir vwar
self service libre-service ⓜ
lee·brer·sair·vees
self-employed indépendant(e) ⓜ/ⓕ
un·day·pon·don(t)
selfish égoïste ay·go·eest
sell vendre von·drer
seminar séminaire ⓜ say·mee·nair
send envoyer on·vwa·yay
sensible raisonnable ray·zo·na·bler
sensual sensuel(le) ⓜ/ⓕ son·swel
separate séparé(e) ⓜ/ⓕ say·pa·ray
September septembre ⓜ sep·tom·brer
series série ⓕ say·ree

serious sérieux/sérieuse ⓜ/ⓕ
say·ree·yer/say·ree·yerz
service service ⓜ sair·vees
service charge service ⓜ sair·vees
service station station-service ⓕ
sta·syon·sair·vees
seven sept set
several plusieurs plew·zyer
sew coudre koo·drer
sex sexe ⓜ seks
sexism sexisme ⓜ sek·see·smer
sexist sexiste sek·seest
sexy sexy sek·see
shade ombre ⓕ om·brer
shadow ombre ⓕ om·brer
shake (something) agiter a·zhee·tay
shallow peu profond ⓜ per pro·fon(d)
shampoo shampooing ⓜ shom·pwung
shape forme ⓕ form
shape façonner fa·so·nay
share (a dorm etc) partager
par·ta·zhay
share (with) partager (avec)
par·ta·zhay (a·vek)
sharp (blade etc) tranchant(e) ⓜ/ⓕ
tron·shon(t)
shave se raser ser ra·zay
shaving cream mousse à raser ⓕ
moos a ra·zay
she elle el
sheep mouton ⓜ moo·ton
sheet (bed) drap ⓜ dra
sheet (of paper) feuille ⓕ fer·yee
shelf étagère ⓕ ay·ta·zhair
shelter abri ⓜ a·bree
ship navire ⓜ na·veer
shirt chemise ⓕ sher·meez
shoe chaussure ⓕ sho·sewr
shoe shop magasin de chaussures ⓜ
ma·ga·zun der sho·sewr
shoot tirer tee·ray
shop magasin ⓜ ma·ga·zun
shop faire des courses fair day koors
shopping centre centre commercial
ⓜ son·trer ko·mair·syal
short (height) court(e) ⓜ/ⓕ koor(t)
shortage manque ⓜ mongk

shorts short ⓜ short
shoulder épaule ⓕ ay·pol
shout crier kree·yay
show montrer mon·tray
show spectacle ⓜ spek·ta·kler
shower douche ⓕ doosh
shrine lieu saint ⓜ lyer sun
shut fermé(e) ⓜ/ⓕ fair·may
shy timide tee·meed
sick malade ma·lad
sickness maladie ⓕ ma·la·dee
side côté ⓜ ko·tay
sign signe ⓜ see·nyer
signature signature ⓕ see·nya·tewr
silk soie ⓕ swa
silver argent ⓜ ar·zhon
similar semblable som·bla·bler
simple simple sum·pler
since (May etc) depuis der·pwee
sing chanter shon·tay
Singapore Singapour sung·ga·poor
singer chanteur/chanteuse ⓜ/ⓕ shon·ter/shon·terz
single (person) célibataire say·lee·ba·tair
single room chambre pour une personne ⓕ shom·brer poor ewn pair·son
singlet maillot de corps ⓜ ma·yo der kor
sister sœur ⓕ ser
sit s'asseoir sa·swar
situation situation ⓕ see·twa·syon
six six sees
size (general) taille ⓕ tai
skateboarding skateboard ⓜ sket·bord
ski skier skee·yay
skiing ski ⓜ skee
skill compétence ⓕ kom·pay·tons
skin peau ⓕ po
skirt jupe ⓕ zhewp
skis skis ⓜ skee
sky ciel ⓜ syel
sleep sommeil ⓜ so·may
sleep dormir dor·meer

sleeping bag sac de couchage ⓜ sak der koo·shazh
sleeping car wagon-lit ⓜ va·gon·lee
sleeping pill somnifère ⓜ som·nee·fair
sleepy (to be sleepy) avoir sommeil a·vwar so·may
slice tranche ⓕ tronsh
slide (film) diapositive ⓕ dya·po·zee·teev
slow lent(e) ⓜ/ⓕ lon(t)
slowly lentement lon·ter·mon
small petit(e) ⓜ/ⓕ per·tee/per·teet
smaller plus petit(e) ⓜ/ⓕ plew per·tee/·teet
smallest le plus petit/la plus petite ⓜ/ⓕ ler plew per·tee/la plew per·teet
smell odeur ⓕ o·der
smell sentir son·teer
smile sourire ⓜ soo·reer
smile sourire soo·reer
smoke fumée ⓕ few·may
smoke fumer few·may
snack casse-croûte ⓜ kas·kroot
snail escargot ⓜ es·kar·go
snake serpent ⓜ sair·pon
snorkel nager avec un tuba na·zhay a·vek un tew·ba
snow neige ⓕ nezh
snow neiger nay·zhay
snowboarding surf (des neiges) ⓜ serf (day nezh)
soap savon ⓜ sa·von
soccer foot(ball) ⓜ foot(bol)
social welfare sécurité sociale ⓕ say·kew·ree·tay so·syal
socialism socialisme ⓜ so·sya·lees·mer
socialist socialiste so·sya·leest
society société ⓕ so·syay·tay
socks chaussettes ⓕ sho·set
soft doux/douce ⓜ/ⓕ doo/doos
software logiciel ⓜ lo·zhee·syel
soldier soldat ⓜ sol·da
solid solide so·leed
some quelques kel·ker
some du/de la/des ⓜ/ⓕ/pl dew/der la/day

S

someone quelqu'un kel·kun
something quelque chose kel·ker shoz
sometimes quelquefois kel·ker·fwa
son fils ⓜ fees
song chanson ⓕ shon·son
soon bientôt byun·to
sore douloureux/douloureuse ⓜ/ⓕ doo·loo·rer/doo·loo·rerz
south sud ⓜ sewd
southern hemisphere hémisphère sud ⓜ ay·mees·fair sewd
souvenir souvenir ⓜ soov·neer
souvenir shop magasin de souvenirs ⓜ ma·ga·zun der soov·neer
space espace ⓜ es·pas
Spain Espagne ⓕ es·pa·nyer
speak parler par·lay
special spécial(e) ⓜ/ⓕ spay·syal
specialist spécialiste ⓜ/ⓕ spay·sya·leest
speech discours ⓜ dees·koor
speed vitesse ⓕ vee·tes
speed limit limitation de vitesse ⓕ lee·mee·ta·syon der vee·tes
speedometer compteur (de vitesse) ⓜ kon·ter (der vee·tes)
spend (money) dépenser day·pon·say
spend (time) passer pa·say
spicy épicé(e) ⓜ/ⓕ ay·pee·say
spider araignée ⓕ a·ray·nyay
spine colonne vertébrale ⓕ ko·lon vair·tay·bral
spirit esprit ⓜ es·pree
spoon cuillère ⓕ kwee·yair
sport sport ⓜ spor
sports ground terrain de sport ⓜ tay·run der spor
sports store/shop magasin de sports ⓜ ma·ga·zun der spor
sportsperson sportif/sportive ⓜ/ⓕ spor·teef/spor·teev
sprain entorse ⓕ on·tors
spring (coil) ressort ⓜ rer·sor
spring (season) printemps ⓜ prun·tom
square (town) place ⓕ plas

stadium stade ⓜ stad
stage scène ⓕ sen
stairway escalier ⓜ es·ka·lyay
stale pas frais/fraîche ⓜ/ⓕ pa fray/fresh
stale (bread) rassis(e) ⓜ/ⓕ ra·see(z)
stamp timbre ⓜ tum·brer
stand-by ticket billet stand-by ⓜ bee·yay stond·bai
stars étoiles ⓕ ay·twal
start commencement ⓜ ko·mons·mon
start commencer ko·mon·say
station gare ⓕ gar
stationer's (shop) papeterie ⓕ pa·pet·ree
stay rester res·tay
steal voler vo·lay
steep raide red
step marche ⓕ marsh
stereo (system) chaîne hi-fi ⓕ shen ee·fee
stockings bas ⓜ ba
stolen volé(e) ⓜ/ⓕ vo·lay
stomach estomac ⓜ es·to·ma
stomach ache (to have a) avoir mal au ventre a·vwar mal o von·trer
stone pierre ⓕ pyair
stop arrêt ⓜ a·ray
stop (doing) s'arrêter sa·ray·tay
stop (something, someone) arrêter a·ray·tay
storm orage ⓜ o·razh
story histoire ⓕ ees·twar
stove réchaud ⓜ ray·sho
straight droit(e) ⓜ/ⓕ drwa(t)
straight ahead tout droit too drwa
strange étrange ay·tronzh
stranger étranger/étrangère ⓜ/ⓕ ay·tron·zhay/ay·tron·zhair
stream ruisseau ⓜ rwee·so
street rue ⓕ rew
street market braderie ⓕ bra·dree
strike (go on strike) se mettre en grève ser may·trer ong grev
string ficelle ⓕ fee·sel
stroller poussette ⓕ poo·set

strong fort(e) ⓜ/ⓕ for(t)
student étudiant(e) ⓜ/ⓕ
ay·tew·dyon(t)
studio atelier ⓜ a·ter·lyay
study étudier ay·tew·dyay
stupid stupide stew·peed
style style ⓜ steel
subtitles sous-titres ⓜ soo·tee·trer
suburb banlieue ⓕ bon·lyer
subway métro ⓜ may·tro
suffer souffrir soo·freer
suitcase valise ⓕ va·leez
summer été ⓜ ay·tay
sun soleil ⓜ so·lay
sunblock écran solaire total ⓜ
ay·kron so·lair to·tal
sunburn coup de soleil ⓜ koo der
so·lay
Sunday dimanche ⓜ dee·monsh
sunglasses lunettes de soleil ⓕ
lew·net der so·lay
sunny ensoleillé(e) ⓜ/ⓕ
on·so·lay·yay
sunrise lever du soleil ⓜ ler·vay dew
so·lay
sunscreen écran solaire ⓜ ay·kron
so·lair
sunset coucher du soleil ⓜ koo·shay
dew so·lay
supermarket supermarché ⓜ
sew·pair·mar·shay
superstition superstition ⓕ
sew·pair·stee·syon
support supporter sew·por·tay
sure sûr(e) ⓜ/ⓕ sewr
surf surfer ser·fay
surface mail (land) voie de terre vwa
der tair
surface mail (sea) voie maritime vwa
ma·ree·teem
surfboard planche de surf ⓕ plonsh
der serf
surname nom de famille ⓜ nom der
fa·mee·yer
surprise surprise ⓕ sewr·preez
survive survivre sewr·vee·vrer
sweater pull ⓜ pewl

Sweden Suède ⓕ swayd
sweet sucré(e) ⓜ/ⓕ sew·kray
swim nager na·zhay
swimming pool piscine ⓕ pee·seen
swimsuit maillot de bain ⓜ ma·yo
der bun
Switzerland Suisse ⓕ swees
synagogue synagogue ⓕ see·na·gog
synthetic synthétique sun·tay·teek
syringe seringue ⓕ ser·rung

T

table table ⓕ ta·bler
table tennis tennis de table ⓜ
tay·nees der ta·bler
tablecloth nappe ⓕ nap
tail queue ⓕ ker
tailor tailleur ⓜ ta·yer
take prendre pron·drer
take a photo prendre en photo
pron·drer on fo·to
talk parler par·lay
talk conversation ⓕ kon·vair·sa·syon
talk (lecture) exposé ⓜ eks·po·zay
tall grand(e) ⓜ/ⓕ gron(d)
tampon tampon hygiénique ⓜ
tom·pon ee·zhay·neek
tanning lotion crème de bronzage ⓕ
krem de bron·zazh
tap robinet ⓜ ro·bee·nay
tasty délicieux/délicieuse ⓜ/ⓕ
day·lees·yer/day·lees·yerz
tax taxe ⓕ taks
taxi taxi ⓜ tak·see
taxi stand station de taxi ⓕ sta·syon
der tak·see
teacher professeur ⓜ pro·fay·ser
team équipe ⓕ ay·keep
teaspoon petite cuillère ⓕ per·teet
kwee·yair
technique technique ⓕ tek·neek
teeth dents ⓕ don
telegram télégramme ⓜ tay·lay·gram
telephone téléphone ⓜ tay·lay·fon
telephone téléphoner tay·lay·fo·nay
telephone box cabine téléphonique
ⓕ ka·been tay·lay·fo·neek

T

telescope télescope ⓜ tay·lay·skop
television télé(vision) ⓕ
tay·lay(vee·zyon)
tell dire deer
tell (a story) raconter ra·kon·tay
teller caissier/caissière ⓜ/ⓕ
kay·syay/kay·syair
temperature (fever) température ⓕ
tom·pay·ra·tewr
temperature (weather) température
ⓕ tom·pay·ra·tewr
temple temple ⓜ tom·pler
ten dix dee(s)
tenant locataire ⓜ/ⓕ lo·ka·tair
tennis tennis ⓜ tay·nees
tennis court court de tennis ⓜ koor
der tay·nees
tent tente ⓕ tont
tent pegs piquets de tente ⓜ pee·kay
der tont
terrible affreux/affreuse ⓜ/ⓕ
a·frer/a·frerz
terrorism terrorisme ⓜ
tay·ro·rees·mer
test essai ⓜ ay·say
thank remercier rer·mair·syay
that ce/cette ⓜ/ⓕ ser/set
that (one) cela ser·la
theatre théâtre ⓜ tay·a·trer
their leur/leurs sg/pl ler
then (at the time) alors a·lor
then (next) puis pwee
there là la
therefore donc dongk
they ils/elles ⓜ/ⓕ eel/el
thick épais/épaisse ⓜ/ⓕ ay·pay/
ay·pes
thief voleur/voleuse ⓜ/ⓕ vo·ler/vo·lerz
thin maigre may·grer
thing chose ⓕ shoz
think penser pon·say
third troisième trwa·zyem
thirsty (to be) avoir soif a·vwar swaf
this ce/cette ⓜ/ⓕ ser/set
this (one) ceci ser·see
three trois trwa
throat gorge ⓕ gorzh

throw jeter zher·tay
thrush (illness) muguet ⓜ mew·gay
Thursday jeudi ⓜ zher·dee
ticket billet ⓜ bee·yay
ticket collector contrôleur ⓜ
kon·tro·ler
ticket machine distributeur de
tickets ⓜ dee·stree·bew·ter der tee·kay
ticket office guichet ⓜ gee·shay
tide marée ⓕ ma·ray
tie (draw) match nul ⓜ matsh newl
tight étroit(e) ⓜ/ⓕ ay·trwa(t)
time heure ⓕ er
time difference décalage horaire ⓜ
day·ka·lazh o·rair
time (general) temps ⓜ tom
timetable horaire ⓜ o·rair
tin (can) boîte ⓕ bwat
tin opener ouvre-boîte ⓜ
oo·vrer·bwat
tiny minuscule mee·new·skewl
tip (gratuity) pourboire ⓜ poor·bwar
tire pneu ⓜ pner
tired fatigué(e) ⓜ/ⓕ fa·tee·gay
tissues mouchoirs en papier ⓜ pl
moo·shwar om pa·pyay
to à a
toast pain grillé ⓜ pung gree·yay
toaster grille-pain ⓜ greey·pun
tobacco tabac ⓜ ta·ba
tobacconist bureau de tabac ⓜ
bew·ro der ta·ba
today aujourd'hui o·zhoor·dwee
toe orteil ⓜ or·tay
together ensemble on·som·bler
toilet toilettes ⓕ pl twa·let
toilet paper papier hygiénique ⓜ
pa·pyay ee·zhyay·neek
tomorrow demain der·mun
tomorrow afternoon demain
après-midi der·mun a·pray·mee·dee
tomorrow evening demain soir
der·mun swar
tomorrow morning demain matin
der·mum ma·tun
tonight ce soir ser swar
too (expensive etc) trop tro

too much/many trop tro

too much (rain etc)/too many (people etc) trop de tro der

tooth dent ① don

toothache mal de dents ⓜ a·vwar mal o don

toothbrush brosse à dents ① bros a don

toothpaste dentifrice ⓜ don·tee·frees

toothpick cure-dent ⓜ kewr·don

torch (flashlight) lampe de poche ① lomp der posh

touch toucher too·shay

touch (sense) toucher too·shay

tour voyage ⓜ vwa·yazh

tourist touriste ⓜ/① too·reest

tourist office office de tourisme ⓜ o·fees·der too·rees·mer

tournament tournoi ⓜ toor·nwa

tow truck dépanneuse ① day·pa·nerz

toward (direction) vers vair

toward (feelings) envers on·vair

towel serviette ① sair·vyet

tower tour ① toor

town ville ① veel

toxic waste déchets toxiques ⓜ pl day·shay tok·seek

toy jouet ⓜ zhway

track (path) chemin (de randonnée) ⓜ sher·mun (der ron·do·nay)

track (sports) piste ① peest

trade commerce ⓜ ko·mairs

traffic circulation ① seer·kew·la·syon

traffic jam bouchon ⓜ boo·shon

traffic lights feux ⓜ fer

trail piste ① peest

train train ⓜ trun

train station gare ① gar

transfer transfert ⓜ trons·fair

transit lounge salle de transit ① sal der tron·zeet

translate traduire tra·dweer

transport transport ⓜ trons·por

travel voyager vwa·ya·zhay

travel agency agence de voyage ① a·zhons der vwa·yazh

travel sickness mal des transports ⓜ mal day trons·por

travellers cheque chèque de voyage ⓜ shek der vwa·yazh

treatment traitement ⓜ tret·mon

tree arbre ⓜ ar·brer

trek randonnée ⓜ ran·do·nay

trick ruse ① rewz

trick tromper trom·pay

trip voyage ⓜ vwa·yazh

trolley chariot ⓜ shar·yo

trouble peine ① pen

trousers pantalon ⓜ pon·ta·lon

truck camion ⓜ ka·myon

true vrai(e) ⓜ/① vray

trust faire confiance à fair kon·fyons a

trust confiance ① kon·fyons

truth vérité ① vay·ree·tay

try essayer ay·say·yay

T-shirt T-shirt ⓜ tee·shert

tube (tyre) chambre à air ① shom·brer a air

Tuesday mardi ⓜ mar·dee

tune air ⓜ air

turn tourner toor·nay

TV télé ① tay·lay

TV series série ① say·ree

tweezers pince à épiler ① puns a ay·pee·lay

twice deux fois der fwa

twin beds lits jumeaux ⓜ pl day lee zhew·mo

twins jumeaux/jumelles ⓜ/① zhew·mo/zhew·mel

two deux der

type type ⓜ teep

typical typique tee·peek

tyre pneu ⓜ pner

U

ugly laid(e) ⓜ/① lay/led

ultrasound ultrason ⓜ ewl·tra·son

umbrella parapluie ① pa·ra·plwee

uncertain incertain(e) ⓜ/① un·sair·tun/un·sair·ten

uncomfortable inconfortable ung·kon·for·ta·bler

230

V

under sous soo
understand comprendre kom·pron·drer
underwater camera appareil photo sous-marin ⓜ a·pa·ray fo·to soo·ma·run
underwear sous-vêtements ⓜ soo·vet·mon
unemployed chômeur/chômeuse ⓜ/ⓕ sho·mer/sho·merz
unemployment chômage ⓜ sho·mazh
unfair injuste un·zhewst
unfurnished non-meublé(e) ⓜ/ⓕ no·mer·blay
uniform uniforme ⓜ ew·nee·form
union union ⓕ ew·nyon
union (trade) syndicat ⓜ sun·dee·ka
universe univers ⓜ ew·nee·vair
university université ⓕ ew·nee·vair·see·tay
unleaded sans plomb son plom
unsafe dangereux/dangereuse ⓜ/ⓕ don·zhrer/don·zhrerz
until (Friday, etc) jusqu'à zhew·ska
unusual peu commun(e) ⓜ/ⓕ per ko·mun/ko·mewn
up en haut on o
uphill (to go) monter mon·tay
upstairs en haut on o
urgent urgent(e) ⓜ/ⓕ ewr·zhon(t)
us nous noo
USA les USA ⓜ lay zew·es·a
use utiliser ew·tee·lee·zay
useful utile ew·teel
usually habituellement a·bee·twel·mon

V

vacancy chambre libre ⓕ shom·brer lee·brer
vacant libre lee·brer
vacation vacances ⓕ pl va·kons
vaccination vaccination ⓕ vak·see·na·syon
vagina vagin ⓜ va·zhun

validate valider va·lee·day
valley vallée ⓕ va·lay
valuable de valeur der va·ler
value (price) valeur ⓕ va·ler
van camionnette ⓕ ka·myo·net
vegetable légume ⓜ lay·gewm
vegetarian végétarien/végétarienne ⓜ/ⓕ vay·zhay·ta·ryun/vay·zhay·ta·ryen
vehicle véhicule ⓜ vay·ee·kewl
vein veine ⓕ ven
venereal disease maladie vénérienne ⓕ ma·la·dee vay·nay·ryen
very très tray
vest maillot de corps ⓜ ma·yo der kor
via via vee·a
video camera caméra vidéo ⓕ ka·may·ra vee·day·yo
view vue ⓕ vew
village village ⓜ vee·lazh
vine vigne ⓕ vee·nyer
vineyard vignoble ⓜ vee·nyo·bler
virus virus ⓜ vee·rews
visa visa ⓜ vee·za
visit (museum etc) visiter vee·zee·tay
visit (person) aller voir a·lay vwar
visitor visiteur/visiteuse ⓜ/ⓕ vee·zee·ter/vee·zee·terz
visitor (guest) invité(e) ⓜ/ⓕ un·vee·tay
vitamin vitamine ⓕ vee·ta·meen
volume volume ⓜ vo·lewm
voluntary (not paid) bénévole bay·nay·vol
volunteer bénévole ⓜ/ⓕ bay·nay·vol
vomit vomir vo·meer
vote voter vo·tay

W

wage salaire ⓜ sa·lair
wait (for) attendre a·ton·drer
waiter serveur/serveuse ⓜ/ⓕ sair·ver/sair·verz
waiting room salle d'attente ⓕ sal da·tont

wake (someone) up réveiller ray·vay·yay

wake up se réveiller ser ray·vay·yay

walk marcher mar·shay

wall (outer) mur ⓜ mewr

want vouloir voo·lwar

war guerre ⓕ gair

wardrobe penderie ⓕ pon·dree

warm chaud(e) ⓜ/ⓕ sho(d)

warn prévenir prayv·neer

warning avertissement ⓜ a·vair·tees·mon

wash (oneself) se laver ser la·vay

wash (something) laver la·vay

washing machine machine à laver ⓕ ma·sheen a la·vay

wasp guêpe ⓕ gep

watch regarder rer·gar·day

watch montre ⓕ mon·trer

water eau ⓕ o

water bottle (hot) bouillotte ⓕ boo·yot

waterfall cascade ⓕ kas·kad

waterproof imperméable um·pair·may·abler

waterskiing ski ⓜ nautique skee no·teek

wave vague ⓕ vag

way direction ⓕ dee·rek·syon

way (manner) façon ⓕ fa·son

way (road) chemin ⓜ sher·mun

we nous noo

weak faible fay·bler

wealthy riche reesh

wear porter por·tay

weather temps ⓜ tom

weather forecast météo ⓕ may·tay·o

wedding mariage ⓜ ma·ree·azh

Wednesday mercredi ⓜ mair·krer·dee

week semaine ⓕ ser·men

weekend week-end ⓜ week·end

weigh peser per·zay

weight poids ⓜ pwa

welcome accueillir a·ker·yeer

welfare (aid) assistance publique ⓕ a·sees·tons pewb·leek

well bien byun

west ouest ⓜ west

wet mouillé(e) ⓜ/ⓕ moo·yay

what quel(le) ⓜ/ⓕ kel

wheel roue ⓕ roo

wheelchair fauteuil ⓜ roulant fo·ter·yee roo·lon

when quand kon

where où oo

which quel(le) ⓜ/ⓕ kel

which lequel/laquelle ⓜ/ⓕ ler·kel/la·kel

which qui kee

whistle siffler see·flay

white blanc/blanche ⓜ/ⓕ blong/blonsh

who qui kee

whole tout entier/toute entière ⓜ/ⓕ too ton·tyay/too ton·tyair

why pourquoi poor·kwa

wide large larzh

widow veuve ⓕ verv

widower veuf ⓜ verf

wife femme ⓕ fam

wild sauvage so·vazh

win gagner ga·nyay

wind vent ⓜ von

window fenêtre ⓕ fer·nay·trer

windscreen/windshield pare-brise ⓜ par·breez

windsurfer planche ⓕ à voile plonsh a vwal

windsurfing (to go) faire de la planche à voile fair der la plonsh a vwal

wine vin ⓜ vun

winery cave viticole ⓕ kaav vee·tee·kol

wings ailes ⓕ el

winner gagnant(e) ⓜ/ⓕ ga·nyon(t)

winter hiver ⓜ ee·vair

wire fil de fer ⓜ feel der fair

wish souhaiter sway·tay

with avec a·vek

withdrawal retrait ⓜ rer·tray

within (an hour etc) avant a·von

without sans son

witness témoin ⓜ tay·mwun

woman femme ⓕ fam

Y

wonderful merveilleux/ merveilleuse ⑩/① mair·vay·yer/ mair·vay·yerz
wood bois ⑩ bwa
wool laine ① len
word mot ⑩ mo
work travail ⑩ tra·vai
work travailler tra·va·yay
work experience stage en entreprise ⑩ stazh on on·trer·preez
work permit permis de travail ⑩ pair·mee der tra·vai
world monde ⑩ mond
World Cup La Coupe du Monde la koop dew mond
worms vers ⑩ vair
worried inquiet/inquiète ⑩/① ung·kyay/ung·kyet
worry s'inquiéter sung·kyay·tay
worse pire peer
worship faire ses dévotions fair say day·vo·syon
worship (someone) adorer a·do·ray
wrist poignet ⑩ pwa·nyay
write écrire ay·kreer
writer écrivain ⑩ ay·kree·vun
wrong faux/fausse ⑩/① fo/fos
wrong (direction) mauvais(e) ⑩/① mo·vay(z)
wrong (to be) avoir tort a·vwar tor

Y

year année ⑩ a·nay
yellow jaune zhon
yes oui wee
yesterday hier ee·yair
yet encore ong·kor
yoga yoga ⑩ yo·ga
you vous pl/pol voo
you tu inf tew
young jeune zhern
your pol votre/vos sg/pl vo·trer/vo
your sg&inf ton/ta/tes ⑩/①/pl ton/ ta/tay
youth hostel auberge de jeunesse ① o·bairzh der zher·nes

Z

zero zéro zay·ro
zip/zipper fermeture éclair ① fair·mer·tewr ay·klair
zoo zoo ⑩ zo

Dictionary

FRENCH *to* ENGLISH

français–anglais

Nouns have their gender indicated by ⓜ or ⓕ. You'll also see sg and pl for singular and plural nouns. Where a word that could be either a noun or a verb has no gender indicated, it's a verb.

A

à a at • to

à bord a bor aboard

à côté de a ko·tay der beside • next to

à droite a drwat right (direction)

à gauche a gosh left (direction)

à la maison a la may·zon home

à l'étranger a lay·tron·zhay abroad

à l'heure a ler on time

à peu près a per pray approximately

à plein temps a plun ton full-time

à temps partiel a tom par·syel part-time

abeille ⓕ a·bay bee

abondance ⓕ a·bon·dons plenty

abri ⓜ a·bree shelter

accepter ak·sep·tay accept

accident ⓜ ak·see·don accident • crash

accueillir a·ker·yeer welcome

accumulation ⓕ a·kew·mew·la·syon collection

acheter ash·tay buy

acte de naissance ⓜ akt der nay·sons birth certificate

acteur/actrice ⓜ/ⓕ ak·ter/ak·trees actor

actualités ak·twa·lee·tay news (on TV etc)

actuel(le) ⓜ/ⓕ ak·twel current

acupuncture ⓕ a·kew·pongk·tewr acupuncture

adaptateur ⓜ a·dap·ta·ter adaptor

addition ⓕ a·dee·syon bill • check

admettre ad·me·trer admit

administration ⓕ ad·mee·nee·stra·syon administration

admirer ad·mee·ray admire

adorer a·do·ray worship (someone)

adresse ⓕ a·dres address

adulte ⓜ/ⓕ a·dewlt adult

adversaire ⓜ/ⓕ ad·vair·sair opponent

aérobic ⓜ a·ay·ro·beek aerobics

aérogramme ⓜ a·ay·ro·gram aerogram

aéroport ⓜ a·ay·ro·por airport

affaires ⓕ a·fair business

affreux/affreuse ⓜ/ⓕ a·frer/a·frerz awful • terrible

Afrique ⓕ a·freek Africa

âge ⓜ azh age

âgé(e) ⓜ/ⓕ a·zhay elderly

agence de voyage ⓕ a·zhons der vwa·yazh travel agency

agence immobilière ① a·zhons ee·mo·bee·lyair estate agency
agenda ⓜ a·zhun·da diary
agent de police ⓜ a·zhon der po·lees officer (police)
agent immobilier ⓜ a·zhon ee·mo·bee·lyay real estate agent
agiter a·zhee·tay shake (something)
agréable a·gray·a·bler nice (pleasant)
agressif/agressive ⓜ/① a·gray·seef/ a·gray·seev aggressive
agriculteur/agricultrice ⓜ/① a·gree·kewl·ter/a·gree·kewl·trees farmer
agriculture ① a·gree·kewl·tewr agriculture
aide ① ed help
aider ay·day help
aiguille ① ay·gwee·yer needle
ailes ① el wings
aimant(e) ⓜ/① ay·mon(t) caring
aimer ay·may like • love
air ⓜ air air • tune
alcool ⓜ al·kol alcohol
Allemagne ① al·ma·nyer Germany
aller a·lay go
aller retour ⓜ a·lay rer·toor return (ticket)
aller voir a·lay vwar visit (person)
allergie ① a·lair·zhee allergy
allocation de chômage ① a·lo·ka·syon der sho·mazh dole
allume-feu anti-moustiques ⓜ a·lewm·fer on·tee·moo·steek mosquito coil
allumettes ① pl a·lew·met matches (for lighting)
alors a·lor then (at the time)
alpinisme ⓜ al·pee·nee·smer mountaineering
alternative ① al·tair·na·teev alternative
altitude ① al·tee·tewd altitude
amant(e) ⓜ/① a·mon(t) lover
amateur ⓜ a·ma·ter amateur
ambassade ① om·ba·sad embassy

ambassadeur/ambassadrice ⓜ/① om·ba·sa·der/om·ba·sa·drees ambassador
ambulance ① om·bew·lons ambulance
améliorer a·may·lyo·ray improve
amende ① a·mond fine (penalty)
amener am·nay bring (a person)
amer/amère ⓜ/① a·mair bitter
ami/amie ⓜ/① a·mee friend
amical(e) ⓜ/① a·mee·kal friendly
amitié ① a·mee·tyay friendship
amour a·moor love
ample om·pler loose (clothes)
ampoule ① om·pool blister • light bulb
analgésique ⓜ a·nal·zhay·zeek painkiller
analyse de sang ① a·na·leez der son blood test
anglais(e) ⓜ/① ong·glay(z) English
Angleterre ① ong·gler·tair England
animal ⓜ a·nee·mal animal
animal familier ⓜ a·nee·mal fa·mee·lyay pet
anneau ⓜ a·no ring (shape)
année ① a·nay year
anniversaire ⓜ a·nee·vair·sair birthday
annuaire ⓜ an·wair phone book
annuel(le) ⓜ/① a·nwel annual
annuler a·new·lay cancel
antibiotiques ⓜ on·tee·byo·teek antibiotics
anti-nucléaire on·tee·new·klay·air antinuclear
antique on·teek ancient
antiquité ① on·tee·kee·tay antique
antiseptique ⓜ on·tee·sep·teek antiseptic
août ⓜ oot August
appareil acoustique ⓜ a·pa·ray a·koos·teek hearing aid
appareil de chauffage ⓜ a·pa·ray der sho·fazh heater

appareil photo ⓜ a·pa·ray fo·to camera

— jetable zhay·ta·bler disposable camera

— numérique new·may·reek digital camera

— sous-marin soo·ma·run underwater camera

appel en PCV ⓜ a·pel on pay·say·vay collect call

appeler a·play call

appendice a·pun·dees appendix

apporter a·por·tay bring (a thing)

apprendre a·pron·drer learn

après a·pray after

après-demain a·pray·der·mun day after tomorrow (the)

après-midi a·pray·mee·dee afternoon

après-rasage ⓜ a·pray·ra·zazh aftershave

après-shampooing ⓜ a·pray·shom·pwung conditioner (hair)

araignée ⓕ a·ray·nyay spider

arbitre ⓜ ar·bee·trer referee

arbre ⓜ ar·brer tree

archéologie ⓕ ar·kay·o·lo·zhee archaeology

architecte(e) ⓜ/ⓕ ar·shee·tekt architect

architecture ar·shee·tek·tewr architecture

argent ⓜ ar·zhon cash • money • silver

arnaque ⓕ ar·nak rip-off

arrêt ⓜ a·ray stop

arrêt d'autobus ⓜ a·ray do·to·bews bus stop

arrêter a·ray·tay stop (something, someone) • arrest

arrière a·ryair rear (seat etc)

arrivées ⓕ a·ree·vay arrivals

arriver a·ree·vay arrive

art ⓜ ar art

artisanat ⓜ ar·tee·za·na crafts

artiste ⓜ/ⓕ ar·teest artist

arts martiaux ⓜ pl ar mar·syo martial arts

ascenseur ⓜ a·son·ser elevator • lift

Asie ⓕ a·zee Asia

aspirine ⓕ as·pee·reen aspirin

assez a·say enough

assiette ⓕ a·syet plate

assistance publique ⓕ a·sees·tons pewb·leek welfare (aid)

assurance ⓕ a·sew·rons insurance

assurer a·sew·ray insure

asthme ⓜ as·mer asthma

atelier ⓜ a·ter·lyay studio

athlétisme ⓜ at·lay·tees·mer athletics

atmosphère ⓕ at·mos·fair atmosphere

attaché(e) ⓜ/ⓕ a·ta·shay attached

atteindre a·tun·drer reach • wait (for)

attraper a·tra·pay catch

au coin o kwun on the corner

au revoir a rer·vwar goodbye

aube ob dawn

auberge de jeunesse ⓕ o·bairzh der zher·nes youth hostel

aucun(e) ⓜ/ⓕ o·kun/o·kewn none

au-dessus o·der·sew above

aujourd'hui o·zhoor·dwee today

aussi o·see also

Australie ⓕ o·stra·lee Australia

autel ⓜ o·tel altar

autobus ⓜ o·to·bews bus (city)

autocar ⓜ o·to·kar bus (intercity)

automatique o·to·ma·teek automatic

automne ⓜ o·ton autumn • fall

autoroute ⓕ o·to·root highway • motorway

autour o·toor around

autre o·trer other

avant a·von before

avant-hier a·von·tyair day before yesterday

avec a·vek with

avenir av·neer future

avenue ⓕ av·new avenue

B

avertissement ⓜ a·vair·tees·mon warning

aveugle a·ver·gler blind

avide a·veed greedy (money)

avion ⓜ a·vyon aeroplane

aviron ⓜ a·vee·ron rowing

avis ⓜ a·vee opinion

avocat(e) ⓜ/ⓕ a·vo·ka(t) lawyer

avoir a·vwar have

— besoin de ber·zwun de need

— de la chance der la shons lucky (to be)

— des hallucinations day za·lew·see·na·syon hallucinate

— faim fum hungry (to be)

— la tête qui tourne la tet kee toorn dizzy (to be dizzy)

— le mal de mer ler mal der mair seasick (to be)

— mal au ventre mal o von·trer stomach ache (to have a)

— mal aux dents mal o don toothache

— raison ray·zon right (to be right)

— soif swaf thirsty (to be)

— sommeil so·may sleepy (to be sleepy)

— tort tor wrong (to be)

avortement ⓜ a·vor·ter·mon abortion

avril ⓜ a·vreel April

B

baby-sitter ⓜ&ⓕ ba·bee·see·ter babysitter

bac ⓜ bak ferry

bagages ⓜ pl ba·gazh baggage • luggage

bagarre ⓕ ba·gar fight

bague ⓕ bag ring (on finger)

baignoire ⓕ be·nywar bath

bail ⓜ ba·yer lease

bain ⓜ bun bath (have a)

baiser bay·zay fuck

baiser ⓜ bay·zay kiss

balcon ⓜ bal·kon balcony

balle (de tennis) ⓕ bal (der tay·nees) (tennis) ball

ballet ⓜ ba·lay ballet

ballon (de football) ⓜ ba·lon (der foot·bol) football • soccer ball

bande ⓕ bond band (music)

bande dessinée ⓕ bond day·see·nay comic (magazine)

banlieue ⓕ bon·lyer suburb

banque ⓕ bonk bank

baptême ⓜ ba·tem baptism

bar ⓜ bar bar • pub

barrière ⓕ bar·yair fence • gate

bas ⓜ ba stockings

bas/basse ⓜ/ⓕ ba(s) low

baseball ⓜ bez·bol baseball

basket(ball) ⓜ bas·ket(bol) basketball

bateau ⓜ ba·to boat

bâtiment ⓜ ba·tee·mon building

batterie ⓕ bat·ree battery (car) • drums

bavarder ba·var·day chat

bavoir ⓜ ba·vwar bib

beau/belle ⓜ/ⓕ bo/bel beautiful • handsome

beaucoup (de) bo·koo (der) a lot (of) • many • plenty

beau-père ⓜ bo·pair father-in-law

bébé ⓜ bay·bay baby

belle-mère ⓕ bel·mair mother-in-law

bénéfice ⓜ bay·nay·fees profit

bénévole ⓜ/ⓕ bay·nay·vol voluntary (not paid) • volunteer

bible ⓕ bee·bler bible

bibliothèque ⓕ bee·blee·o·tek library

bien byun well

bien déterminé byun day·tair·mee·nay definite

bientôt byun·to soon

bière ⓕ byair beer

bijoux ⓜ pl bee·zhoo jewellery

billard américain ⓜ bee·yar a·may·ree·kun pool (game)

billet ⓜ bee·yay ticket

— de banque der bonk banknote

— stand-by stond·bai stand-by ticket

blanc/blanche ⓜ/ⓕ blong/blonsh white

blanchisserie ⓕ blon·shees·ree laundry (place)

blessé(e) ⓜ/ⓕ blay·say hurt • injured

blessure ⓕ blay·sewr injury

bleu ⓜ bler bruise

bleu(e) ⓜ/ⓕ bler blue

bloqué(e) ⓜ/ⓕ blo·kay blocked

bœuf ⓜ berf ox

bohémien/bohémienne ⓜ/ⓕ bo·ay·myun/bo·ay·myen Bohemian • hippie

boire bwar drink

bois ⓜ bwa wood

bois de chauffage ⓜ bwa der sho·fazh firewood

boisson ⓕ bwa·son drink

boîte ⓕ bwat box • can (tin) • carton (for ice cream) • nightclub

boîte aux lettres ⓕ bwat o lay·trer mailbox

bol ⓜ bol bowl

bon/bonne ⓜ/ⓕ bon/bon good

bon marché ⓜ bon mar·shay cheap

bonde ⓕ bond plug (bath)

bondé(e) ⓜ/ⓕ bon·day crowded

bord ⓜ bor edge

— de la mer der la mair seaside

— du trottoir dew tro·twar kerb

botte ⓕ bot boot (footwear)

bouche ⓕ boosh mouth

boucherie ⓕ boosh·ree butcher's shop

bouchon ⓜ boo·shon traffic jam

boucles d'oreille ⓕ boo·kler do·ray earrings

bouddhiste boo·deest Buddhist

boue ⓕ boo mud

bouger boo·zhay move

bougie ⓕ boo·zhee candle

bouillie ⓕ boo·yee baby food

bouillotte ⓕ boo·yot water bottle (hot)

boulangerie ⓕ boo·lon·zhree bakery

boulevard ⓜ bool·var boulevard

boussole ⓕ boo·sol compass

bout ⓜ boo end

bouteille ⓕ boo·tay bottle

bouton ⓜ boo·ton button

boxe ⓕ boks boxing

boxer-short ⓜ bok·sair·short boxer shorts

braderie ⓕ bra·dree street market

braille ⓜ bra·yer Braille

bras ⓜ bra arm

briquet ⓜ bree·kay cigarette lighter

brochure ⓕ bro·shewr brochure

broderie ⓕ bro·dree embroidery

bronchite ⓕ bron·sheet bronchitis

brosse ⓕ bros brush

— à cheveux a shver hairbrush

— à dents a don toothbrush

brûler brew·lay burn

brûlure ⓕ brew·lewr burn

brumeux/brumeuse ⓜ/ⓕ brew·mer/brew·merz foggy

brun/brune ⓜ/ⓕ brun/brewn brown

bruyant(e) ⓜ/ⓕ brew·yon(t) noisy

budget ⓜ bewd·zhay budget

buffet ⓜ bew·fay buffet

bureau ⓜ bew·ro office

— de poste der post post office

— de tabac der ta·ba tobacconist

— des objets trouvés day zob·zhay troo·vay lost property office

bus ⓜ bews bus (city)

but ⓜ bewt goal

C

cabine téléphonique ⓕ ka·been tay·lay·fo·neek telephone box

câble ⓜ ka·bler cable

cache-sexe ⓜ kash·seks G-string

cadeau ⓜ ka·do gift • present

cadenas ⓜ kad·na padlock

cafard ⓜ ka·far cockroach

café ⓜ ka·fay cafe • coffee

caisse (enregistreuse) ⓕ kes (on·rer·zhee·strerz) cash register

caissier/caissière ⓜ/ⓕ kay·syay/kay·syair cashier • teller

C

calculatrice ⓕ kal·kew·la·trees
calculator
calendrier ⓜ ka·lon·dree·yay calendar
caméra vidéo ⓜ ka·may·ra
vee·day·yo video camera
camion ⓜ ka·myon lorry • truck
camionnette ⓕ ka·myo·net van
camp ⓜ kon camp
campagne ⓕ kom·pa·nyer
countryside
camping ⓜ kom·peeng camping
ground
Canada ⓜ ka·na·da Canada
canard ⓜ ka·nar duck
cancer ⓜ kon·sair cancer
canif ⓜ ka·neef penknife
canot automobile ⓜ ka·no
o·to·mo·beel motorboat
cape ⓕ kap cloak
capitalisme ⓜ ka·pee·ta·lees·mer
capitalism
car ⓜ kar bus (intercity)
caravane ⓕ ka·ra·van caravan
carnet ⓜ kar·nay notebook
carrefour ⓜ kar·foor intersection
carrière ⓕ kar·ryair career
carte ⓕ kart menu
carte ⓕ kart map (of country)
— de crédit kart der kray·dee credit
card
— d'embarquement kart
dom·bar·ker·mon boarding pass
— d'identité kart dee·don·tee·tay
identification card (ID)
— grise kart greez car owner's title
— postale kart pos·tal postcard
— routière kart roo·tyair road map
cartouche de gaz ⓕ kar·toosh der
gaz gas cartridge
cas urgent ⓜ ka ewr·zhon emergency
cascade ⓕ kas·kad waterfall
casher ka·shair kosher
casque ⓜ kask helmet
cassé(e) ⓜ/ⓕ ka·say broken
casse-croûte ⓜ kas·kroot snack
casser ka·say break

casserole ⓕ kas·rol pan
cassette ⓕ ka·set cassette
cathédrale ⓕ ka·tay·dral cathedral
catholique ka·to·leek Catholic
cause ⓕ koz cause
CD ⓜ say·day CD
ce ⓜ ser that • this
ce soir ser swar tonight
ceci ser·see this (one)
ceinture de sécurité ⓕ sun·tewr der
say·kew·ree·tay seatbelt
cela ser·la that (one)
célèbre say·leb·rer famous
célibataire say·lee·ba·tair single
(person)
cendrier ⓜ son·dree·yay ashtray
cent son hundred
cent ⓜ sent cent
centimètre ⓜ son·tee·me·trer
centimetre
centre ⓜ son·trer centre
centre commercial ⓜ son·trer
ko·mair·syal shopping centre
centre-ville ⓜ son·trer·veel city
centre
céramique ⓕ say·ra·meek ceramic
cercle ⓜ sair·kler circle
certain(e) ⓜ/ⓕ sair·tun/·ten certain
certificat ⓜ sair·tee·fee·ka certificate
cette ⓕ set that • this
chaîne ⓕ shen chain • channel
— de bicyclette der bee·see·klet
bike chain
— de montagnes der mon·ta·nyer
mountain range
— hi-fi ee·fee stereo (system)
chaise ⓕ shez chair
chaleur ⓕ sha·ler heat
chambre ⓕ shom·brer room
— à air a air air tube (tyre)
— à coucher a koo·shay bedroom
— libre lee·brer vacancy
— pour deux personnes poor der
pair·son double room
— pour une personne poor ewn
pair·son single room

champ ⓜ shom field

champ de courses ⓜ shon der koors racetrack

champagne ⓜ shom·pa·nyer Champagne

championnat ⓜ shom·pyo·na championship

chance ⓕ shons luck

changer shon·zhay change

chanson ⓕ shon·son song

chanter shon·tay sing

chanteur/chanteuse ⓜ/ⓕ shon·ter/shon·terz singer

chapeau ⓜ sha·po hat

chaque shak each • every

charcuterie ⓕ shar·kew·tree delicatessen

chariot ⓜ shar·yo trolley

charmant(e) ⓜ/ⓕ shar·mon(t) charming

chasse ⓕ shas hunting

chat ⓜ sha cat

château ⓜ sha·to castle

chaton ⓜ sha·ton kitten

chaud(e) ⓜ/ⓕ sho(d) hot • warm

chauffé(e) ⓜ/ⓕ sho·fay heated

chaussettes ⓕ sho·set socks

chaussure ⓕ sho·sewr shoe

chaussures de marche ⓕ pl sho·sewr der marsh hiking boots

chef ⓜ shef leader

chef de cuisine ⓜ shef der kwee·zeen chef

chemin ⓜ shmun path • lane • way

— de fer der dair railway

— de montagne der mon·ta·nyer mountain path

chemise ⓕ sher·meez shirt

chèque ⓜ shek check (banking) • cheque

chèque de voyage ⓜ shek der vwa·yazh travellers cheque

cher/chère ⓜ/ⓕ shair expensive

chercher shair·shay look for

cheval ⓜ shval horse

cheveux ⓜ shver hair

cheville ⓕ sher·vee·yer ankle

chèvre ⓕ shev·rer goat

chien ⓜ shyun dog

chien d'aveugle ⓜ shyun da·ver·gler guide dog

chiot ⓜ shyo puppy

chocolat ⓜ sho·ko·la chocolate

choisir shwa·zeer choose

choix ⓜ shwa choice

chômage ⓜ sho·mazh unemployment

chômeur/chômeuse ⓜ/ⓕ sho·mer/sho·merz unemployed

chose ⓕ shoz thing

chrétien(ne) ⓜ/ⓕ kray·tyun/kray·tyen Christian

ciel ⓜ syel sky

cigare ⓜ see·gar cigar

cigarette ⓕ see·ga·ret cigarette

cime ⓕ seem peak

cimetière ⓜ seem·tyair cemetery

cinéma ⓜ see·nay·ma cinema

cinq sungk five

circulation ⓕ seer·kew·la·syon traffic

cirque ⓜ seerk circus

ciseaux ⓜ pl see·zo scissors

citoyen(ne) ⓜ/ⓕ see·twa·yun/see·twa·yen citizen

citoyenneté ⓕ see·twa·yen·tay citizenship

clair(e) ⓜ/ⓕ klair clear • light (of colour)

classe ⓕ klas class

— affaires klas a·fair business class

— touriste klas too·reest economy class

classique kla·seek classical

clavier ⓜ kla·vyay keyboard

clé ⓕ klay key

client(e) ⓜ/ⓕ klee·on(t) client • customer

clignotant ⓜ klee·nyo·ton indicator (on car)

climatisé kee·ma·tee·zay air-conditioned

C

clinique privée ① klee·neek pree·vay private hospital

cocaïne ① ko·ka·een cocaine

cochon ⓜ ko·shon pig

cocktail ⓜ kok·tel cocktail

code postal ⓜ kod pos·tal post code

cœur ⓜ ker heart

coffre-fort ⓜ kof·rer·for safe

coiffeur/coiffeuse ⓜ/① kwa·fer/ kwa·ferz hairdresser

coin ⓜ kwun corner

colis ⓜ ko·lee parcel

collant ⓜ ko·lon pantyhose

colle ① kol glue

collectionner ko·lek·syo·nay collect (stamps etc)

collègue ⓜ/① ko·leg colleague

collier ⓜ ko·lyay necklace

colline ① ko·leen hill

colloque ⓜ ko·lok conference (small)

colonne vertébrale ① ko·lon vair·tay·bral spine

combinaison ① kom·bee·nay·zon combination

comédie ① ko·may·dee comedy

comme kom as • like

commencement ⓜ ko·mons·mon start

commencer ko·mon·say begin • start

comment ko·mon how

commerce ⓜ ko·mairs trade

commissariat ⓜ ko·mee·sar·ya police station

commission ① ko·mee·syon commission

commotion cérébrale ① ko·mo·syon say·ray·bral concussion

commun(e) ⓜ/① ko·mun/ko·mewn common

communauté ① ko·mew·no·tay community

communisme ⓜ ko·mew·nees·mer communism

communiste ko·mew·neest communist

compagnon/compagne ⓜ/① kom·pa·nyon/kom·pa·nyer companion

compétence ① kom·pay·tons skill

compétition ① kom·pay·tees·yon competition

complet/complète ⓜ/① kom·play/ kom·plet booked up • no vacancy

composition directe ① kom·po·zees·yon dee·rekt direct-dial

comprendre kom·pron·drer understand

compris(e) ⓜ/① kom·pree(z) included

compte ⓜ kont account

compte bancaire ⓜ kont bong·kair bank account

compter kon·tay count

compteur (de vitesse) ⓜ kon·ter (der vee·tes) speedometer

comptoir ⓜ kon·twar counter (at bar)

concert ⓜ kon·sair concert

concessionnaire ⓜ kon·say·syo·nair distributor

concevoir kon·ser·vwar design

conduire kon·dweer drive

confession ① kon·fay·syon confession (religious)

confiance ① kon·fyons trust

confirmer kon·feer·may confirm (a booking)

confondre kon·fon·drer mix up (confuse)

confortable kon·for·ta·bler comfortable

congrès ⓜ kong·gray conference (big)

connaître ko·nay·trer know (be familiar with)

conseil ⓜ kon·say advice

conservateur/conservatrice ⓜ/① kon·sair·va·ter/kon·sair·va·trees conservative

consigne ① kon·see·nyer left luggage (office)

consigne automatique ①
kon·see·nyer o·to·ma·teek luggage
lockers
constiptation ① kon·stee·pa·syon
constipation
construire kon·strweer build
consulat ⓜ kon·so·la consulate
contraceptif ⓜ kon·trer·sep·teef
contraceptive
contrat ⓜ kon·tra contract
contre kon·trer against
contrôle ⓜ kon·trol checkpoint
contrôleur ⓜ kon·tro·ler ticket
collector
conversation ① kon·vair·sa·syon
conversation
coopérer ko·o·pay·ray cooperate
coq ⓜ kok rooster
coquillage ⓜ ko·kee·yazh seashell
corde ① kord rope
corde à linge ① kord a lunzh clothes
line
corps ⓜ kor body
correct(e) ⓜ/① ko·rekt correct
corrompu(e) ⓜ/① ko·rom·pew
corrupt
côté ⓜ ko·tay side
côte ① kot coast
coton ⓜ ko·ton cotton
couche ① koosh diaper • nappy
couche d'ozone ① koosh do·zon
ozone layer
coucher du soleil ⓜ koo·shay dew
so·lay sunset
coudre koo·drer sew
couleur ① koo·ler colour
couloir ⓜ koo·lwar aisle (on plane)
coup de soleil ⓜ koo der so·lay
sunburn
coupable koo·pa·bler guilty
coupe ① koop haircut
coupe-ongles ⓜ koop·ong·gler nail
clippers
couper koo·pay cut
coupon ⓜ koo·pon coupon

courageux/courageuse ⓜ/①
koo·ra·zher/koo·ra·zherz brave
courant ⓜ koo·ron current
(electricity)
courir koo·reer run
courrier ⓜ koo·ryay mail (letters)
courroie de ventilateur ① koor·wa
der von·tee·la·ter fanbelt
course ① koors race (sport)
court ⓜ koor court (tennis)
court(e) ⓜ/① koor(t) short (height)
court de tennis ⓜ koor der tay·nees
tennis court
coût ⓜ koo cost
couteau ⓜ koo·to knife
coutume ① koo·tewm custom
couvent ⓜ koo·von convent
couvert ⓜ koo·vair cover charge
couverts ⓜ koo·vair cutlery
couverture ① koo·vair·tewr blanket
crayon ⓜ kray·yon pencil
crèche ① kresh creche
crédit ⓜ kray·dee credit
crème ① krem cream
— de bronzage der bron·zazh tanning
lotion
— hydratante ee·dra·tont
moisturiser
crevaison ① krer·vay·zon puncture
crier kree·yay shout
crique ① kreek creek
critique ① kree·teek review (article)
croire krwar believe
croix ① krwa cross (religious)
croyance ① krwa·yons belief
cru(e) ⓜ/① krew raw
cueillette de fruits ① ker·yet der
frwee fruit picking
cuillère ① kwee·yair spoon
cuir ⓜ kweer leather
cuire kweer cook
cuisine ① kwee·zeen kitchen
cuisinier/cuisinière ⓜ/①
kwee·zee·nyay/kwee·zee·nyair cook
cul ⓜ kew ass (bum)
culture ① kewl·tewr crop (grown)

D

cure-dent ⓜ kewr·don toothpick
CV ⓜ say·vay CV • resumé
cybercafé ⓜ see·bair·ka·fay Internet cafe
cyclisme ⓜ see·klee·smer cycling
cycliste ⓜ/ⓕ see·kleest cyclist

D

dangereux/dangereuse ⓜ/ⓕ don·zhrer/don·zhrerz dangerous
dans don in • into
danse ⓕ dons dancing
danser don·say dance
date ⓕ dat date (day)
date de naissance ⓕ dat der nay·sons date of birth
de der from
— droite drwat right-wing
— gauche gosh left-wing
— la la some
— l'autre côté de lo·trer ko·tay der across
— luxe lewks luxury
— seconde classe skond klas second class
— valeur va·ler valuable
débat ⓜ day·ba argument
déboisement ⓜ day·bwaz·mon deforestation
décalage horaire ⓜ day·ka·lazh o·rair time difference
décembre ⓜ day·som·brer December
décharge ⓕ day·sharzh rubbish dump
déchets nucléaires ⓜ day·shay new·klay·air nuclear waste
déchets toxiques ⓜ pl day·shay tok·seek toxic waste
décision ⓕ day·see·zyon decision
découvrir day·koov·reer discover
déçu(e) ⓜ/ⓕ day·sew disappointed
dedans der·don inside
défectueux/défectueuse ⓜ/ⓕ day·fek·twer/day·fek·twerz faulty
dégâts ⓜ day·ga damage

dehors der·or outside
déjà day·zha already
déjeuner ⓜ day·zher·nay lunch
délicieux/délicieuse ⓜ/ⓕ day·lees·yer/day·lees·yerz tasty
délit ⓜ day·lee crime
demain der·mun tomorrow
— après-midi a·pray·mee·dee tomorrow afternoon
— matin ma·tun tomorrow morning
— soir swar tomorrow evening
demander der·mon·day ask for (something)
démangeaison ⓕ day·mon·zhay·zon itch
demi-litre ⓜ der·mee·lee·trer half a litre
démocratie ⓕ day·mo·kra·see democracy
dent ⓕ don tooth
dentelle ⓕ don·tel lace
dentifrice ⓜ don·tee·frees toothpaste
dentiste ⓜ don·teest dentist
dents ⓕ don teeth
déodorant ⓜ day·o·do·ron deodorant
dépanneuse ⓕ day·pa·nerz tow truck
départ ⓜ day·par departure
dépendance ⓕ day·pon·dons addiction
dépenser day·pon·say spend (money)
dépôt ⓜ day·po deposit
depuis der·pwee since (May etc)
déranger day·ron·zhay disturb
dernier/dernière ⓜ/ⓕ dair·nyay/dair·nyair last (previous)
derrière dair·yair behind
des pl day some
désastre ⓜ day·zas·trer disaster
descendant(e) ⓜ/ⓕ day·son·don(t) descendent
descendre day·son·drer get off (a train, etc) • go down (stairs, etc)
désert ⓜ day·zair desert
désinfectant ⓜ day·zun·fek·ton disinfectant

D

dessert ⓜ day·sair dessert

dessin animé ⓜ day·sun a·nee·may cartoon

dessiner day·see·nay draw (picture)

destin ⓜ des·tun fate

destination ⓕ des·tee·na·syon destination

détail ⓜ day·tai detail

détaillé(e) ⓜ/ⓕ day·ta·yay itemised

détester day·tes·tay hate

détruire day·trweer destroy

deux der two

deux fois der fwa twice

devant der·von in front of

développement ⓜ day·vlop·mon development

devenir derv·neer become

deviner der·vee·nay guess

devoir ⓜ der·vwar duty

devoir der·vwar owe

devoirs ⓜ der·vwar homework

diabète ⓜ dya·bet diabetes

diaphragme ⓜ dya·frag·mer diaphragm

diapositive ⓕ dya·po·zee·teev slide (film)

diarrhée ⓕ dya·ray diarrhoea

dictionnaire ⓜ deek·syo·nair dictionary

dieu ⓜ dyer god

différent(e) ⓜ/ⓕ dee·fay·ron(t) different

difficile dee·fee·seel difficult

dimanche ⓜ dee·monsh Sunday

dîner ⓜ dee·nay dinner

diplôme ⓜ dee·plom degree • diploma

dire deer say • tell

direct(e) ⓜ/ⓕ dee·rekt direct

directeur/directrice ⓜ/ⓕ dee·rek·ter/dee·rek·trees manager

direction ⓕ dee·rek·syon direction

diriger dee·ree·zhay manage (business)

discours ⓜ dees·koor speech

discrimination ⓕ dee·skree·mee·na·syon discrimination

discuter dee·skew·tay discuss

diseuse de bonne aventure ⓕ dee·zerz der bon a·von·tewr fortune teller

disponible dees·po·nee·bler free (available)

dispute ⓕ dees·pewt quarrel

disquaire ⓜ dee·skair music shop

disquette ⓕ dees·ket disk (floppy)

distance ⓕ dees·tons distance

distributeur de tickets ⓜ dee·stree·bew·ter der tee·kay ticket machine

divorcé(e) ⓜ/ⓕ dee·vor·say divorced

dix dee(s) ten

doigt ⓜ dwa finger

dollar ⓜ do·lar dollar

donc dongk therefore

donner do·nay deal (cards) • give

dormir dor·meer sleep

dos ⓜ do back (body)

dose ⓕ doz dose

douane ⓕ dwan customs

double doo·bler double

douche ⓕ doosh shower

douleur ⓕ doo·ler ache • pain

douloureux/douloureuse ⓜ/ⓕ doo·loo·rer/doo·loo·rerz painful • sore

doux/douce ⓜ/ⓕ doo/doos soft

douzaine ⓕ doo·zen dozen

draguer dra·gay chat up

drap ⓜ dra sheet (bed)

drapeau ⓜ dra·po flag

draps ⓜ dra bed linen

drogué dro·gay addicted (to drugs)

drogue ⓕ drog drug • drugs

droit ⓜ drwa law (study, professsion)

droit(e) ⓜ/ⓕ drwa(t) straight

droite ⓕ drwat right (entitlement)

droits civils ⓜ pl drwa see·veel civil rights

droits de l'homme ⓜ pl drwa der lom human rights

drôle drol funny

du ⓜ dew some

dur(e) ⓜ/ⓕ dewr hard (not soft)

E

E

eau ① o water
eau minérale ① o mee·nay·ral
mineral water
échange ⓜ ay·shonzh exchange
échanger ay·shon·zhay change
(money) • exchange
échapper ay·sha·pay escape
écharpe ① ay·sharp scarf
échec ⓜ ay·shek failure
échecs ⓜ ay·shek chess
échiquier ⓜ ay·shee·kyay chess
board
école ① ay·kol school
école professionnelle ① ay·kol
pro·fay·syo·nel college (vocational)
économie ① ay·ko·no·mee economy
Ecosse ① ay·kos Scotland
écouter ay·koo·tay listen (to)
écran ⓜ ay·kron screen
— solaire so·lair sunscreen
— solaire total so·lair to·tal sunblock
écrire ay·kreer write
écrivain ⓜ ay·kree·vun writer
ecstasy ⓜ ek·sta·zee ecstasy (drug)
eczéma ⓜ eg·zay·ma eczema
éducation ① ay·dew·ka·syon
education
effet ⓜ ay·fay effect
effrayé(e) ⓜ/① ay·fray·yay scared
égale ay·gal equal
égalité ① ay·ga·lee·tay equality
égalité des chances ① ay·ga·lee·tay
day shons equal opportunity
église ① ay·gleez church
égoïste ay·go·eest selfish
élection ① ay·lek·syon election
électricité ① ay·lek·tree·see·tay
electricity
elle ① el she
elles ① pl el they (women)
éloigné(e) ⓜ/① ay·lwa·nyay remote
e-mail ⓜ ay·mel email
embrasser om·bra·say kiss
embrayage om·bray·yazh clutch

empêcher om·pay·shay prevent
employé/employée ⓜ/①
om·plwa·yay/om·plwa·yay employee
employé(e) de bureau ⓜ/①
om·plwa·yay der bew·ro office worker
employeur ⓜ om·plwa·yer employer
emprunter om·prun·tay borrow
en on made of (cotton, wood etc)
— avant a·von ahead
— bas ba down
— désordre day·zor·drer messy
— face de fas der opposite
— grève grev on strike
— haut o up • upstairs
— panne pan broken down
— recommandé rer·ko·mon·day
registered mail/post (by)
— retard rer·tar late
encaisser ong·kay·say cash (a
cheque)
enceinte on·sunt pregnant
encore ong·kor again • yet
endroit ⓜ on·drwa spot (place)
énergie ① ay·nair·zhee energy
énergie nucléaire ① ay·nair·zhee
new·klay·air nuclear energy
enfant ⓜ&① on·fon child
enfants ⓜ&① pl on·fon children
ennuyeux/ennuyeuse ⓜ/①
on·nwee·yer/on·nwee·yerz boring
énorme ay·norm huge
enregistrement ⓜ
on·rer·zhee·strer·mon check-in (desk)
enregistrer on·rer·zhees·tray record
ensemble on·som·bler together
ensoleillé(e) ⓜ/① on·so·lay·yay
sunny
entendre on·ton·drer hear
enterrement ⓜ on·tair·mon funeral
enthousiaste on·tooz·yast
enthusiastic
entorse ① on·tors sprain
entracte ⓜ on·trakt intermission
entraîneur ⓜ on·tray·ner coach
entre on·trer between
entrée ① on·tray entry

entreprise ① on·trer·preez company
entrer on·tray enter
entrevue ① on·trer·vew interview
enveloppe ① on·vlop envelope
envers on·vair toward (feelings)
environ on·vee·ron about
environnement ⓜ on·vee·ron·mon environment
envoyer on·vwa·yay send
épais/épaisse ⓜ/① ay·pay/ay·pes thick
épaule ① ay·pol shoulder
épicé(e) ⓜ/① ay·pee·say spicy
épicerie ① ay·pee·sree grocery
épilepsie ① ay·pee·lep·see epilepsy
épingle ① ay·pung·gler pin
épouser ay·poo·zay marry
épuisé(e) ⓜ/① ay·pwee·zay exhausted
équipe ① ay·keep team
équipement ⓜ ay·keep·mon equipment
équipement de plongée ⓜ ay·keep·mon der plon·zhay diving equipment
équitation ① ay·kee·ta·syon horse riding
erreur ① ay·rer mistake
escalier ⓜ es·ka·lyay stairway
escalier roulant ⓜ es·ka·lyay roo·lon escalator
escargot ⓜ es·kar·go snail
escrime ① es·kreem fencing
espace ⓜ es·pas space
Espagne ① es·pa·nyer Spain
espèce menacée de disparition ① es·pes mer·na·say der dees·pa·rees·yon endangered species
espérer es·pay·ray hope
espoir ⓜ es·pwar hope
esprit ⓜ ay·spree mind • spirit
essai ⓜ ay·say test
essayer ay·say·yay try
essence ① ay·sons gas • petrol
est ⓜ est east

estomac ⓜ es·to·ma stomach
et ay and
établissement d'enseignement secondaire ⓜ ay·ta·blees·mon don·say·nyer·mon zgon·dair high school
étage ⓜ ay·tazh floor (storey)
étagère ① ay·ta·zhair shelf
étang ⓜ ay·tong pond
été ⓜ ay·tay summer
étiquette ① ay·tee·ket luggage tag
étoiles ① ay·twal stars
étrange ay·tronzh strange
étranger/étrangère ⓜ/① ay·tron·zhay/ay·tron·zhair foreign • stranger
être e·trer be
être d'accord e·trer da·kor agree
être enrhumé e·trer on·rew·may have a cold
étroit(e) ⓜ/① ay·trwa(t) tight
étudiant(e) ⓜ/① ay·tew·dyon(t) student
étudier ay·tew·dyay study
euro ⓜ er·ro euro
Europe ① er·rop Europe
euthanasie ① er·ta·na·zee euthanasia
événement ⓜ ay·ven·mon event
évident(e) ⓜ/① ay·vee·don(t) obvious
exactement eg·zak·ter·mon exactly
examen ⓜ eg·za·mun exam
excédent ek·say·don excess (baggage)
excellent(e) ⓜ/① ek·say·lon excellent
exemple ⓜ eg·zom·pler example
exercice ⓜ eg·zair·sees exercise
exiger eg·zee·zhay demand
expérience ① eks·pair·yons experience
expliquer eks·plee·kay explain
exploitation ① eks·plwa·ta·syon exploitation
exporter eks·por·tay export

F

exposé ⓜ eks·po·zay talk (lecture)
exposition ⓕ ek·spo·zee·syon exhibition
exprès eks·pres express (mail)
expression ⓕ ek·spray·syon phrase

F

fâché(e) ⓜ/ⓕ fa·shay angry
facile fa·seel easy
facilement ému fa·seel·mon ay·mew emotional (person)
façon ⓕ fa·son way (manner)
facteur ⓜ fak·ter postman
faible fay·bler weak
faire fair do • make
— attention a·ton·syon look out
— confiance à kon·fyons a trust
— de la planche à voile der la plonsh a vwal windsurfing (to go)
— des courses day koors shop
— du lèche-vitrines dew lesh·vee·treen go window-shopping
— du stop dew stop hitchhike
— du vélo dew vay·lo cycle
— frire freer fry
— la randonnée la ron·do·nay hike
— les courses lay koors go shopping
— semblant som·blon pretend
— ses dévotions say day·vo·syon worship
— une fausse couche ewn fos koosh miscarriage (to have a)
fait ⓜ fet fact
fait/faite à la main ⓜ/ⓕ fay/fet a la mun handmade
falaise ⓕ fa·lez cliff
famille ⓕ fa·mee·yer family
fan ⓜ/ⓕ fan fan (of person)
fasciste fa·sheest fascist
fatigué(e) fa·tee·gay tired
faute ⓕ fot foul (football) • fault
fauteuil ⓜ fo·ter·yee armchair
fauteuil roulant ⓜ fo·ter·yee roo·lon wheelchair

faux/fausse ⓜ/ⓕ fo/fos false • wrong
fax ⓜ faks fax machine
félicitations fay·lee·see·ta·syon congratulations
femelle fer·mel female
femme ⓕ fam wife • woman
— au foyer o fwa·yay homemaker
— d'affaires da·fair business woman
fenêtre ⓕ fer·nay·trer window
fer à repasser ⓜ fair a rer·pa·say iron (for clothes)
ferme ⓕ ferm farm
fermé(e) ⓜ/ⓕ fair·may closed
fermé(e) à clé ⓜ/ⓕ fair·may a klay locked
fermer fair·may close
fermer à clé fair·may a klay lock
fermeture éclair ⓕ fair·mer·tewr ay·klair zip • zipper
fête ⓕ fet celebration • festival
feu ⓜ fer fire
feuille ⓕ fer·yee leaf • sheet (of paper)
feux ⓜ fer traffic lights
février ⓜ fayv·ree·yay February
fiançailles ⓕ fyon·sai engagement
fiancé ⓜ fyon·say fiancé
fiancé(e) ⓜ/ⓕ fyon·say engaged
fiancée ⓕ fyon·say fiancée
ficelle ⓕ fee·sel string
fiction ⓕ feek·syon fiction
fièvre ⓕ fyev·rer fever
fil de fer ⓜ feel der fair wire
fil dentaire ⓜ feel don·tair dental floss
filet ⓜ fee·lay net
fille ⓕ fee·yer daughter • girl
film ⓜ feelm film (cinema) • movie
fils ⓜ fees son
fines herbes ⓕ feen zairb herbs
fini(e) ⓜ/ⓕ fee·nee over (finished)
finir fee·neer end • finish
fleur ⓕ fler flower
fleuriste ⓜ&ⓕ fler·reest florist
flic ⓜ fleek cop

foi ① fwa faith

foie ⓜ fwa liver

foncé(e) ⓜ/① fon·say dark (of colour)

fondamental fon·da·mon·tal basic

foot(ball) ⓜ foot(bol) football • soccer

forêt ① fo·ray forest

forme ① form shape

fort(e) ⓜ/① for(t) loud • strong

fortune ① for·tewn fortune (money)

fou/folle ⓜ/① foo/fol crazy

foule ① fool crowd

four ⓜ foor oven

four à micro-ondes ⓜ foor a mee·kro·ond microwave (oven)

fourchette ① foor·shet fork

fourmi ① foor·mee ant

fragile fra·zheel fragile

frais/fraîche ⓜ/① fray/fresh cool • fresh

franchise ① fron·sheez baggage allowance

freins ⓜ frun brakes

fréquent(e) ⓜ/① fray·kon(t) frequent

frère ⓜ frair brother

froid(e) ⓜ/① frwa(d) cold

frontière ① fron·tyair border

frottis ⓜ fro·tee pap smear

fruit ⓜ frwee fruit

fumée ① few·may smoke

fumer few·may smoke

G

gagnant(e) ⓜ/① ga·nyon(t) winner

gagner ga·nyay earn • win

galerie ① gal·ree art gallery (private)

gamin/gamine ⓜ/① ga·mun/ga·meen kid (boy or girl)

gant de toilette ⓜ gon der twa·let face cloth

gants ⓜ pl gon gloves

garage ⓜ ga·razh garage

garanti(e) ⓜ/① ga·ron·tee guaranteed

garçon ⓜ gar·son boy

garde-fou ⓜ gard·foo rail

garderie ① gard·ree childminding

gardien de but ⓜ gar·dyun der bewt goalkeeper

gare ① gar train station

gare routière ① gar roo·tyair bus station

garer (une voiture) ga·ray (ewn vwa·tewr) park (a car)

gas-oil ⓜ gaz·wal diesel

gastro-entérite ① gastro·on·tay·reet gastroenteritis

gaz ⓜ gaz gas (for cooking)

gazon ⓜ ga·zon grass (lawn)

gel ⓜ zhel frost

gelé(e) ⓜ/① zher·lay frozen

geler zher·lay freeze

gênant(e) ⓜ/① zhay·non(t) embarrassing

gendarme ⓜ zhon·darm police officer (in country)

gêné(e) ⓜ/① zhay·nay embarrassed

gêner zhay·nay embarrass

général(e) ⓜ/① zhay·nay·ral general

généreux/généreuse ⓜ/① zhay·nay·rer/zhay·nay·rerz generous

génial(e) ⓜ/① zhay·nyal brilliant

genou ⓜ zhnoo knee

genre ⓜ zhon·rer kind (type)

gens ⓜ pl zhon people

gentil/gentille ⓜ/① zhon·tee kind • nice

gérant(e) ⓜ/① zhay·ron(t) manager (restaurant, hotel)

gilet de sauvetage ⓜ zhee·lay der sov·tazh life jacket

glace ① glas ice • ice cream

gorge ① gorzh throat

gourmand(e) ⓜ/① goor·mon(d) greedy (food)

goût ⓜ goo flavour

gouvernement ⓜ goo·vair·ner·mon government

grâce ① gras blessing

gramme ⓜ gram gram

grand lit ⓜ gron lee double bed

grand magasin ⓜ gron ma·ga·zun department store

grand(e) ⓜ/ⓕ gron(d) big • large • tall

grande route ⓕ grond root main road

grand-mère ⓕ grom·mair grandmother

grand-père ⓜ grom·pair grandfather

grands-parents ⓜ pl grom·pa·ron grandparents

gras/grasse ⓜ/ⓕ gra/gras fat

gratuit(e) ⓜ/ⓕ gra·twee(t) free (gratis)

grenouille ⓕ grer·noo·yer frog

grille-pain ⓜ greey·pun toaster

grippe ⓕ greep flu

gris(e) ⓜ/ⓕ gree(z) gray • grey

grosseur ⓕ gro·ser lump

grotte ⓕ grot cave

groupe ⓜ **de rock** groop der rok rock group

groupe ⓜ **sanguin** groop song·gun blood group

guêpe ⓕ gep wasp

guerre ⓕ gair war

guichet ⓜ gee·shay ticket office

guichet automatique de banque (GAB) ⓜ gee·shay o·to·ma·teek der bonk automatic teller machine (ATM)

guide ⓜ geed guide (person) • guidebook

guidon ⓜ gee·don handlebars

guitare ⓕ gee·tar guitar

gym ⓕ zheem gym (activity)

gymnase ⓜ zheem·naz gym (place)

gym(nastique) ⓕ zheem(na·steek) gymnastics

gynécologue ⓜ/ⓕ zhee·nay·ko·log gynaecologist

H

habiter a·bee·tay live (in a place)

habitude ⓕ a·bee·tewd habit

habituellement a·bee·twel·mon usually

halal a·lal Halal

hall ⓜ ol foyer (of cinema)

hamac ⓜ a·mak hammock

handicapé(e) ⓜ/ⓕ on·dee·ka·pay disabled

harcèlement ⓜ ar·sel·mon harassment

hasard ⓜ a·zar chance

haut(e) ⓜ/ⓕ o(t) high

hauteur ⓕ o·ter height

hémisphère nord ⓜ ay·mees·fair nor northern hemisphere

hémisphère sud ⓜ ay·mees·fair sewd southern hemisphere

hépatite ⓕ ay·pa·teet hepatitis

herbe ⓕ airb grass (marijuana)

herboriste ⓜ/ⓕ air·bo·reest herbalist

héroïne ⓕ ay·ro·een heroin

heure ⓕ er hour • time

heures d'ouverture ⓕ pl lay zer doo·vair·tewr opening hours

heureux/heureuse ⓜ/ⓕ er·rer/er·rerz happy

hier ee·yair yesterday

hindou(e) ⓜ/ⓕ un·doo Hindu

histoire ⓕ ees·twar history • story

historique ees·to·reek historical

hiver ⓜ ee·vair winter

hockey ⓜ o·kay hockey

hockey sur glace ⓜ o·kay sewr glas ice hockey

homme ⓜ om man

homme d'affaires ⓜ om da·fair business man

homme/femme politique ⓜ/ⓕ om/fam po·lee·teek politician

homosexuel(le) ⓜ/ⓕ o·mo·sek·swel gay • homosexual

honnête o·net honest

hôpital ⓜ o·pee·tal hospital

horaire ⓜ o·rair timetable

horoscope ⓜ o·ro·skop horoscope

hors jeu or·zher offside (sport)

hors service or sair·vees out of order

hospitalité ⓕ os·pee·ta·lee·tay hospitality

hôtel m o·tel hotel
huile f weel oil
huit weet eight
humain m ew·mun human
humour m ew·moor humour

I

ici ee·see here
idée f ee·day idea
idiot(e) m/f ee·dyo(t) idiot
ignorant(e) m/f ee·nyo·ron(t) ignorant
il eel he
île f eel island
illégal(e) m/f ee·lay·gal illegal
ils eel they (men)
image f ee·mazh picture
imagination f ee·ma·zhee·na·syon imagination
immatriculation ee·ma·tree·kew·la·syon car registration
immédiatement ee·may·dyat·mon immediately/right now
immigration f ee·mee·gra·syon immigration
imperméable um·pair·may·abler raincoat • waterproof
impoli(e) m/f um·po·lee rude • impolite
important(e) m/f um·por·ton(t) important
importer um·por·tay import
impossible um·po·see·bler impossible
impôt sur le revenu m um·po sewr ler rerv·new income tax
imprimante f um·pree·mont printer (computer)
incertain(e) m/f un·sair·tun/ un·sair·ten uncertain
inconfortable ung·kon·for·ta·bler uncomfortable
Inde f und India
indépendant(e) m/f un·day·pon·don(t) independent • self-employed

indigestion f un·dee·zhes·tyon indigestion
indiquer un·dee·kay point
individu m un·dee·vee·dew individual
industrie f un·dews·tree industry
industriel/industrielle m/f un·dews·tree·el industrial
infection f un·fek·syon infection
infirmier/infirmière m/f un·feer·myay/un·feer·myair nurse
inflammation f un·fla·ma·syon inflammation
influence f un·flew·ons influence
informatique f un·for·ma·teek IT
ingénierie un·zhay·nee·ree engineering
ingénieur m un·zhay·nyer engineer
ingrédient m ung·gray·dyon ingredient
injecter un·zhek·tay inject
injuste un·zhewst unfair
innocent(e) m/f ee·no·son(t) innocent
inondation f ee·non·da·syon flood
inopportun(e) m/f ee·no·por·tun/ ee·no·po·tewn inconvenient
inquiet/inquiète m/f ung·kyay/ ung·kyet worried
insecte m un·sekt bug • insect
institut universitaire m un·stee·tew ew·nee·vair·see·tair college
intelligent(e) m/f un·tay·lee·zhon(t) intelligent
intéressant(e) m/f un·tay·ray·son(t) interesting
international(e) m/f un·tair·na·syo·nal international
Internet m un·tair·net Internet
interprète m/f un·tair·pret interpreter
intime un·teem intimate
invité(e) m/f un·vee·tay visitor (guest)
inviter un·vee·tay invite
Irlande f eer·lond Ireland

J

itinéraire ⓜ ee·tee·nay·rair itinerary • route

itinéraire de randonnée ⓜ ee·tee·nay·rair der ron·do·nay hiking route

ivre ee·vrer drunk

J

jaloux/jalouse ⓜ/ⓕ zha·loo/zha·looz jealous

jamais zha·may never

jambe ⓕ zhomb leg

jambon ⓜ zhom·bon ham

janvier ⓜ zhon·vyay January

Japon ⓜ zha·pon Japan

jardin ⓜ zhar·dun garden

— botanique bo·ta·neek botanic garden

— d'enfants don·fon kindergarten

jardinage ⓜ zhar·dee·nazh gardening

jaune zhon yellow

je zher I

jean ⓜ zheen jeans

jeep ⓕ zheep jeep

jeter zher·tay throw

jeu ⓜ zher game

jeu électronique ⓜ zher ay·lek·tro·neek computer game

jeudi ⓜ zher·dee Thursday

jeune zhern young

jockey ⓜ zho·kay jockey

jogging ⓜ zho·geeng jogging

joie ⓕ zhwa joy

joindre zhwun·drer join

joli(e) ⓜ/ⓕ zho·lee pretty

jouer zhoo·ay act • play

jouet ⓜ zhway toy

jour ⓜ zhoor day

— de l'An der lon New Year's Day

— de Noël der no·el Christmas Day

journal ⓜ zhoor·nal newspaper

journaliste ⓜ/ⓕ zhoor·na·leest journalist

juge ⓜ zhewzh judge

juif/juive ⓜ/ⓕ zhweef/zhweev Jewish

juillet ⓜ zhwee·yay July

juin ⓜ zhwun June

jumeaux/jumelles ⓜ/ⓕ pl zhew·mo/zhew·mel twins

jupe ⓕ zhewp skirt

jusqu'à zhew·ska until (Friday, etc)

justice ⓕ zhew·stees justice

K

kascher ka·shair kosher

kilo ⓜ kee·lo kilo

kilogramme ⓜ kee·lo·gram kilogram

kilomètre ⓜ kee·lo·may·trer kilometre

kinésithérapeute ⓜ/ⓕ kee·nay·zee·tay·ra·pert physiotherapist

kinésithérapie ⓕ kee·nay·zee·tay·ra·pee physiotherapy

kiosque ⓜ kyosk kiosk

L

là la there

lac ⓜ lak lake

laid(e) ⓜ/ⓕ lay/led ugly

laine ⓕ len wool

laisser lay·say leave (something)

laisser tomber lay·say tom·bay drop

lait ⓜ lay milk

lame de rasoir ⓕ lam der ra·zwar razor blade

lampe ⓕ lomp lamp

— de poche der posh torch (flashlight)

langue ⓕ long language

lapin ⓜ la·pun rabbit

large larzh wide

laver la·vay wash (something)

laverie ⓕ lav·ree launderette

laxatif ⓜ lak·sa·teef laxative

le/la plus grand(e) ⓜ/ⓕ ler/la plew gron(d) biggest

le plus petit/la plus petite ⓜ/ⓕ ler plew per·tee/la plew per·teet smallest

le/la plus proche ⓜ/ⓕ ler/la plew prosh nearest

le/la meilleur(e) ⓜ/ⓕ ler/la may·yer best

légal(e) ⓜ/ⓕ lay·gal legal

léger/légère ⓜ/ⓕ lay·zhay/lay·zhair light (not heavy)

législation ⓕ lay·zhee·sla·syon legislation

légume ⓜ lay·gewm vegetable

lent(e) ⓜ/ⓕ lon(t) slow

lentement lon·ter·mon slowly

lequel/laquelle ⓜ/ⓕ ler·kel/la·kel which

Les Jeux Olympiques lay zher zo·lum·peek Olympic Games

lesbienne ⓕ les·byen lesbian

lettre ⓕ lay·trer letter

lettres classiques ⓕ pl le·trer kla·seek humanities

leur/leurs sg/pl ler their

lever ler·vay lift (arm)

lever du soleil ⓜ ler·vay dew so·lay sunrise

lèvre ⓕ lay·vrer lip

lézard ⓜ lay·zar lizard

liaison ⓕ lyay·zon affair

liberté ⓕ lee·bair·tay freedom

librairie ⓕ lee·bray·ree bookshop

libre lee·brer free (at liberty) • vacant

libre-service ⓜ lee·brer·sair·vees self service

lieu ⓜ lyer place

— de naissance der nay·sons place of birth

— saint sun shrine

lièvre ⓜ lyev·rer hare

ligne ⓕ lee·nyer line

ligne aérienne ⓕ lee·nyer a·ay·ryen airline

limitation de vitesse ⓕ lee·mee·ta·syon der vee·tes speed limit

lin ⓜ lun linen (material)

linge ⓜ lunzh laundry (clothes) • linen

lingerie ⓕ lun·zhree lingerie

lire leer read

lit ⓜ lee bed

literie ⓕ leet·ree bedding

lits jumeaux ⓜ pl day lee zhew·mo twin beds

livre ⓜ leev·rer book

livre ⓕ leev·rer pound (money, weight)

livrer leev·ray deliver

local(e) ⓜ/ⓕ lo·kal local

locataire ⓜ/ⓕ lo·ka·tair tenant

location de voitures ⓕ lo·ka·syon der vwa·tewr car hire

logement ⓜ lozh·mon accommodation

logiciel ⓜ lo·zhee·syel software

loi ⓕ lwa law

lointain(e) ⓜ/ⓕ lwun·tun/·ten far

long ⓜ long long

long-courrier long·koo·ryay long-distance (flight)

longue ⓕ long long

longueur ⓕ long·ger length

louer loo·ay hire • rent

louer à bail loo·way a ba·yer lease

lourd(e) ⓜ/ⓕ loor(d) heavy

loyal(e) ⓜ/ⓕ lwa·yal loyal

lubrifiant ⓜ lew·bree·fyon lubricant

lumière ⓕ lew·myair light

lundi ⓜ lun·dee Monday

lune de miel ⓕ lewn der myel honeymoon

lunettes ⓕ pl lew·net glasses (spectacles) • goggles (skiing)

— de soleil der so·lay sunglasses

luxe ⓜ lewks luxury

M

ma ⓕ ma my

machine ⓕ ma·sheen machine

machine à laver ⓕ ma·sheen a la·vay washing machine

mâchoire ⓕ ma·shwar jaw

Madame ma·dam Mrs • Ms

Mademoiselle mad·mwa·zel Miss

M

M

magasin ⓜ ma·ga·zun shop
— de chaussures der sho·sewr shoe shop
— de souvenirs der soov·neer souvenir shop
— de sports der spor sports store/shop
— de vêtements der vet·mon clothing shop
— de vins et spiritueux der vun ay spee·ree·twer liquor store
— pour équipement de camping poor ay·keep·mon der kom·peeng camping store
— qui vend des appareils électriques kee von day za·pa·ray ay·lek·treek electrical store
magazine ⓜ ma·ga·zeen magazine
magicien/magicienne ⓜ/ⓕ ma·zhee·syun/ma·zhees·yen magician
mai ⓜ may May
maigre may·grer thin
maillot de bain ⓜ may·yo der bun bathing suit
maillot de corps ⓜ ma·yo der kor singlet • vest
main ⓕ mun hand
maintenant mun·ter·non now
maire ⓜ mair mayor
mairie ⓕ may·ree city hall
mais may but
maison ⓕ may·zon house
majorité ⓕ ma·zho·ree·tay majority
mal à la tête ⓜ mal a la tet headache
mal des transports ⓜ mal day trons·por travel sickness
malade ma·lad ill • sick
maladie ⓕ ma·la·dee disease • sickness
— de cœur der ker heart condition
— vénérienne vay·nay·ryen venereal disease
malhonnête mal·o·net dishonest
maman ⓕ ma·mon mum

mammographie ⓕ ma·mo·gra·fee mammogram
manger mon·zhay eat
manif(estation) ⓕ ma·neef(ay·sta·syon) protest
manifester ma·nee·fay·stay protest
manoeuvre ⓜ ma·ner·vrer labourer
manque ⓜ mongk shortage
manquer mong·kay miss
manquer de mong·kay der run out of
manteau ⓜ mon·to coat
maquillage ⓜ ma·kee·yazh make-up
marchand ⓜ mar·shon shopkeeper
— de journaux mar·shon der zhoor·no newsagent
— de légumes mar·shon der lay·gewm greengrocer
marche ⓕ marsh step
marché ⓜ mar·shay market
marché aux puces ⓜ mar·shay o pews fleamarket
marcher mar·shay walk
mardi ⓜ mar·dee Tuesday
marée ⓕ ma·ray tide
mari ⓜ ma·ree husband
mariage ⓜ ma·ryazh marriage • wedding
marié(e) ⓜ/ⓕ ma·ryay married
marihuana ⓕ ma·ree·wa·na marihuana
mars ⓜ mars March
marteau ⓜ mar·to hammer
massage ⓜ ma·sazh massage
masser ma·say massage
masseur/masseuse ⓜ/ⓕ ma·ser/ma·serz masseur/masseuse
match ⓜ matsh game (sports)
match nul ⓜ matsh newl tie (draw)
matelas ⓜ mat·la mattress
matériel ⓜ ma·tay·ryel material
matin ⓜ ma·tun morning
mauvais(e) ⓜ/ⓕ mo·vay(z) bad • off (meat) • wrong (direction)
mécanicien/mécanicienne ⓜ/ⓕ may·ka·nee·syun/may·ka·nee·syen mechanic

médecin ⓜ mayd·sun doctor
médecine ⓕ med·seen medicine
médias ⓜ pl may·dya media
médicament ⓜ may·dee·ka·mon medicine (medication)
méditation ⓕ may·dee·ta·syon meditation
meilleur(e) ⓜ/ⓕ may·yer better
mélanger may·lon·zhay mix
membre ⓜ mom·brer member
même mem same
mémoire ⓕ may·mwar memory (ability to remember)
ménage ⓜ may·nazh housework
mensonge ⓜ mon·sonzh lie
menstruation ⓕ mon·strew·a·syon menstruation
menteur/menteuse ⓜ/ⓕ mon·ter/ mon·terz liar
mentir mon·teer lie (tell lies)
menuisier ⓜ mer·nwee·zyay carpenter
mer ⓕ mair sea
mercredi ⓜ mair·krer·dee Wednesday
mère ⓕ mair mother
merveilleux/merveilleuse ⓜ/ⓕ mair·vay·yer/mair·vay·yerz wonderful
mes pl may my
message ⓜ may·sazh message
messe ⓕ mes mass (Catholic)
métal ⓜ may·tal metal
météo ⓕ may·tay·o weather forecast
mètre ⓜ may·trer metre
métro ⓜ may·tro subway
mettre may·trer put
meublé(e) ⓜ/ⓕ mer·blay furnished
meubles ⓜ mer·bler furniture
midi mee·dee midday · noon
mignon/mignonne ⓜ/ⓕ mee·nyon/ mee·nyon cute
migraine ⓕ mee·gren migraine
militaire mee·lee·tair military
militant/militante ⓜ/ⓕ mee·lee·ton(t) activist
millénaire ⓜ mee·lay·nair millennium

millimètre ⓜ mee·lee·may·trer millimetre
million ⓜ mee·lyon million
minorité ⓕ mee·no·ree·tay minority
minuit mee·nwee midnight
minuscule mee·new·skewl tiny
minute ⓕ mee·newt minute
miroir ⓜ mee·rwar mirror
mode ⓕ mod fashion
modem ⓜ mo·dem modem
moderne mo·dairn modern
moi mwa me
moins mwun least
moins de mwun der less
mois ⓜ mwa month
moitié ⓕ mwa·tyay half
mon ⓜ mon my
monarchie ⓕ mo·nar·shee monarchy
monastère ⓜ mo·na·stair monastery
monde ⓜ mond world
monnaie ⓕ mo·nay change (coins)
mononucléose infectieuse ⓕ mo·no·new·klay·oz un·fek·syerz glandular fever
Monsieur mer·syer Mr
montagne ⓕ mon·ta·nyer mountain
monter mon·tay climb
— à bord de a bor der board (a plane, ship)
— à (cheval) a (shval) ride (horse)
montre ⓕ mon·trer watch
montrer mon·tray show
monument ⓜ mo·new·mon monument
morceau ⓜ mor·so piece
mordre mor·drer bite
morsure ⓕ mor·sewr bite (dog)
mort ⓕ mor death
mort(e) ⓜ/ⓕ mor(t) dead
mosquée ⓕ mo·skay mosque
mot ⓜ mo word
motel ⓜ mo·tel motel
moteur ⓜ mo·ter engine
moto ⓕ mo·to motorcycle
mouche ⓕ moosh fly
mouchoir ⓜ moo·shwar handkerchief

N

mouchoirs en papier ⓜ pl
moo·shwar om pa·pyay tissues
mouillé(e) ⓜ/ⓕ moo·yay wet
mourir moo·reer die
mousse à raser ⓕ moos a ra·zay
shaving cream
moustiquaire ⓕ moo·stee·kair
mosquito net
moustique ⓜ moo·steek mosquito
mouton ⓜ moo·ton sheep
muguet ⓜ mew·gay thrush (illness)
mur ⓜ mewr wall (outer)
muscle ⓜ mews·kler muscle
musée ⓜ mew·zay museum •
art gallery (state)
musicien/musicienne ⓜ/ⓕ
mew·zees·yun/mew·zees·yen
musician
musicien(ne) des rues ⓜ/ⓕ
mew·zee·syun/mew·zee·syen day
rew busker
musique ⓕ mew·zeek music
musulman(e) ⓜ/ⓕ mew·zewl·mon/
mew·zewl·man Muslim

N

nager na·zhay swim
nager avec un tuba na·zhay a·vek un
tew·ba snorkel
nappe ⓕ nap tablecloth
nationalité ⓕ na·syo·na·lee·tay
nationality
nature ⓕ na·tewr nature
naturopathe ⓜ&ⓕ na·tew·ro·pat
naturopath
nausée ⓕ no·zay nausea
nausées matinales ⓕ pl no·zay
ma·tee·nal morning sickness
navire ⓜ na·veer ship
né(e) ⓜ/ⓕ nay born
nécessaire nay·say·sair necessary
neige ⓕ nezh snow
neiger nay·zhay snow
nettoyage ⓜ net·wa·yazh cleaning
nettoyer net·wa·yay clean
neuf nerf nine

nez ⓜ nay nose
ni nee neither
nier nee·ay deny
n'importe où num·port oo
anywhere
n'importe quel/quelle ⓜ/ⓕ
num·port kel any
n'importe qui num·port kee
anyone
n'importe quoi num·port kwa
anything
niveau ⓜ nee·vo level (tier, height)
Noël ⓜ no·el Christmas
noir(e) ⓜ/ⓕ nwar black
noir et blanc nwar ay blong B&W
(film)
nom ⓜ nom name
— de famille der fa·mee·yer family
name • surname
non non no
non-direct non·dee·rekt nondirect
non-fumeur non·few·mer
nonsmoking
non-meublé(e) ⓜ/ⓕ no·mer·blay
unfurnished
nord ⓜ nor north
normal(e) ⓜ/ⓕ nor·mal regular
nostalgique nos·tal·zheek homesick
notre no·trer our
nourrir noo·reer feed
nourriture ⓕ noo·ree·tewr food
nous noo us • we
nouveau/nouvelle ⓜ/ⓕ noo·vo/
noo·vel new
Nouvelle-Zélande ⓕ noo·vel·zay·lond
New Zealand
nuage ⓜ nwazh cloud
nuageux/nuageuse ⓜ/ⓕ nwa·zher/
nwa·zherz cloudy
nuit ⓕ nwee night
numéro ⓜ new·may·ro number
— de chambre der shom·brer room
number
— de passeport der pas·por passport
number

O

objectif ⓜ ob·zhek·teef lens
objet ⓜ ob·zhay purpose
objets artisanaux ⓜ pl ob·zhay ar·tee·za·no handicrafts
obscur(e) ⓜ/ⓕ ob·skewr dark
obtenir op·ter·neer obtain
occasion ⓕ o·ka·zyon opportunity
occupation ⓕ o·kew·pa·syon occupation
occupé(e) ⓜ/ⓕ o·kew·pay busy
océan ⓜ o·say·on ocean
odeur ⓕ o·der smell
œil ⓜ er·yee eye
office de tourisme ⓜ o·fees·der too·rees·mer tourist office
officier ⓜ o·fees·yay officer
oiseau ⓜ wa·zo bird
ombre ⓕ om·brer shade • shadow
opéra ⓜ o·pay·ra opera
opérateur/opératrice ⓜ/ⓕ o·pay·ra·ter/o·pay·ra·trees operator
opération ⓕ o·pay·ra·syon operation
or ⓜ or gold
orage ⓜ o·razh storm
orange o·ronzh orange (colour)
ordinaire or·dee·nair ordinary
ordinateur ⓜ or·dee·na·ter computer
ordinateur portable ⓜ or·dee·na·ter por·ta·bler laptop
ordonnance ⓕ or·do·nons prescription
ordonner or·do·nay order
ordre ⓜ or·drer order
ordures ⓕ pl or·dewr garbage • rubbish
oreille ⓕ o·ray ear
oreiller ⓜ o·ray·yay pillow
organisation ⓕ or·ga·nee·za·syon organisation
organiser or·ga·nee·zay organise
orgasme ⓜ or·gas·mer orgasm
original(e) ⓜ/ⓕ o·ree·zhee·nal original
orteil ⓜ or·tay toe

os ⓜ os bone
ou oo or
où oo where
ouate de coton ⓕ wat der ko·ton cotton balls
oublier oo·blee·yay forget
ouest ⓜ west west
oui wee yes
outre-mer oo·trer·mair overseas
ouvert(e) ⓜ/ⓕ oo·vair(t) open
ouvre-boîte ⓜ oo·vrer·bwat can/tin opener
ouvre-bouteille ⓜ oo·vrer·boo·tay bottle opener
ouvrier/ouvrière ⓜ/ⓕ oo·vree·yay/oo·vree·yair manual worker
ouvrier d'usine ⓜ oo·vree·yay dew·zeen factory worker
ouvrière d'usine ⓕ oo·vree·yair dew·zeen factory worker
ouvrir oo·vreer open
overdose ⓕ o·vair·doz overdose
oxygène ⓜ ok·see·zhen oxygen

P

pacemaker ⓜ pes·may·ker pacemaker
page ⓕ pazh page
paiement ⓜ pay·mon payment
pain ⓜ pun bread
pain grillé ⓜ pung gree·yay toast
paire ⓕ pair pair (couple)
paix ⓕ pay peace
palais ⓜ pa·lay palace
panier ⓜ pan·yay basket
panne pan break down
pansement ⓜ pons·mon bandage
pantalon ⓜ pon·ta·lon pants • trousers
papa ⓜ pa·pa dad
paperasserie ⓕ pa·pras·ree paperwork
papeterie ⓕ pa·pet·ree stationer's (shop)
papier ⓜ pa·pyay paper

papier hygiénique ⓜ pa·pyay ee·zhyay·neek toilet paper
papillon ⓜ pa·pee·yon butterfly
Pâques pak Easter
paquet ⓜ pa·kay package • packet
par par by • per (day)
— avion a·vyon airmail
— exprès eks·pres express mail (by)
— voie de terre vwa der tair surface mail (by land)
— voie maritime vwa ma·ree·teem surface mail (by sea)
parade ⓕ pa·rad parade (ceremony)
paraplégique pa·ra·play·zheek paraplegic
parapluie ⓜ pa·ra·plwee umbrella
parc ⓜ park park
parc national ⓜ park na·syo·nal national park
parce que pars ker because
par-dessus par·der·sew over (above)
pardonner par·do·nay forgive
pare-brise ⓜ par·breez windscreen • windshield
parents ⓜ pl pa·ron parents
paresseux/paresseuse ⓜ/ⓕ pa·ray·ser/pa·ray·serz lazy
parfait(e) ⓜ/ⓕ par·fay(t) perfect
parfum ⓜ par·fum perfume
pari ⓜ pa·ree bet
parier par·yay bet
parking ⓜ par·keeng carpark
parler par·lay speak • talk
parmi par·mee among
partager par·ta·zhay share
parti ⓜ par·tee party (politics)
participer par·tee·see·pay participate
particulier/particulière ⓜ/ⓕ par·tee·kew·lyay/par·tee·kew·lyair particular
partie ⓕ par·tee part
partir par·teer depart • leave
pas compris pa kom·pree excluded
pas encore pa zong·kor not yet
pas frais/fraîche ⓜ/ⓕ pa fray/fresh stale

pas mal pa mal not bad
passe ⓕ pas pass (football)
passé pa·say past
passeport ⓜ pas·por passport
passer pa·say pass • spend (time)
passe-temps ⓜ pas·ton hobby
pâtisserie ⓕ pa·tees·ree cake shop
pauvre po·vrer poor
pauvreté ⓕ po·vrer·tay poverty
payer pay·yay pay
pays ⓜ pay·ee country
paysage ⓜ pay·yee·zazh scenery
Pays-Bas ⓜ pl pay·ee·ba Netherlands
peau ⓕ po skin
pêche ⓕ pesh fishing
pédale ⓕ pay·dal pedal
peigne ⓜ pe·nyer comb
peine ⓕ pen trouble
peintre ⓜ pun·trer painter
peinture ⓕ pun·tewr painting (the art)
pellicule ⓕ pay·lee·kewl film (for camera)
pendant pon·don during
pendant la nuit pon·don la nwee overnight
penderie ⓕ pon·dree wardrobe
pendule ⓕ pon·dewl clock
pénicilline ⓕ pay·nee·see·leen penicillin
pénis ⓜ pay·nees penis
penser pon·say think
pension ⓕ pon·syon boarding house
pension (de famille) ⓕ pon·syon (der fa·mee·yer) guesthouse
perdant(e) ⓜ/ⓕ par·don(t) loser
perdre pair·drer lose
perdu(e) ⓜ/ⓕ pair·dew lost
père ⓜ pair father
permanent(e) ⓜ/ⓕ pair·ma·non(t) permanent
permettre pair·me·trer allow
permis ⓜ pair·mee permit
— de conduire der kon·dweer driver's licence
— de travail der tra·vai work permit

permission ① pair·mee·syon permission

personnalité ① pair·so·na·lee·tay personality

personne ① pair·son person

personnel(le) ⓜ/① pair·so·nel personal

perte ① pairt loss

pertinent(e) ⓜ/① pair·tee·non(t) relevant

peser per·zay weigh

petit(e) ⓜ/① per·tee(t) little • small

— ami ⓜ per·tee ta·mee boyfriend

— amie ① per·teet a·mee girlfriend

— cuillère ① per·teet kwee·yair teaspoon

— déjeuner ⓜ per·tee day·zher·nay breakfast

— monnaie ① per·teet mo·nay loose change

— tapis ⓜ per·tee ta·pee mat

petite-fille ① per·teet fee·yer granddaughter

petit-fils ⓜ per·tee fees grandson

pétition ① pay·tees·yon petition

pétrole ⓜ pay·trol oil (petrol)

peu ⓜ per little bit

— commun(e) ⓜ/① ko·mun/ ko·mewn unusual

— profond(e) ⓜ/① pro·fon(d) shallow

peur ① per fear

peut-être per·tay·trer maybe

phares ⓜ pl far headlights

pharmacie ① far·ma·see chemist • pharmacy

pharmacien(ne) ⓜ/① far·ma·syun/ far·ma·syen chemist (person)

photo ① fo·to photo

photographe ⓜ/① fo·to·graf photographer

photographie ① fo·to·gra·fee photography

pièce (de théâtre) ① pyes (der tay·a·trer) play (theatre)

pièce d'identité ① pyes dee·don·tee·tay identification

pièces ① pyes coins

pied ⓜ pyay foot

pierre ① pyair stone

piéton ⓜ pyay·ton pedestrian

pile ① peel battery

pilule ① pee·lewl pill

pince à épiler ① puns a ay·pee·lay tweezers

pipe ① peep pipe

pique-nique ⓜ peek·neek picnic

piquets de tente ⓜ pee·kay der tont tent pegs

piqûre ① pee·kewr bite (insect) • injection

pire peer worse

piscine ① pee·seen swimming pool

piste ① peest track (sports) • trail

piste cyclable ① peest see·kla·bler bike path

pistolet ⓜ pees·to·lay gun

placard ⓜ pla·kar cupboard

place ① plas seat (place) • square (town)

place centrale ① plas son·tral main square

plage ① plazh beach

plainte ① plunt complaint

plaisanterie ① play·zon·tree joke

plan ⓜ plon map (of town)

planche à voile ① plonsh a vwal windsurfer

planche de surf ① plonsh der serf surfboard

plancher ⓜ plon·shay floor

planète ① pla·net planet

plaque d'immatriculation ① plak dee·ma·tree·kew·la·syon license plate number

plastique ⓜ plas·teek plastic

plat ⓜ pla dish

plat(e) ⓜ/① pla(t) flat

plein(e) ⓜ/① plun/plen full

pleurer pler·ray cry

pleuvoir pler·vwar rain

P

plongée (sous-marine) ① plon·zhay (soo·ma·reen) diving

plonger plon·zhay dive

pluie ① plwee rain

plus ⓜ plews most

plus de plews der more

plus grand(e) ⓜ/① plew gron(d) bigger

plus petit(e) ⓜ/① plew per·tee/·teet smaller

plus tard plew·tar later

plusieurs plew·zyer several

pneu ⓜ pner tyre

poche ① posh pocket

poêle ① pwal frying pan

poésie ① po·ay·zee poetry

poids ⓜ pwa weight

poignet ⓜ pwa·nyay wrist

pointe ① pwunt point

poisson ⓜ pwa·son fish

poissonnerie ① pwa·son·ree fish shop

poitrine ① pwa·treen chest

police ① po·lees police

policier ⓜ po·lee·syay police officer (in city)

politique ① po·lee·teek policy · politics

pollen ⓜ po·len pollen

pollution ① po·lew·syon pollution

pommade pour les lèvres ① po·mad poor lay lay·vrer lip balm

pompe ① pomp pump

pont ⓜ pon bridge

populaire po·pew·lair popular

port ⓜ por harbour · port

porte ① port door

porte-monnaie ⓜ port·mo·nay purse

porter por·tay carry · wear

posemètre ⓜ poz·may·trer light meter

poser po·zay ask (a question)

positif/positive ⓜ/① po·zee·teef/ po·zee·teev positive

possible po·see·bler possible

poste ① post mail (postal system)

pot ⓜ po carton · jar · pot

pot d'échappement ⓜ po day·shap·mon exhaust (car)

pot-de-vin ⓜ po·der·vun bribe

poterie ① po·tree pottery

poubelle ① poo·bel garbage/ rubbish can

poulet ⓜ poo·lay chicken

poumon ⓜ poo·mon lung

poupée ① poo·pay doll

pour poor for

— cent son percent

pourboire ⓜ poor·bwar tip (gratuity)

pourquoi poor·kwa why

pousser poo·say grow · push

poussette ① poo·set pushchair · stroller

poussière ① poo·syair dust

pouvoir poo·vwar can (be able or have permission)

pouvoir ⓜ poo·vwar power

poux ⓜ pl poo lice

pratique pra·teek practical

pratiquer pra·tee·kay practise

précédent(e) ⓜ/① pray·say·don(t) previous

préférer pray·fay·ray prefer

premier/première ⓜ/① prer·myay/ prer·myair first

premier ministre ⓜ prer·myay mee·nee·strer prime minister

première classe ① prer·myair klas first class

prendre pron·drer take

prendre en photo pron·drer on fo·to take a photo of (someone)

prénom ⓜ pray·non first/given name

préparer pray·pa·ray prepare

près de pray der near

présent ⓜ pray·zon present (time)

présenter pray·zon·tay introduce (people)

préservatif ⓜ pray·zair·va·teef condom

président ⓜ pray·zee·don president

presque pres·ker almost

pressé(e) ⓜ/ⓕ pray·say in a hurry
pression ⓕ pray·syon pressure
prêt(e) ⓜ/ⓕ pray/pret ready
prêtre ⓜ pray·trer priest
prévenir prayv·neer warn
prévision ⓕ pray·vee·zyon forecast
prévoir pray·vwar forecast
prière ⓕ pree·yair prayer
principal(e) ⓜ/ⓕ prun·see·pal main
printemps ⓜ prun·tom spring (season)
prise ⓕ preez plug (electricity)
prison ⓕ pree·zon jail • prison
prisonnier/prisonnière ⓜ/ⓕ pree·zo·nyay/pree·zo·nyair prisoner
privé(e) ⓜ/ⓕ pree·vay private
prix ⓜ pree price
prix d'entrée ⓜ pree don·tray admission (price)
probable pro·ba·bler probable
problème ⓜ pro·blem problem
prochain(e) ⓜ/ⓕ pro·shun/pro·shen next (month)
proche prosh close
produire pro·dweer produce
professeur ⓜ pro·fay·ser teacher
professeur (à l'université) ⓜ pro·fay·ser (a lew·nee·vair·see·tay) lecturer
professionnel(le) ⓜ/ⓕ pro·fay·syo·nel professional
profond(e) ⓜ/ⓕ pro·fon(d) deep
programme ⓜ pro·gram programme
programme des spectacles ⓜ pro·gram day spek·tak·ler entertainment guide
projecteur ⓜ pro·zhek·ter projector
prolongation ⓕ pro·long·ga·syon extension (visa)
promenade ⓕ prom·nad ride
promesse ⓕ pro·mes promise
promettre pro·may·trer promise
promouvoir pro·moo·vwar promote
propre pro·prer clean
propriétaire ⓜ&ⓕ pro·pree·ay·tair landlady • landlord • owner

prostituée ⓕ pro·stee·tway prostitute
protection ⓕ pro·tek·syon protection
protégé(e) ⓜ/ⓕ pro·tay·zhay protected (species)
protéger pro·tay·zhay protect
protège-slips ⓜ pl pro·tezh·sleep panty liners
provisions ⓕ pl pro·vee·zyon food supplies • provisions
prudence ⓕ prew·dons caution
psychothérapie ⓕ psee·ko·tay·ra·pee psychotherapy
public ⓜ pewb·leek public
publicité ⓕ pewb·lee·see·tay advertisement
puce ⓕ pews flea
puis pwee then (next)
puissance nucléaire ⓕ pwee·sons new·klay·air nuclear power
pull ⓜ pewl jumper • sweater
punir pew·neer punish
pur(e) ⓜ/ⓕ pewr pure

Q Q

Q

quai ⓜ kay platform
qualification ⓕ ka·lee·fee·ka·syon qualification
qualité ⓕ ka·lee·tay quality
quand kon when
quantité ⓕ kon·tee·tay quantity
quarantaine ⓕ ka·ron·ten quarantine
quart ⓜ kar quarter
quatre ka·trer four
quel/quelle ⓜ/ⓕ kel what • which
quelque chose kel·ker shoz something
quelquefois kel·ker·fwa sometimes
quelques kel·ker some
quelqu'un kel·kun someone
question ⓕ kay·styon question
queue ⓕ ker queue • tail
qui kee which • who
quincaillerie ⓕ kung·kay·ree hardware store

R

R

quitter kee·tay quit

quotidien(ne) ⓜ/ⓕ ko·tee·dyun/ ko·tee·dyen daily

race ⓕ ras race

racisme ⓜ ra·sees·mer racism

raconter ra·kon·tay tell (a story)

radiateur ⓜ ra·dya·ter radiator

radical(e) ⓜ/ⓕ ra·dee·kal radical

radio ⓕ ra·dyo radio

raide red steep

raison ⓕ ray·zon reason

raisonnable ray·zo·na·bler sensible

ramasser ra·ma·say pick up (something)

randonnée ⓕ ron·do·nay hiking

rapide ra·peed fast • quick

rapport ⓜ ra·por connection

rapports sexuels protégés ⓜ pl ra·por seks·wel pro·tay·zhay safe sex

raquette ⓕ ra·ket racquet

rare rar rare

rasoir ⓜ ra·zwar razor

rassis(e) ⓜ/ⓕ ra·see(z) stale (bread)

rat ⓜ ra rat

rave ⓕ raiv rave

réalisateur/réalisatrice ⓜ/ⓕ ray·a·lee·za·ter/ray·a·lee·za·trees director (film)

réaliser ray·a·lee·zay direct (a film)

réaliste ray·a·leest realistic

réalité ⓕ ray·a·lee·tay reality

rebord ⓜ rer·bor ledge

récemment ray·sa·mon recently

receveur ⓜ rer·ser·ver conductor (bus)

recevoir rer·ser·vwar receive

réchaud ⓜ ray·sho stove

recherches ⓕ pl rer·shairsh research

récolte ⓕ ray·kolt crop (gathered)

recommander rer·ko·mon·day recommend

reconnaissant(e) ⓜ/ⓕ rer·ko·nay·son(t) grateful

reconnaître rer·ko·nay·trer recognise

reçu ⓜ rer·sew receipt

recueil d'expressions ⓜ rer·ker·yer dek·spray·syon phrasebook

recyclable rer·see·kla·bler recyclable

recyclage ⓜ rer·see·klazh recycling

recycler rer·see·klay recycle

rédacteur/rédactrice ⓜ/ⓕ ray·dak·ter/ray·dak·trees editor

réduire ray·dweer reduce

référence ⓕ ray·fay·rons reference

réfrigérateur ⓜ ray·free·zhay·ra·ter refrigerator

réfugié(e) ⓜ/ⓕ ray·few·zhyay refugee

refuser rer·few·zay refuse

regarder rer·gar·day look • look at • watch

régime ⓜ ray·zheem diet

région ⓕ ray·zhyon region

règles ⓕ ray·gler rules

règles douloureuses ⓕ pl ray·gler doo·loo·rerz period pain

reine ⓕ ren queen

relation ⓕ rer·la·syon relationship

religieuse ⓕ rer·lee·zhyerz nun

religieux/religieuse ⓜ/ⓕ rer·lee·zhyer/rer·lee·zhyerz religious

religion ⓕ rer·lee·zhyon religion

remboursement ⓜ rom·boor·ser·mon refund

remercier rer·mair·syay thank

remise ⓕ rer·meez discount

remplir rom·pleer fill

rencontrer ron·kon·tray meet

rendez-vous ⓜ ron·day·voo appointment • date

renseignements ⓜ pl ron·sen·yer·mon information

réparer ray·pa·ray repair

repas ⓜ rer·pa meal

repasser rer·pa·say iron (clothes)

répondre ray·pon·drer answer • reply

réponse ⓕ ray·pons answer • response

repos ⓜ rer·po rest

représenter rer·pray·zon·tay represent

république ① ray·pewb·leek republic

réseau ⓜ ray·zo network

réservation ① ray·zair·va·syon reservation

réserver ray·zair·vay book (make a booking)

respirer res·pee·ray breathe

ressort ⓜ rer·sor spring (coil)

restaurant ⓜ res·to·ron restaurant

rester res·tay stay

retard ⓜ rer·tard delay

retrait ⓜ rer·tray withdrawal

retrait des bagages ⓜ rer·tray day ba·gazh baggage claim

retraité(e) ⓜ/① rer·tray·tay pensioner • retired

réussite ① ray·ew·seet achievement

réveil ⓜ ray·vay alarm clock

réveiller ray·vay·yay wake (someone) up

revenir rerv·neer return

revenus ⓜ pl rerv·new income

rêver ray·vay dream

révolution ① ray·vo·lew·syon revolution

rhume ⓜ **des foins** rewm day fwun hay fever

riche reesh rich • wealthy

rien ryun nothing

rire reer laugh

risque ⓜ reesk risk

rivière ① ree·vyair river

riz ⓜ ree rice

robe ① rob dress

robinet ⓜ ro·bee·nay faucet • tap

rocher ⓜ ro·shay rock

rock ⓜ rok rock (music)

roi ⓜ rwa king

roller ⓜ ro·lair rollerblading

roman ⓜ ro·mon novel

romantique ro·mon·teek romantic

rond(e) ⓜ/① ron(d) round

rond-point ⓜ rom·pwun roundabout (traffic)

rose roz pink

roue ① roo wheel

rouge roozh red

rouge à lèvres ⓜ roozh a lay·vrer lipstick

rougeole ① roo·zhol measles

rougeur ① roo·zher rash

route ① root road

royaume ⓜ rwa·yom kingdom

rue ① rew street

ruelle ① rwel lane (city)

rugby ⓜ rewg·bee rugby

ruines ① pl rween ruins

ruisseau ⓜ rwee·so stream

ruse ① rewz trick

rythme ⓜ reet·mer rhythm

S

sa ① sa her • his

sabbat ⓜ sa·ba Sabbath

sable ⓜ sa·bler sand

sac ⓜ sak bag

— à dos a do backpack

— à main a mun handbag

— de couchage der koo·shazh sleeping bag

saint(e) ⓜ/① sun(t) saint

Saint-Sylvestre ① sun·seel·ves·trer New Year's Eve

saison ① say·zon season

salaire ⓜ sa·lair salary • wage

salaud ⓜ sa·lo bastard

sale sal dirty

salle ① sal room

— d'attente sal da·tont waiting room

— de bain sal der bun bathroom

— de transit sal der tron·zeet transit lounge

salon de beauté ⓜ sa·lon der bo·tay beauty salon

s'allonger sa·lon·zhay lie (not stand)

salope ① sa·lop bitch

samedi ⓜ sam·dee Saturday

s'amuser sa·mew·zay enjoy (oneself) • fun (have fun)

sandales ① son·dal sandals

S

sang ⓜ son blood
sans son without
sans plomb son plom unleaded
sans-abri son·za·bree homeless
santé ⓕ son·tay health
s'arrêter sa·ray·tay stop (doing)
s'asseoir sa·swar sit
satisfait(e) ⓜ/ⓕ sa·tees·fay/
sa·tees·fet satisfied
sauf sof except
sauna ⓜ so·na sauna
sauter so·tay jump
sauvage so·vazh wild
sauver so·vay save
savoir sa·vwar know
savon ⓜ sa·von soap
scénario ⓜ say·na·ryo script
scénariste ⓜ/ⓕ say·na·reest
scriptwriter
scène ⓕ sen stage
science ⓕ syons science
science-fiction ⓕ syons·feek·syon
science fiction
scientifique ⓜ&ⓕ syon·tee·feek
scientist
score ⓜ skor score
sculpture ⓕ skewl·tewr sculpture
se coucher ser koo·shay go to bed
se décider ser day·see·day decide
se disputer ser dees·pew·tay argue
se laver ser la·vay wash (oneself)
se mettre à genoux ser may·trer a
zher·noo kneel
se mettre en grève ser may·trer ong
grev strike (go on strike)
se plaindre ser plun·drer complain
se raser ser ra·zay shave
se rendre compte de ser ron·drer
kont der realise
se reposer ser rer·po·zay relax (rest)
se réveiller ser ray·vay·yay wake up
se souvenir ser soo·ver·neer
remember
seau ⓜ so bucket
sec/sèche ⓜ/ⓕ sek/sesh dry
sécher say·shay dry (clothes)

second(e) ⓜ/ⓕ skon/skond
second
seconde ⓕ skond second (clock)
secret ⓜ ser·kray secret
secrétaire ⓜ/ⓕ ser·kray·tair
secretary
sécurité ⓕ say·kew·ree·tay safety •
security
sécurité sociale ⓕ say·kew·ree·tay
so·syal social welfare
sein ⓜ sun breast
sel ⓜ sel salt
selle ⓕ sel saddle
semaine ⓕ ser·men week
semblable som·bla·bler similar
séminaire ⓜ say·mee·nair seminar
s'ennuyer son·nwee·yay bored (be)
sensation ⓕ son·sa·syon feeling
(physical)
sensibilité de la pellicule ⓕ
son·see·bee·lee·tay der la pay·lee·kewl
film speed
sensuel(le) ⓜ/ⓕ son·swel sensual
sentier ⓜ son·tyay footpath
sentiment ⓜ son·tee·mon feeling
(emotion)
sentir son·teer smell
séparé(e) ⓜ/ⓕ say·pa·ray separate
sept set seven
septembre ⓜ sep·tom·brer
September
série ⓕ say·ree series
sérieux/sérieuse ⓜ/ⓕ say·ree·yer/
say·ree·yerz serious
seringue ⓕ ser·rung syringe
séropositif/séropositive ⓜ/ⓕ
say·ro·po·zee·teef/say·ro·po·zee·teev
HIV positive
serpent ⓜ sair·pon snake
serrer dans ses bras say·ray don say
bra hug
serrure ⓕ say·rewr lock
serveur/serveuse ⓜ/ⓕ sair·ver/
sair·verz waiter
service ⓜ sair·vees service • service
charge

service militaire ⓜ sair·vees mee·lee·tair military service

serviette ⓕ sair·vyet briefcase • napkin • towel

serviette hygiénique ⓕ sair·vyet ee·zhyay·neek sanitary napkin

ses pl say her • his

seul(e) ⓜ/ⓕ serl only

sexe ⓜ seks sex

sexisme ⓜ sek·see·smer sexism

sexiste sek·seest sexist

sexy sek·see sexy

s'habiller sa·bee·yay dress (oneself)

shampooing ⓜ shom·pwung shampoo

short ⓜ short shorts

si see if

SIDA ⓜ see·da AIDS

siège pour enfant ⓜ syezh poor on·fon child seat

siffler see·flay whistle

signature ⓕ see·nya·tewr signature

signe ⓜ see·nyer sign

simple sum·pler simple

Singapour sung·ga·poor Singapore

singe ⓜ sunzh monkey

s'inquiéter sung·kyay·tay worry

situation ⓕ see·twa·syon situation

situation ⓕ **familiale** see·twa·syon fa·mee·lyal marital status

six sees six

skateboard ⓜ sket·bord skate-boarding

ski ⓜ skee skiing

ski nautique ⓜ skee no·teek waterskiing

skier skee·yay ski

skis ⓜ skee skis

slip ⓜ sleep panties • underpants

s'occuper de so·kew·pay der look after

socialisme ⓜ so·sya·lees·mer socialism

socialiste so·sya·leest socialist

société ⓕ so·syay·tay society

sœur ⓕ ser sister

soie ⓕ swa silk

soigner swa·nyay care for (someone)

soigneux/soigneuse ⓜ/ⓕ swa·nyer/ swa·nyerz careful

soir ⓜ swar evening

soirée ⓕ swa·ray night out • party

soldat ⓜ sol·da soldier

solde ⓜ sold balance (account)

soleil ⓜ so·lay sun

solide so·leed solid

somme ⓕ som amount (money)

sommeil ⓜ so·may sleep

somnifère ⓜ som·nee·fair sleeping pill

son ⓜ son her • his

sonner so·nay ring (of phone)

sortie ⓕ sor·tee exit

sortir sor·teer go out

sortir avec sor·teer a·vek date (go out with)

souffrir soo·freer suffer

souhaiter sway·tay wish

soulever sool·vay lift • raise

sourd(e) ⓜ/ⓕ soor(d) deaf

sourire soo·reer smile

sourire ⓜ soo·reer smile

souris ⓕ soo·ree mouse

sous soo below • under

sous-titres ⓜ soo·tee·trer subtitles

sous-vêtements ⓜ soo·vet·mon underwear

soutien-gorge ⓜ soo·tyung·gorzh bra

souvenir ⓜ soov·neer memory (recollection) • souvenir

souvent soo·von often

sparadrap ⓜ spa·ra·dra Band-Aid

spécial(e) ⓜ/ⓕ spay·syal special

spécialiste ⓜ/ⓕ spay·sya·leest specialist

spectacle ⓜ spek·ta·kler performance • show

sport ⓜ spor sport

sportif/sportive ⓜ/ⓕ spor·teef/ spor·teev sportsperson

stade ⓜ stad stadium

T

stage en entreprise ⓜ stazh on on·trer·preez work experience
station de métro ⓕ sta·syon der may·tro metro station
station de taxi ⓕ sta·syon der tak·see taxi stand
station-service ⓕ sta·syon·sair·vees petrol station
stérilet ⓜ stay·ree·lay IUD
stupéfiant ⓜ stew·pay·fyon narcotic
stupéfiant(e) ⓜ/ⓕ stew·pay·fyon(t) amazing
stupide stew·peed stupid
style ⓜ steel style
stylo ⓜ stee·lo pen (ballpoint)
suborner sew·bor·nay bribe
sucré(e) ⓜ/ⓕ sew·kray sweet
sud ⓜ sewd south
suivre swee·vrer follow
supérette de quartier ⓕ sew·pay·ret der kar·tyay convenience store
supermarché ⓜ sew·pair·mar·shay supermarket
superstition ⓕ sew·pair·stee·syon superstition
supplémentaire sew·play·mon·tair additional • extra
supporter sew·por·tay support
sur sewr on
sûr(e) ⓜ/ⓕ sewr sure
surf (des neiges) ⓜ serf (day nezh) snowboarding
surfer ser·fay surf
surnom ⓜ sewr·nom nickname
surprise ⓕ sewr·preez surprise
survivre sewr·vee·vrer survive
synagogue ⓕ see·na·gog synagogue
syndicat ⓜ sun·dee·ka union (trade)
syndrome prémenstruel ⓜ sun·drom pray·mon·strwel premenstrual tension
synthétique sun·tay·teek synthetic
syrop contre la toux ⓜ see·ro kon·trer la too cough medicine

T

ta ⓕ sg inf ta your
tabac ⓜ ta·ba tobacco
table ⓕ ta·bler table
tableau ⓜ ta·blo painting (a work)
tableau d'affichage ⓜ ta·blo da·fee·shazh scoreboard
taie d'oreiller ⓕ tay do·ray·yay pillowcase
taille ⓕ tai size (general)
tailleur ⓜ ta·yer tailor
talc ⓜ talk baby powder
tambour ⓜ tom·boor drum
tampon hygiénique ⓜ tom·pon ee·zhyay·neek tampon
tante ⓕ tont aunt
tapis ⓜ ta·pee rug
tarif ⓜ ta·reef fare
tarifs postaux ⓜ pl ta·reef pos·to postage
tasse ⓕ tas cup
taux de change ⓜ to der shonzh currency exchange • exchange rate
taxe ⓕ taks tax
— à la vente a la vont sales tax
— d'aéroport da·ay·ro·por airport tax
taxi ⓜ tak·see taxi
technique ⓕ tek·neek technique
télé ⓕ tay·lay TV
télécarte ⓕ tay·lay·kart phone card
télécommande ⓕ tay·lay·ko·mond remote control
télégramme ⓜ tay·lay·gram telegram
téléphérique ⓜ tay·lay·fay·reek cable car
téléphone ⓜ tay·lay·fon telephone
téléphone portable ⓜ tay·lay·fon por·ta·bler mobile phone
téléphone public ⓜ tay·lay·fon pewb·leek public telephone
téléphoner tay·lay·fo·nay telephone
télescope ⓜ tay·lay·skop telescope
télésiège ⓜ tay·lay·syezh chairlift (skiing)

télévision ① tay·la·vee·zyon television

témoin ⑩ tay·mwun witness

température ① tom·pay·ra·tewr temperature

temple ⑩ tom·pler temple

temps ⑩ tom time (general) • weather

tennis ⑩ tay·nees tennis

tennis de table ⑩ tay·nees der ta·bler table tennis

tension artérielle ① ton·syon ar·tay·ryel blood pressure

tente ① tont tent

terrain ⑩ tay·rung ground

— de camping der kom·peeng campsite

— de golf der golf golf course

— de jeux der zher playground

— de sport der spor sports ground

Terre ① tair Earth

terre ① tair earth • land

terrorisme ⑩ tay·ro·rees·mer terrorism

tes pl inf tay your

test de grossesse ⑩ test der gro·ses pregnancy test kit

tête ① tet head

tétine ① tay·teen pacifier • dummy

teush ⑩ tersh hash

théâtre ⑩ tay·a·trer drama (theatre)

timbre ⑩ tum·brer stamp

timide tee·meed shy

tire-bouchon ⑩ teer·boo·shon corkscrew

tirer tee·ray pull • shoot

tissu ⑩ tee·sew fabric

toilettes ① pl twa·let public toilet

toit ⑩ twa roof

tombe ① tomb grave

tomber tom·bay fall

ton ⑩ sg inf ton your

tonalité ① to·na·lee·tay dial tone

tôt to early

toucher too·shay feel • touch

toujours too·zhoor always

tour ① toor tower

touriste ⑩&① too·reest tourist

tourner toor·nay turn

tournoi ⑩ toor·nwa tournament

tous les deux too lay der both

tous les jours too lay zhoor every day

tout too all • everything

— droit drwa straight ahead

— le monde ler mond everyone

— près pray nearby

tout(e) seul(e) ⑩/① too(t) serl alone

toux ① too cough

toxicomanie ① tok·see·ko·ma·nee drug addiction

traduire tra·dweer translate

trafiquant de drogue ⑩ tra·fee·kon der drog drug dealer

train ⑩ trun train

traite bancaire ① tret bong·kair bank draft

traitement ⑩ tret·mon treatment

tranchant(e) ⑩/① tron·shon(t) sharp (blade, etc)

tranche ① tronsh slice

tranquille trong·keel quiet

transfert ⑩ trons·fair transfer

transport ⑩ trons·por transport

travail ⑩ tra·vai job • work

— dans un bar don zun bar bar work

— intermittent un·tair·mee·ton casual work

travailler tra·va·yay work

traverser tra·vair·say cross

tremblement de terre ⑩ trom·bler·mon der tair earthquake

très tray very

tribunal ⑩ tree·bew·nal court (legal)

tricheur/tricheuse ⑩/① tree·sher/tree·sherz cheat

tricot ⑩ tree·ko knitting

triste treest sad

trois trwa three

troisième trwa·zyem third

tromper trom·pay trick

trop tro too (expensive etc)

trop de tro der too much (rain etc) • too many (people etc)

trou ⑩ troo hole

trousse à pharmacie ⓕ troos a far·ma·see first-aid kit
trouver troo·vay find
T-shirt ⓜ tee·shert T-shirt
tu inf tew yo
tuer tew·way kill
type ⓜ teep type
typique tee·peek typical

U

ultrason ⓜ ewl·tra·son ultrasound
un peu um per a little
un(e) ⓜ/ⓕ un/ewn un • one
une fois ewn fwa once
uniforme ⓜ ew·nee·form uniform
union ⓕ ew·nyon union
univers ⓜ ew·nee·vair universe
université ⓕ ew·nee·vair·see·tay university
urgent(e) ⓜ/ⓕ ewr·zhon(t) urgent
usine ⓕ ew·zeen factory
utile ew·teel useful
utiliser ew·tee·lee·zay use

V

vacances ⓕ pl va·kons holidays • vacation
vaccination ⓕ vak·see·na·syon vaccination
vache ⓕ vash cow
vagin ⓜ va·zhun vagina
vague ⓕ vag wave
valeur ⓕ va·ler value (price)
valider va·lee·day validate
valise ⓕ va·leez suitcase
vallée ⓕ va·lay valley
varappe ⓕ va·rap rock climbing
végétarien/végétarienne ⓜ/ⓕ vay·zhay·ta·ryun/vay·zhay·ta·ryen vegetarian
véhicule ⓜ vay·ee·kewl vehicle
veine ⓕ ven vein
vélo ⓜ vay·lo bicycle
vélo tout terrain (VTT) ⓜ vay·lo too tay·run (vay·tay·tay) mountain bike

vendre von·drer sell
vendredi von·drer·dee Friday
venimeux/venimeuse ⓜ/ⓕ ver·nee·mer/ver·nee·merz poisonous
venir ver·neer come
vent ⓜ von wind
vente ⓕ vont sale
vente aux enchères ⓕ vont o zon·shair auction
ventilateur ⓜ von·tee·la·ter fan (machine)
vérifier vay·ree·fyay check
vérité ⓕ vay·ree·tay truth
verre ⓜ vair drink (alcoholic) • glass
verres de contact ⓜ vair der kon·takt contact lenses
vers vair toward (direction)
vers ⓜ vair worms
vert(e) ⓜ/ⓕ vair(t) green
veste ⓕ vest jacket
vestiaire ⓜ vays·tyair cloakroom
vêtements ⓜ vet·mon clothing
veuf ⓜ verf widower
veuve ⓕ verv widow
via vee·a via
viande ⓕ vyond meat
vide veed empty
vie ⓕ vee life
vieux/vieille ⓜ/ⓕ vyer/vyay old
vigne ⓕ vee·nyer vine
vignoble ⓜ vee·nyo·bler vineyard
VIH (virus immunodéficitaire humain) ⓜ vay·ee·ash (vee·rews ee·mew·no·day·fee·see·tair ew·mun) HIV
village ⓜ vee·lazh village
ville ⓕ veel city • town
vin ⓜ vun wine
violer vyo·lay rape
violet(te) ⓜ/ⓕ vyo·lay/vyo·let purple
virus ⓜ vee·rews virus
visa ⓜ vee·za visa
visage ⓜ vee·zazh face
visite guidée ⓕ vee·zeet gee·day guided tour
visiter vee·zee·tay visit (museum etc)

visiteur/visiteuse ⓜ/ⓕ vee·zee·ter/
vee·zee·terz visitor
vitamine ⓕ vee·ta·meen vitamin
vitesse ⓕ vee·tes speed
vivant(e) ⓜ/ⓕ vee·von(t) alive
vivre vee·vrer live
voile ⓕ vwal sail • sailing
voir vwar see
voiture ⓕ vwa·tewr car
voiture de police ⓕ vwa·tewr der
po·lees police car
vol ⓜ vol flight • robbery
volé(e) ⓜ/ⓕ vo·lay stolen
voler vo·lay fly • rob • steal
voleur/voleuse ⓜ/ⓕ vo·ler/vo·lerz
thief
volume ⓜ vo·lewm volume
vomir vo·meer vomit
vos pl/pol vo your
voter vo·tay vote
votre sg pol vo·trer/vo your
vouloir voo·lwar want
vous pl pol voo you
voyage ⓜ vwa·yazh journey • tour •
trip
voyage d'affaires ⓜ vwa·yazh da·fair
business trip
voyager vwa·ya·zhay travel
voyageur/voyageuse ⓜ/ⓕ
vwa·ya·zher/vwa·ya·zherz passenger

vrai(e) ⓜ/ⓕ vray real • true
vraiment vray·mon really
vue ⓕ vew view

W

wagon-lit ⓜ va·gon·lee sleeping car
wagon-restaurant ⓜ
va·gon·res·to·ron dining car
week-end ⓜ week·end weekend

Y

yeux ⓜ yer eyes
yoga ⓜ yo·ga yoga

Z

zéro zay·ro zero
zoo ⓜ zo zoo

Index

l'indice

For topics that are covered in several sections of this book, we've indicated the most relevant page number in bold.

INDEX